LESSONS FOR SCHOOLS?

# Lessons for Schools?

## A Comparison of Business and Educational Management

*Mike Bottery*

CASSELL

371.2
B659L

Cassell                              387 Park Avenue South
Villiers House                       New York
41/47 Strand                         NY 10016-8810
London WC2N 5JE

© Mike Bottery 1994

First published 1994

**British Library Cataloguing-in-Publication Data**
A catalogue record for this book is available from the British Library.

ISBN 0-304-32722-0 (hardback)
     0-304-32724-7 (paperback)

Typeset by York House Typographic Ltd, Ealing W13 8NT
Printed and bound in Great Britain by Redwood Books, Trowbridge, Wiltshire

# Contents

# *Preface*

This is a book about business practices written by an educationalist. It consists of case studies of five very different businesses, and discussions arising from them about the relationship between business and education. The businesses considered are:

- Marks & Spencer, a renowned High Street retailer
- BP Chemicals, an industrial giant
- Fabricast, a small engineering firm
- Anglo Motors, a medium-sized car dealership

Finally, Castle Hill, part of a new Trust Hospital complex, is included because it, like schools, is entering into the challenges of a market situation.

The book aims to do four things. Firstly, it tries to bring each company to life for the reader, by relating the story of each one's development, and its present methods of working. Secondly, it asks what structures and practices are common to all organizations, and therefore may be suitable for adoption by schools. Thirdly, by identifying what, if anything, is unique to the enterprises in question, it attempts to defend schools against transfers which may be invalid and damaging. Finally, it asks whether the lessons are all one-way, and whether schools have something to teach other organizations.

The research method was simple, but, I hope, not simplistic. Initial choice and structuring was followed by reading the literature, job-shadowing, and then semi-structured interviews with key individuals, some identified for me, other identified by me through experience at the company. The visits were spaced over periods of time which ranged from two weeks to two months, with a regular, if gentle, updating from individuals within the companies about the latest developments.

Each company was approached with as open a mind as possible, though not with a blank one.

- Marks & Spencer was chosen because of its reputation for professionalism, and for the way it developed its staff.

- BP Chemicals was approached because of my need to see a large multinational company with an area of concern – chemicals – as far from education as possible.
- Fabricast was chosen because of its suitability as an example of a small but enterprising firm.
- Anglo Motors was chosen because of my desire to see an area of business famous (or infamous) for selling.
- Castle Hill was approached because of the need for comparability with another public service entering into the marketplace.

As it turned out, for the reasons given, but also through unexpected bonuses, the companies turned out to be excellent choices.

- Marks & Spencer raised questions regarding the transferability of practices to schools in terms of deciding on product range and maintaining product quality.
- BP Chemicals raised questions on the concept of quality.
- Fabricast highlighted the dilemmas of paternalism and organizational growth.
- Anglo Motors illustrated in quite profound ways the problems of organizational change.
- The NHS study raised questions of the role of the professional in a bureaucratized and accountable world.

The studies also enabled me to place schools within the larger picture *vis-à-vis* their role in a technologically developed society in the late twentieth century.

These were bonuses adding a richness to the investigations, which increased their depth, and made them both pleasurable and educational. I hope the reader finds the same.

# *Acknowledgements*

This book has depended heavily upon other people's goodwill and time: without them it would not have happened. There really have been too many people who have helped to list them all by name, but to all I say a large 'thank you'. I would, however, like to single out some for giving help above and beyond the call of duty. In particular, I would like to thank John Lloyd at Marks & Spencer, Tony Hunt at BP, Steve Hilton and Dave Langton at Fabricast, Roger at Anglo Motors, and Jeff Crawshaw at Castle Hill, as well as Malcolm Thompson who set up a number of the initial visits. To all I am indebted. I would also like to mention my colleagues at the University of Hull, in particular Derek Webster and Nigel Wright, who gave me advice, support and coffee at important moments. My thanks also go to the Editors of *Educational Studies* and *Aspects of Education*, for permission to utilize some material previously published in those journals. Last but not least, and as always, my thanks and love to Jill, for being Jill.

# Introduction

There seems little doubt that schools *do* have lessons to learn from the business world. Certainly, teachers' experiences of the management of education by western governments over the last few years have not inspired confidence in ministerial recommendations; so when politicians advocate that educationalists should adopt more businesslike practices, it is perhaps of little wonder that teachers are less than keen to pay them attention. Nevertheless, this really is a case of listening to the message, not the messenger. Indeed, the individual in education who is confident enough to assert that schools have nothing to learn from business and industry must know little about them. Even a nodding acquaintance with businesses makes one conscious of the host of functions which *all* organizations must perform. There can be little argument that schools, like other organizations, need to decide on what they should be doing, on recruiting and training the right people, on deciding who does what (see Handy and Aitken, 1986: 32–3 on this). Some non-educational organizations do these things extraordinarily well. Schools, then, would be missing an opportunity if they failed to look at how these excellent performers went about such tasks.

A further reason for looking at business and industry, however, lies in the fact that recent changes in legislation throughout the western world have meant that schools have had to become more businesslike. Taking their cue from businesses and industry, governments in the UK, the USA, Canada, Australia, New Zealand and beyond have employed three principles to underpin a series of dramatic changes in the way in which educationalists look at their institutions. These principles are:

- that to maintain their existence, schools must balance their books – their incomings must minimally equal their outgoings;
- that there must be a clear purchaser–provider split: the decision to use the institution must rest with the purchaser rather than the provider, and the purchaser must have the information and the finance to carry through that decision;
- finally, that the purchaser must have a choice between various providers in order to improve the quality of what is provided.

Thus, in the UK for example, devolved management to schools (known as LMS), open enrolment and the publication of results have all in their various ways been intended to force schools to plan in accordance with financial restraints, to listen to the customer and, increasingly, to advertise themselves. As the current 'businesslike' climate is not going to change for the foreseeable future, educationalists would be prudent to look for advice and help from a sector which has for long faced the stresses of the marketplace.

A third reason for examining this area lies in the constraining of perspective caused by working within only one kind of organization. Organizations which seek change, do so in part by hiring from outside. For, with the best will in the world, an individual immersed in one culture, whatever strengths derive from this experience, will have his or her concept of possibilities limited by it. If this goes for working within one institution, how much more will it be for individuals working within one *kind* of institution? No matter how convinced one may be that schools do some things differently, and that these differences need to be held on to, the danger in such a belief, with no real points of comparison, is that too much is retained. Long-cherished beliefs are not challenged; things that could be more efficient, effective, and acceptable are not scrutinized out of ignorance of the possibilities. Change does not take place. Even more dangerously, because too much is defended, those from outside the educational world who see the outdated and ineffective being championed may well assume that the rest is indefensible as well. In so doing, the baby gets thrown out with the bath water. Educationalists need to confront that which is different, they need to justify that which they think is indispensable.

So a final reason is that, by asking these questions, educationalists need to go back to first principles, and ask what schools *should* be doing. In so doing, they ask what is unique to education, and what needs to be nurtured, to be protected. Ultimately, then, this book suggests ways in which schools might improve their practice, but it also asks schools to think of what they should defend, what they might even export. They then cease to be junior partners in any study of organizations, a move is made beyond one-way transfers and a real dialogue begins.

Yet if there *are* transferabilities, there is also need for thought regarding the complicating factors which make simple and total transference a problematical matter. Any investigation of this area needs to be cautious on a number of issues. An initial one is for any tendency to assume that there is some such beast as 'business'. A second caution concerns the assumption that writers in this area adopt one coherent and unambiguous approach to their subject. Finally, a word of caution needs to be said about the suitability of such approaches: whilst they may perform similar functions at the most general level, to what extent do businesses have the same purposes as schools when it comes to their specific missions? The answers to all are neither simple nor straightforward. This does not mean that educationalists should simply ignore the area of business. But neither should they adopt an attitude of total acceptance. Any lessons for schools should be critically evaluated before adoption of their principles is considered. This is the purpose of this introductory chapter: to lay out some of the issues which need to be considered when each of the case studies is described.

## IS THERE A BEAST CALLED 'BUSINESS'?

There seems little doubt that there are dominant trends in theories about how businesses and industries operate, which may incline some to believe that there is a beast called 'business'. Thus, for example, a recent trend, which will be referred to throughout this book, and which is well described and explored by Gilbert *et al.* (1992), has been the movement from a 'Fordist' to a 'post-Fordist' style of industrial relationships, which has been largely dictated by changes in technology and the workplace. The Fordist approach was predicated upon assembly lines, mass production and mass consumption. Industrial relationships were then based upon the structures created by management and unions: strong central control, trade union negotiations, with many layers of management ensuring that implementation was carried out as the centre directed it.

From such beginnings, a very different model has arisen, based upon a different set of demands and realizations: the realization that motivation is more than just the administration of reward and punishment, but crucially involves strong individual involvement; that developments based around the information technology explosion mean that smaller production units are viable; that the consumer is less interested in the mass-produced, and more in the individualistic; that the workforce therefore has to be specialized and flexible; that the new technology allows for considerable surveil-lance without the need for intermediate layers of management. Post-Fordism, then, means the devolution of responsibility (though not necessarily power), the breakup of large companies into smaller, self-managing units, and a core of flexible, self-motivated workers, with others being de-skilled by technology, others being hired only if and when required.

These two very different models suggest dominant trends in the running of business and industry, which, as we shall see, may also have implications for schools. Nevertheless, one still needs caution in deriving lessons for schools, because, despite such movements, there may still be major differences between different kinds of businesses. Thus, at a superficial level at least, it is possible to identify three different kinds of businesses:

- service industries, such as banks, solicitors and health services, which really sell you nothing save themselves;
- commercial enterprises, such as retailers, which certainly sell tangible products but which produce nothing themselves;
- industrial enterprises which turn raw materials into finished or part-finished products.

Now, as they are doing different things, it shouldn't be too surprising if their management practices are different as well. Indeed it would seem sensible to assume this: they will probably not adopt the same practices to achieve different ends.

Moreover, any examination of companies suggests that even those in the same sector do not always operate for the same reasons. Some may place almost exclusive emphasis upon the maximization of profits, and will do everything within the law (and a little without) to achieve this end. Others may see their role as that of providing a quality service to customers, the achievement of profit being regarded as little more than the way to stay afloat. Others may be noted for the high priority they give to the consideration of their employees' welfare. Others may adopt a 'stakeholder' model, and attempt to balance all of these, and more. Finally, some may be very much a reflection of the chairperson, and have aspects which some would call decidedly unbusinesslike.

So one might be sensible in being cautious when politicians, books or people in business lump business and industrial organizations together. Most educationalists' experiences of their own sector would lead them to believe that such views were as wrong as those which described schools as clones of some master plan. Whilst there are similarities between schools, what also impresses is their variety. If businesses and industries are similarly diverse, won't it be dangerous for anyone to claim that schools can learn 'from business and industry' – as if there was a single model to be consulted?

## IS THERE ONE ACCEPTED APPROACH TO THE INVESTIGATION AND DESCRIPTION OF ORGANIZATIONS?

The simple answer to this is 'no'. This area of study is characterized by differences of viewpoint, and ambiguity of expression. There simply is no one accepted perspective from which to look at organizations. Now, there is little doubt that having a variety of ways of looking at them is valuable, for, as Morgan (1993) suggests, different perspectives can act as aids in the reframing of personal experience, heightening one's consciousness, one's understanding of this experience. The more perspectives, then, in one's armoury, the less likelihood there is of parochialism and insularity, the more likely one is to be able to resonate with other people's feelings, perceptions and understandings.

Nevertheless, there is a bewildering variety of perspectives, and they run under different names, and sometimes different meanings. There are, for instance, different *paradigms*, usually based upon the level of the organization at which one prefers to focus. Aldrich (1993), for instance, suggests that there are three such dominant paradigms at the present time – the *ecological* (which views the organization as one of many in the marketplace), the *institutional* (which views it as a social system of values for its participants) and the *interpretive* (which views it as a location for widely differing personal meanings). Reed (1989), on the other hand, in his description of managerial functions, describes them as located within (*a*) a *critical* perspective (concerned with the control function of subordinating labour to the demands of capital); (*b*) a *political* perspective (concerned with the reconciliation of conflict between interest groups within the organization); or (*c*) a *technical* perspective (concerned with the realization of instrumental objectives). Both the Aldrich and Reed paradigms have commonalities, but both have their distinctive orientations, which will affect their ultimate conclusions. Clearly, what level, and what factors within each level, you focus on will give you different perspectives of what is happening.

But not only are there different paradigms, there are also different *metaphors* for how organizations function. Handy (1985), for instance, describes organizational functioning in terms of four Greek gods:

- Zeus, the paternalist autocrat
- Apollo, the bureaucratic rationalist

- Athena, the problem-solving group-worker
- Dionysus, the anarchic individualist

Morgan (1986), on the other hand, describes eight different *images* of how and why an organization functions, which he describes as

- organizations as machines
- organizations as organisms
- organizations as brains
- organizations as cultures
- organizations as political systems
- organizations as psychic prisons
- organizations as flux and transformation
- organizations as instruments of domination

Such metaphors may be helpful in understanding what an organization is doing, or what its members are trying to make it do, but they are only metaphors. So, whilst they may help our understanding, they may also constrain our imaginations as to the possibilities of organizations.

Finally, and not surprisingly after what has just been described, there is little likelihood of agreement over appropriate *methodologies*. Here, a basic difference lies between objective, quantitative methods of investigation and subjective, qualitative ones. The former position argues that organizations can be viewed as objectively existing entities, which can be studied as they react and adapt to their environments, and, further, that when one comes to studying their internal workings, a similarly 'scientific' approach may be used. Griffiths (1957: 388), for instance, makes a powerful case for a 'hard' science of administrative behaviour when he argues:

> The great task of science has been to impose an order upon the universe. . . . This is the great task of theory in the field of educational administration. Within a set of principles, yet to be formulated, it will be possible to predict the behaviour of individuals within the organisation framework, and it will be possible to make decisions that will result in a more efficient and effective enterprise. Research will have more meaning because it will be directed towards the solution of problems, have clear definitions, and will contribute to the whole concept of administration.

A more qualitative and subjective position is taken by writers like Greenfield (in Greenfield and Ribbins, 1993), who argues that 'the organization' is a fiction, for it is no more than the sum of the individuals who work within it, with their own points of view, aspirations, hopes and fears. The possibility of objectively meaningful concepts, or the use of objective quantitative analysis of anything meaningful, in the organization is therefore a chimera, made political by the way in which those with power in the organization – normally the management – assert their own position as the one true and objective assessment of a situation, rather than, as it is, one particular, if dominant, view of things.

In such circumstances, Greenfield argues, the search for some timeless and value-free organizational meaning is bound to fail, and the best we can hope for is to provide others with our understandings and our meanings, and hope that these raise others' consciousness of the possibilities around them. In so doing, we all become Schon's (1983) 'reflective practitioners', being open to, and capable of, framing and reframing our experiences in the light of dialogue with others about their experiences.

Clearly, then, what you believe you *can* study will say a lot about *how* and *what* you go about studying. This last dispute in many ways characterizes much of my own perspective and methodology. However, whilst I accept many of Greenfield's thoughts on difference and partiality, it still seems to me important to keep in mind that there are *degrees* of subjectivity, in terms of understanding, and in terms of organizational interpretation. There is no need to draw the conclusion from the above that one opinion is as good as another. As Morgan (1993: 302) argues, it does seem that there are roughly three kinds of data available to the researcher, which have different levels of trustworthiness. A first, and most trustworthy level is that of the public 'facts' about the company: things like the historical data, the numbers of people within it and the financial details. Needless to say, whilst these 'facts' may be more trustworthy than others, they are nevertheless capable of falsification and misinterpretation.

A second level is that of the recording of what people inside and outside of the company say about it. Clearly, what they say need not be true (in any sense), but it does at least provide a record of what people think, and a rough map of the varieties of opinion about the company, even if the researcher then has problems of interpretation regarding what is said.

A final level is that of the researcher's own construction of what is going on. Underpinning this, as with level two findings, are all kinds of assumptions, acknowledged and unacknowledged, as well as individual differences in understanding levels one and two. Different researchers use different perspectives, metaphors and methodologies, for they may be trying to describe different aspects of the same organizations or different kinds of organization, or simply begin from different value bases. It therefore should not be too surprising to find that different authors find different purposes in the same kind of organization, and the same author finds similar purposes in different kinds of organization!

It will be apparent that none of these levels can be totally trustworthy, but a continual process of comparison, reflection and discussion with others over all three levels does provide a degree of protection against bias or inaccurate interpretation, even if they can never provide us with a final 'true' paradigm, perspective, metaphor or image.

## DO ORGANIZATIONS SHARE THE SAME PURPOSES?

It *is* possible to say that organizations share the same purposes, but the validity of such descriptions depends very much upon the *level* at which the organization is viewed. Thus, if a researcher goes into an organization and simply describes how different individuals feel about it, such an approach barely touches organizational purposes, except as individuals see them. This level is the 'interpretive' paradigm of Aldrich (1993) mentioned above, an approach which sees institutions as being no more than geographical locations for a wide variety of individual meanings. This kind of paradigm leaves the researcher to fill in what these individual meanings might be, what in total they might amount to. It allows for the possibility of very different value bases and purposes in organizations. No assumptions about purposes are initially made, no particular focus is insisted upon. Because of this, such an approach could be used in any kind of organization. Its problem, however, lies precisely in that, by focusing upon individuals, it may fail to see the wood for the trees – the central purpose or mission for which the organization exists.

Aldrich's next level, the 'institutional' paradigm, has many of the same advantages but the same kinds of problems. It suggests that we move beyond individual subjectivities to view the organization at least as a coherent system of values for its participants. However, like the previous paradigm, it imposes no particular kinds of purposes on how the researcher initially approaches the study, and thus allows the researcher to impute different value systems, different kinds of purposes, for the organization. So, like the 'interpretive' paradigms, it sets a level for the investigation, but doesn't suggest how we view that level. What it can't do, however, is provide a comparative analysis of different kinds of organizations, simply because it asks us to look at only one at a time. And if organizations do have different purposes, such comparisons can be very useful in bringing them out.

The problems are in many ways reversed when one comes to Aldrich's final level, the 'ecological' paradigm. Here, comparison between organizations is possible, but in a great deal of literature the focus of this comparison is preset, the organization to be viewed as one of many in the marketplace. This will not be a problem for a shop, a manufacturer or a commercial television station, for this focus accurately reflects their location and their purpose. But where it is possible to argue that an organization like a school has primary purposes different from, even antithetical to, market purposes, such a focus frames schools in a way which, at best, diverts their attention from educational to financial or managerial purposes, at worst perverts their mission statements.

Present policies in the UK, and across much of the western world, are designed to place schools in some kind of marketplace. However, if one of the major aims of this book is to see what can be borrowed from organizations located within a marketplace situation, another is precisely to reflect upon the validity of the transference of such assumptions to schools, rather than, as the adoption of an ecological paradigm normally does, making the assumption seem unproblematical. It is with such cautions that the case studies begin.

# Chapter 1

## Marks & Spencer: The Professional Company

### THE ORGANIZATION

I followed Jenny, the administration manager, around the store as she 'counted tills' – assessing whether the actual till receipts matched what was recorded. As we came down the stairs on to the shop floor, she reached into a box and put on a pair of glasses. I didn't understand. I'd never seen her wear glasses, and, anyway, these didn't look like personal glasses. As I continued to watch, she went from till to till, doing her job, wearing these glasses. My attempts to guess why she wore them took on bizarre, almost science fiction, overtones. Was there some light, harmful to the eyes if looked at too long, which came from these cash registers? Did the glasses magnify the notes so that they could be seen more easily and thereby prevent mistakes? Nothing so extra-ordinary. It was, Jenny explained later, a standard company precaution. There was always the outside possibility of an ammonia attack by thieves. Wearing glasses prevented such attacks causing damage to the eyes. So simple, so thoughtful, so thorough, and a good example of the professionalism at Marks & Spencer (M&S), where the attempt is made to think of virtually every eventuality and to counter it before it occurs. A good beginning for an explanation of why M&S is the largest and the most profitable retailer in the UK, with 303 stores and over 52,000 employees, a turnover for the year ending 31 March 1993 of £5.9 billion, a profit of £737 million, over fifteen million customers every week, and having the distinction of its Marble Arch store in London featuring annually in the *Guinness Book of Records* for taking more money per square foot than any other retailer in the world.

Indeed, for a company which spends practically nothing on advertising, it has in its century-long history established an almost astonishing reputation with the average shopper, who will tell you that he or she *knows* not only that M&S produces top-quality merchandise and that the service is both courteous and efficient, but that the way they treat their workforce is caring, thoughtful and generous. There is, it is believed, an affectionate paternalism at the top of the company which means that the staff are well treated, motivated and loyal. The end result of all of this is that if you want a company which you can trust, then M&S, so the general feeling goes, is probably your best bet.

How did the company get such an enviable reputation? This reputation is built, I believe, upon four interrelated factors. The first, *its business principles*, were developed out of the experiences of its founder, Michael Marks, and subsequent chairmen. The second, *the balance between centralization and decentralization*, is a crucial debate happening in most organizations at the present time. The third, *the development of the people within the organization*, stems in part from these business principles but also from an ethical commitment to people. The fourth, *the search for a meaning and application of quality*, is an outcome of the pursuit of the first three. It will be necessary, then, to examine all four in an understanding of the company, before moving on to investigate the possibilities of educational transferabilities.

## Business principles

An understanding of these is best gained by examining the history and development of the company policy over the years.

The story of the company begins in 1882 when the 19-year-old Michael Marks arrived in London from Bialystock, in Russian Poland. He quickly moved north to Leeds which already had a thriving Jewish community specializing in the clothing trade. One of his earliest meetings there was fortuitous in the extreme. As Alistair Dewhirst, chairman of I. J. Dewhirst Ltd, and still a supplier to Marks & Spencer, recounts:

> One day my grandfather was walking down Kirkgate when he was addressed by a stranger with the single word 'Barons'. My grandfather spoke to the man and quickly realised that he did not speak or understand English. With my grandfather, however, was his manager, who spoke a little Yiddish, and was able to talk to the man in that language. He discovered that he was a Polish refugee, who had come to Leeds looking for the firm of Barran Clothiers, whose generosity in giving work to refugees was known as far afield as Poland.
>
> My grandfather was fascinated by the stranger. He took him back to his warehouse, where he learned he was looking for work and had no money. He offered to lend him £5, and Michael Marks asked if he might use it to buy goods from the warehouse. My grandfather agreed, and as Michael Marks paid off the debt in instalments, he was allowed to make further purchases to the same amount. This was my grandfather's first contact with Michael Marks.
> (quoted in Tse, 1985: 14)

Beginning as a 'licensed hawker', a peddler, tramping the dales and villages of West Yorkshire, Michael Marks opened a stall in Leeds market in 1884, first on the open site, and then the covered site, and in so doing could now trade all week, irrespective of the weather. It was in the closed market that he developed the innovation of dividing his stall into two sections, one part for individually priced items over a penny, the other part for those all costing a penny. Above this part he hung a slogan, 'Don't Ask the Price, it's a Penny.' (A life-size model of such a stall can be found in the foyer of Head Office.) The practice became so popular that he quickly abandoned the more expensive items and sold just those at a penny. His business rapidly expanded, and he began to run other stalls as well. The simplicity for customer and stallholder alike of penny-only items was a major factor in his success. As everything was a penny, customers could self-select and self-serve, a considerable attraction to a working class whose real income increased by over 50 per cent between 1880 and 1900 but who preferred not to be embarrassed by constantly having to ask to view goods. Moreover, by the use of such a technique Marks's own business calculations were greatly streamlined, and allowed for easy expansion and co-ordination between his different stalls. Whilst clearly this policy has had to be modified over the years, the concept of *operational simplicity* has been stressed and re-stressed throughout the company's history – a notion which, on the negative side, prohibits the over-use of rules and procedures, and on the positive side, enlists the initiative of employees, and trusts and empowers them to make the right decisions without constant recourse to higher authority.

Crucially as well, this penny-only policy forced Marks to seek constantly for as wide a choice of goods as possible, and also to strive for the highest quality, which meant looking for the most efficient and highest quality suppliers, and for both he and they to accept very modest profit margins. This latter feature is a major principle of retailing at M&S today – one begins not by calculating what are the costs of producing a product, adding a profit margin and then retailing it to customers, but rather by determining what the customer can and will afford, and then finding ways of producing high-quality goods at that price. Marks & Spencer are not alone in this seeming back-to-front method of retailing. Henry Ford did the same thing. As Ford said:

> Our policy is to reduce the price, extend the operations, and improve the article. You will notice that the reduction of the price comes first. We have never considered any cost as fixed. Therefore we first reduce the price to the point where we believe more sales will result. Then we go ahead and try to make the price.
> (1923: 146)

Levitt put it succinctly when he said:

> His [Ford's] real genius was marketing. We think he was able to cut his selling price and therefore sell millions of $500 cars because his invention of the assembly line had reduced the costs. Actually he invented the assembly line because he had concluded that at $500 he could sell millions of cars. Mass production was the *result* not the cause of his low prices.
> (1960: 45–56).

By 1894, Michael Marks had established seven stalls, one shop and a warehouse for centralized distribution, and it was apparent that the business was rapidly becoming too large for one man. Marks approached Isaac Dewhirst with a view to a partnership, but Dewhirst's own business was sufficiently prosperous for him to refuse the offer. Instead he suggested as partner his cashier, Thomas Spencer, and on 28 September 1894 the firm of Marks & Spencer was founded. The partnership worked: by the time of Spencer's retirement in 1903, there were forty branches of the company. Two years later, however, Spencer died, and Marks, having to take up the reins again, became overburdened with the work, and died in 1907. There followed a period of turbulence and disagreement, with no one person taking charge overall, which was only settled when Michael Marks's son, Simon, became chairman in 1917 at the age of 28.

Simon Marks's tenure as chairman saw large changes in the company. The stalls gradually disappeared, and the shops became the dominant feature. Increased competition from other stores like F. W. Woolworth led to Marks visiting America in 1924 to improve his understanding of business practices. As he said:

> It was there that I learned many new things. I learned the value of more imposing, commodious premises, modern methods of administration and the statistical control of stocks in relation to sales. I learned that new accounting machines could help reduce the time to give the necessary information to hours instead of weeks . . . I learned the value of counter footage, that is, that each counter foot of space had to pay wages, rent, overhead

expenses, and earn a profit. There could be no blind spots on the counters in so far as goods are concerned. This meant a much more exhaustive study of the goods we were selling and the needs of the public. It meant that the staff who were operating with me had to be re-educated and retrained.
(Tse: 20–1)

Marks's visit convinced him that the company had to move away from being at the mercy of what the manufacturer, through the medium of the wholesaler, supplied it with. He realized that selling to the public probably gave the stores a better insight into what the public wanted than either the manufacturers or the wholesalers, provided of course that the retailer kept up-to-date and accurate records of sales. If, then, a retailer could place sufficiently large orders with a manufacturer, the retailer could actually begin to dictate to the manufacturer what it should produce. Whilst the 'nothing more than a penny' policy had to be abandoned through inflationary pressures, the new price limit of 5s (25p) still ensured that the company strove to improve quality where merchandise was available at that price, and, if it was not available, sought to find ways of bringing the goods within the price range without sacrificing quality.

What happened was that two things were eliminated. The first was, after much resistance, the wholesaler. The benefits were obvious. In an early example of this, M&S was able to buy stockings from Corah's at 1s (5p) per dozen less than through the wholesaler. This saving, though, was used not to reduce the price to the customer but instead, in consultation with Corah's, to find ways of improving the quality of the product. This example illustrates an important principle in Marks & Spencer's philosophy – that lower price is not necessarily beneficial to anyone: quality of goods is just as important. Lord Sieff, the next chairman after Simon Marks, argues that:

> The reduction in cost *was* passed on to the customer, but in the form of higher value for the same amount of money paid. We benefited because our reputation for quality was increased. Our suppliers benefited because they were now producing a superior article with better methods of production which they had not had to finance themselves. The customer benefited. And, last but not least, the workers benefited because fresh capital had gone into giving them better plant and improved working conditions.
> (1970: 151)

There are of course those who have questioned the advantage of such a policy. The wholesaler is the most obvious, but it is also argued that a manufacturer's dependence on M&S, because of the company's enormous buying power, not only gives M&S great influence over the manufacturer's policy, but also over the prices negotiated. There is an element of truth to this: where M&S ceases to be supplied by a company, that company may well have been so closely tied to M&S that it may have great difficulty finding new outlets, and may go under. That being said, it is also argued that M&S's loyalty to British clothing manufacturers has kept them in business when many others have failed.

The attention to reducing costs for the variety of benefits described above goes on today. Anyone visiting the backrooms of one of the M&S stores will be struck by the attention to little savings – like the ubiquitous paper stickers exhorting the individual to switch off unnecessary lights – small savings which build quickly into large ones and which benefit a large number of people.

The second elimination resulting from Michael Marks's visit to America was, through the concept of counter footage, the disappearance of those goods which did not sell well enough to justify their place in the store. This led, reversing earlier policy, to a reduction in the range of goods sold – hence to the elimination of seventeen of the company's stores between 1928 and 1932 as it sought to rationalize its selling policy.

A number of things followed. After initial loss of stores, numbers began to increase rapidly again simply because merchandise displayed was only that which was known to be what customers wanted; and when it failed to sell, it disappeared. Those goods that stayed were sold in large numbers, and larger orders were able to be placed with manufacturers, thus allowing Marks to do what he had planned for some time – to begin to turn the relationship between retailer and manufacturer round. More and more, M&S reached back and dictated to the manufacturer what the stores wanted, what price they wanted, and at what level of quality. It was the reason that so much of the company's stock (over 80 per cent) is produced in Britain – for the necessarily intimate relationship between manufacturer and retailer has necessitated a geographical proximity. It also goes some way to explaining why the company sells only one brand of goods – the St Michael brand – in all of its 303 stores. Having just one brand name – the brainchild of Simon Marks and Israel Sieff – means in practice that it is relatively simple to adopt a policy whereby goods are designed by the company, or jointly designed by the company and the manufacturer, to exacting specifications; and M&S employs over 350 technical staff to further this endeavour. Now whilst this one-brand policy means that the customer has a somewhat limited choice, in comparison with the variety of brands offered at other retail stores, this limitation to one brand does mean that more time and effort can be spent on ensuring that what goes out under the brand name is of consistently high quality and priced very reasonably. It also means that less advertising needs to be paid for – and this money can be used to advantage elsewhere, such as in the employment of the technical staff mentioned above.

Starting with Michael Marks, and progressing through the personalities of the succeeding chairmen, what M&S did was, as Drucker (1977: 86) points out, no less than a small revolution. For, by the use of the business principles outlined above, particularly the defining of standards and the reduction of costs to make them affordable by the average buyer, the company was involved in 'the subversion of the class structure of nineteenth-century England by making available to the working and lower middle classes goods of upper-class quality, at prices the working and lower-middle class customer could well afford'.

## Centralization and decentralization

A constant theme in the history of the management of M&S has been that of strong control from the centre. Certainly, a strong centre makes sense; a genuinely strong centre is necessary for the group to retain a sense of corporate identity; and to ensure continuity and communication between its various branches it is essential that they are talking the same language. Moreover, individual stores cannot be expected to work out between them the personnel requirements of the entire group, or to create interviewing techniques of a professional standard. The present company graduate application form, for instance, is a carefully researched document based upon analysis by experts in the field of the major factors M&S is seeking in its applicants, and of the manner in which it can be most efficiently and usefully evaluated; personnel managers are then in a position to know where to look on the form, and what to look for. This ensures that people are selected for the next stage on the basis of the same objective criteria, and not for any subjective personal preference.

Nevertheless, it is clear that a balance must be struck between maintaining an identifiable company policy on major issues and allowing individual store autonomy. In this respect, Marks & Spencer has begun to follow the post-Fordist tendencies described in the introduction. Whilst the company has continued to co-ordinate and standardize a large number of its operations, three of the more interesting developments at M&S over the last few years have been precisely in line with trends seen in many other businesses – a move away from centralist tendencies, the greater use of information technology and the increased motivation of, and placing of responsibility upon, the individual. Thus, the first development has been a devolution of responsibility through the regional grouping of stores. Seldom now do stores stand alone: they work in groups, with a senior management team overseeing a number of stores. This reduces the number of senior managers, but allows for closer links at the local level. A second movement has been at the store level, where the use of electronic stock inventory systems, such as the Food Stock Adjustment System, and the Textile Assisted Stock Replenishment system, both of which automatically reorder goods sold, are adjustable at store level, allowing those on the ground to make their input into the balance between goods on sale.

Finally, there has been a change in culture away from a paternalism in career development to one which places the responsibility and onus upon individuals to pursue their own careers. In many respects this parallels the movement in Conservative thought generally away from the paternalistic Toryism of the past, which with its *noblesse oblige* orientation accepted a responsibility for those below in return for their acceptance of its right to rule and command. Free marketeers stress much more the responsibility of the individual to carve out personal career paths, in the belief that this leads to greater freedom and motivation. The process also self-selects those most useful to the company. Under such a system, a company would no longer sponsor individuals, and in so doing perhaps sponsor the wrong ones; now the best would come to the top simply because they showed the capacity to do so. This is a tough, almost social Darwinist, conception of the survival of the fittest, and is a long way from the M&S's traditional paternalism. Nevertheless it is early days in its inception, and curiously, appears to be coming from the bottom up. As more junior ranks are encouraged by management, primarily through the appraisal system, to develop personal development plans, with the back-up and counselling of their line managers, increasingly the executive level is beginning to see this as an opportunity for them to reflect and consider their own career paths as well, rather than to leave this more to chance and the paternalism of the company. If the acceptance of a greater responsibility for one's career path becomes the norm, there will probably be another culture change within the company, and that will be towards a greater openness: for, paradoxically, personal development plans, undergirded by appraisal systems, encourage the individual to share his or her concerns and thoughts about the future, rather than keeping these under wraps, or simply leaving them to someone senior to deal with. However, such culture changes take time: it will be interesting to see whether this move towards decentralization becomes effective.

**The care and development of people**

Perhaps as renowned as the Marks & Spencer reputation for quality merchandise has been its reputation for looking after and developing its people. Will this be affected by the probable culture changes ahead? The probable answer is: not necessarily, for, if personal development plans are structured, and back-up in terms of time and money is provided for their realization, then M&S may achieve the best of both worlds: a workforce motivated to push their own careers forward, but also feeling that the company is still interested and supportive of them. Look at what Tse (1985: 118) said on this a few years ago:

> One would find almost inescapably the general pattern of feeling as something like this: that the company not only looks after the staff well, but, more importantly, the staff feel they are being treated as individuals; that they are given opportunities continuously to train and develop themselves; that management is on their side, not against and above them; and that they see very little gap between what top management preaches and what is being practised.

Certainly, there are some issues which need not be materially affected by the new culture. At the most public level, the company offers the best pay and benefits package of any major retailer in the UK, whilst employees also benefit from a non-contributory pension scheme. However, the impression of employee care continues as one moves behind the scenes. First impressions of the backrooms of the stores are uniformly impressive: as neat, well-equipped and clean as the shopping area. The toilets are spotless and well provisioned, the men's for instance normally containing after-shave, anti-perspirant, shaver talc, body spray and a variety of brushes. The eating area is carpeted, and looks and feels more like a well-provisioned restaurant than a store canteen. Stores have a consultant chiropodist and doctor or nurse, a dental inspection and education service, and used to have a hairdresser, though, as buying power and the capacity for choice by staff has increased, this service has decreased in popularity and is now being discontinued. Unusually enlightened in a company top-heavy with male board members is the practice of offering to all permanent female members of staff *and* wives of male employees the opportunity of having a cervical smear test and routine breast cancer screenings. Other little extras add to the loyalty of employees – such as the wedding gifts given to staff who get married after three or more years' service. Even little services not generally known by the public increase worker morale and commitment: the end of the store day is completed when customers have left with the sale of 'waste', which is anything but, to employees. This is the sale at considerably reduced prices to staff of foodstuffs which have reached their 'sell-by' date but which are still eminently eatable. This can lead to a considerable reduction in the food bills of staff, and it is of interest to note that other large stores tend to cut costs by selling off such produce to *customers*. Not so at M&S: it is a service greatly appreciated by staff: it was very noticeable to me on my visits that the management saw this as a perk for the staff, and I was (quite rightly) not invited to partake.

Marcus Sieff, chairman and chief executive from 1972 to 1983, wrote (1990: 55) that good human relations involves what he calls a 'moral attitude': 'the chief executive has a duty to treat his employees as he would like to be treated himself, to do as he would be done by.' He went on, however, to state (p. 59) that this is not the only motive at work. The provision of good facilities for workers 'make for a more pleasant, healthy and comfortable staff, who are that much better at their work; they look after the customer better, and, if you can add good service, to goods of high quality and value, more are sold and, as a result, profits increase.'

This description of employee care, plus the genuine commitment in terms of time and money that go to developing staff, is a good example of an apparent – but not necessarily correct – belief in a single dominating reason for effective human relations policies within businesses. Thus it could be believed *either* that caring for staff and encouraging their development are done out of altruistic or ethical motives, *or* that they are done because it is believed that such a policy actually favours company development. Sieff argued (1990: 60) that the two motives are not incompatible: 'Life is not about this motive as opposed to that, this objective in distinction to that one. . . . Reconciling and directing these motives and objectives is what enlightened management is about.'

A good example of this lies in the establishment of the staff restaurant in the 1930s by Israel Sieff and Simon Marks. Sieff (1970) recounts how he and Marks, in conversation with one of their staff, were informed by her that she would not be having a lunch break because she could not afford it. They both felt that, whilst the wages they were paying were very fair, there would still be counter staff who through wishing to save money would go without food at lunchtime, and the only way to resolve this was 'to provide a hot meal at a cost so low that an employee would have to recognize it as uneconomical not to pay for it and eat it' (p. 158). Such altruism undoubtedly had pay-offs for the company in terms of the motivation and morale, but that does not affect the original basis for the commitment, nor the fact that both altruistic and business motives ran side by side.

Having said this, whilst staff still have a favourable attitude towards the company, they do detect a harder, less paternalistic streak to its operations, particularly since the chairmanships of Lord Rayner and Sir Richard Greenbury, and associated, one might argue, with general post-Fordist tendencies. Some look back with regret to the loss of what they see as M&S's golden age. A number attribute this loss pure and simply to the recessions of the 1980s and early 1990s; others think that a change in attitude and culture is inevitable, and that it is in the long run healthy for the company to take a harder-headed look at its operations. Indeed, both points of view could be right: writers like Hartley (1993) argue that companies aiming to maintain profits in a harsher climate have employed post-Fordist changes precisely to maintain a competitive edge. This harder edge has been seen in the 1990s with heavy cuts in personnel at Head Office in London in 1991, as well as quite radical dismissals of management trainees. This has had its effects in quiet but possibly fundamental ways. Having contact with managers both before and after these cuts, it was apparent to me that morale was badly dented. Anthony (1977: 297) places such feelings in a wider context when he says of managerial commitment: 'It is destroyed as soon as the managers who were recruited partly to apply it in the control of their subordinates, begin to see it applied to themselves.' This seems to me to be a little too apocalyptic: but it does indicate the possible changes in perception of a company, at all levels, when the axe is wielded.

On top of such issues, there has also been a more general demand of employees at M&S to do more for the same amount of money, as the regionalization of the company and a considerable degree of de-layering around the country has taken place, mostly achieved by early retirement and natural wastage. Indeed, there are those in the company who believe that such losses will be to the company's detriment when the economy takes an upturn. Finally, some smaller stores have been closed, and this has not always gone down too well with the general public. I visited as a customer one such store in 1990 and saw at first hand the bitterness publicly displayed by staff being 'outplaced' (fired). The reputation of M&S as the 'caring company' was not enhanced in this small northern town.

Nevertheless, it is fair to say that there was *much* agonizing by Sir Richard Greenbury and his board over the Head Office redundancies, and it is still a sensitive subject (not least because many other companies were doing much the some thing but never got the publicity which M&S did). However, the two other major options – leaving the company with a structure no longer in keeping with its needs (and therefore with individuals in jobs which were not needed), or simply not bringing in new staff for several years until natural wastage had reduced numbers to acceptable levels (as Lord Sieff did in the 1950s), were not seen as viable options if the company wished to remain competitive and healthy. Moreover, M&S does normally do its very best for those it makes redundant. Those whose services were no longer wanted at Central Office were given considerable counselling and advice on planning new directions and on finding a new position with another company, or on the problems and possibilities of setting up their own companies. The strategy has worked rather well – the vast majority of those helped by it have already entered new employment. There seems no reason to doubt that such help was genuinely offered by a company doing better than most in a very difficult financial climate but still finding times hard. This seems to me to be an aspect of paternalism which it would be sad were M&S to lose: yet it is clear that the public and valuable perception of M&S's caring reputation, acquired over the years, has taken a real knock in a bruising era of free-market theory and practice.

Nevertheless, the vast majority of M&S employees who remain still regard the company as more caring than most, and one which is quite remarkable in the degree to which it develops its staff. Such development is not only beneficial to staff themselves, in that it stretches and finds out their potentialities, it is also clearly good for the organization to get the best out of its employees. Individual talents are spotted, abilities are strengthened, by means of a comprehensive and detailed staff development policy. A good example of this is the case of Lynn, the store detective. I spent a fascinating morning with Lynn as she showed me how she worked, and how the mind of the shoplifter worked as well. A basic strategy is the combating of the use of blind spots by the thieves, by the store detective's use of mirrors. 'Never, ever, let the suspect see you are looking at them,' Lynn told me. 'Never make eye contact. If you're looking the other way, they think you're not looking at them. But you can be using the mirrors installed around the store, and in the food section, you can use the glass doors on the frozen food compartments to see what they're up to.' Here, as elsewhere in the store, was a real professional at work, someone committed to and enjoying her job. And how did she come to be doing it? An ex-policewoman perhaps? Not a bit of it. She had started work at sixteen as a shop assistant at M&S, and had begun spotting the shoplifter almost from the word go. Whilst others would be concerned with getting the stock on the shelves, and making sure those packages with the nearest sell-by date were to the front, Lynn was spotting the half-open bag, the jacket only half done up, the furtive look round in a quiet corner. Within two years, she was taking an M&S training course, and before long her career was launched. I saw this time and time again – an ability by the company to spot talent in a particular area and bring it out.

This company strength must in large measure be attributed to the emphasis it gives to personnel work. Whilst many companies espouse a strong personnel philosophy, they may not carry it through into practice either because senior management does not really regard it as central to the success of the company, or because the function is seen as one performed exclusively by distinct personnel staff, or, and in addition to these, not enough people are trained and employed actually to do the work well. Where, on the other hand, you have a company which deliberately makes sure that its trainee managers do not specialize too early but are comfortable in all the major aspects of the company's activities, you stand a much better chance of alleviating or even eliminating these problems both at Central Office and in the stores. Not only does the commercial manager then understand personnel problems and is more able to resolve them, but, and as importantly, personnel managers are conversant with commercial problems and can understand the pressures and problems of that side of the business. It is, in fact, accepted good practice not only for the store and commercial managers to make tours of the sales areas on a regular basis each day, it is also the case for personnel managers as well. It is this day-to-day familiarity with the commercial side that gives the personnel manager his or her strength.

A crucial part of personnel work is in the development of staff. This consists firstly of the highlighting of deficiencies and weaknesses and their remediation by counselling, training courses or work attachments. Secondly, it trains the employee to increasingly higher levels of skills and competencies, it gives each one the opportunity to exercise these skills, and rewards upon adequate performance. This can be stressful, but for those who welcome rather than fear critiquing themselves, it is immensely challenging and exciting. This is all closely tied in with ongoing appraisal throughout the individual's career, where specific behavioural objectives are identified with one's appraiser, and then returned to jointly at some specified later date to determine whether these objectives have been reached.

Not all survive this process. The attrition rate is high with trainee managers, and whilst being selected by Marks & Spencer is as high an accolade as a young person in the retail trade can be given, the disappointment at not making the grade can be nearly as great. It is some consolation to know that, having been initially selected by the company and then given the training described above, rejected trainees can still look forward to a good career with another company. But having been initially selected by the best, there must always be the thought of what might have been. M&S goes to great pains to 'save' recruits, but its standards are high because it will settle only for the best. In this respect, the famed paternalism of the company does not come into consideration.

If managers make the grade, they will be of quite exceptional calibre. It will then be clear that the training of such self-critical, adaptable all-rounders make the transition to teamwork – an increasingly popular option in businesses – that much easier. Whilst every effort is made to remedy identifiable weaknesses in an individual's performance, it is recognized that individuals are not completely malleable superpeople; they have their idiosyncrasies, their strengths, their predilections. Far better, then, to construct teams with a mixed balance of personalities. As Belbin (1981), who wrote probably *the* seminal book on the subject, said:

> The useful people to have in teams are those who possess strengths or characteristics which serve a need without duplicating those already there. Teams are a question of balance. What is needed is not well-balanced individuals, but individuals who balance well with one another. In that way, human frailties can be underpinned and strengths used to full advantage.
> (p. 77)

The result of such an approach – the selection of the best people, the induction of them into the company philosophy, and their continual and career-long appraisal, development and training – is an unmistakable feeling when one deals with the company for any period of time of being in the hands of professionals. This was brought home when I became aware of the steps that John, the personnel manager, who had been responsible for structuring and monitoring my visit, had taken for the final two days of my placement, during which he was going to be away. He had from the beginning delegated the responsibility for the hour-by-hour planning of the placement to a trainee manager, Justine, so that if he were to be away, as was the case, someone was quite capable of taking over. Moreover, he had calculated, as a professional would, that after an initial orientation course I would be in a better position to judge the pace and direction of the final stages of my visit. Furthermore, he had arranged his own timetable so that on the afternoon before he went away he could spend time discussing with me the placement so far, and my thoughts on future directions. He then made the arrangements with Justine to structure my plans for the rest of my time there. This experience – of my being given large amounts of precious time for activities which could seemingly have little benefit to M&S itself – was typical rather than unique. Here was a job – me – assigned to a particular individual, and it was going to be dealt with in the same high-quality professional manner as any other assignment.

**The search for quality**

Marks & Spencer does not claim to sell the best quality products on the market: only that its products represent the best value for money at that price in the High Street. 'Quality' is, however, in many ways the byword of M&S, even more so than 'profit'. Profit has an enticing appeal for a businessperson, as the Sirens had for Odysseus and his men. But, also like the Sirens, too great an absorption can lead the unsuspecting to their doom. Achieving a profit is clearly a requirement of a business if it is to remain in existence, but it has never been conceived by the company as an objective to be pursued for its own sake. Profit, for M&S, comes from pursuing other goals, the first of which is probably the search for quality. As Drucker (1977: 89) puts it, 'Profit . . . is the result of doing things right, rather than the purpose of business activity'.

So doing things right – in terms of selling the right kind of product, ensuring a consistently high standard in manufacture and in service, and in promoting the development of individuals within the organization to further these aims – *results* in profit. Any attempt to turn the relationship round would almost certainly produce shorter-term perspectives, a lowering of standards and morale, and reduced profits. Quality, therefore, is a much more conscious aim.

Tse (1985) suggests that there are four possible concepts of quality, which broadly correspond to four stages of quality control development. The first, *quality control*, consists of establishing standards within a company, comparing the product with the standard, and then, when product does not meet these standards, taking action to correct this mismatch. M&S first reached this stage in a systematic way in 1935 by establishing a textile laboratory to test samples of merchandise. This ensured that quality was uniform and any faults were detected in the materials. This was fine as far as it went, but was little more than an attempt to control quality after the event. The next stage, *quality assurance*, reaches back into the process and attempts to eradicate defects all along the production process, so that there is much greater likelihood of the product being right the first time. M&S began to move to this stage when, in 1936, the Merchandise Development Department was set up, the technical staff employed by the company was greatly expanded and the company began to specify to manufacturers the quantity, quality and types of material to be used for its goods, as well as, in some cases, the method of manufacture. It was then in a much better position to locate problems, being much more intimately connected with the initial processes.

This was well illustrated for me when I observed the manager of one store dealing with an incident in which he spotted that the display sign above certain clothing items indicated that they were reduced but the individual garments themselves had not had their tickets changed. This initially looked to be the fault of the floor staff, and appeared to be compounded by the fact that they were off the floor on a coffee break. However, his first reaction was not to tear a strip off them but rather to work back systematically and attempt to trace the problem to its source. In fact it transpired that the fault lay as much with Central Office and the store office, as London had informed the store office only the night before of the change in price, and had sent insufficient copies of the price changes to the store. One of the office staff had then sent out the copies of the price changes but, because of insufficient numbers, these had not reached the particular floor staff involved. The manager informed Central Office of the problem, asking them to send sufficient copies on future occasions. Finally, he informed the office staff from then on to check the number of copies sent, in order to make sure that enough had come through. The issue was dealt with quickly, efficiently and thoroughly. Rather than merely asking the floor staff to change the individual tickets as soon as possible, steps were taken to ensure that a similar problem would not happen again by tracing the process back to its source and by instituting policies for subsequent occasions.

Whilst quality control, then, is essentially reactive in nature, quality assurance is much more proactive. However, it is still possible for quality assurance to be regarded as the responsibility of a department devoted exclusively to the pursuit of quality. *Total quality control*, then, is that stage at which the organization recognizes that all departments must be engaged in the pursuit of quality assurance. This objective is helped by all employees being conversant with the running and problems of all departments, and by a continued and reiterated commitment to the concept of quality. Both of these are standard company policy at M&S. From here it is a logical step to *company-wide quality control*, in which employees at all levels of the company, and in all departments, are asked to commit themselves and to participate in this continual search for better and better quality assurance. Whilst this undergirds M&S's general approach, it would be fair to say that specific mechanisms for implementing this approach, such as modified forms of the Japanese practice of quality circles, are still in their early stages.

## LESSONS FOR SCHOOLS?

### The cart before the horse?

It was mentioned earlier in this chapter that M&S does not begin by calculating the costs of producing a product, adding a profit margin and then retailing to customers, but begins instead by determining what the customer can and will afford, and then finding ways of producing high-quality goods at that price. For many retailers, this practice may seem back to front. The results indicate differently. In effect, what M&S has done is to set out a list of objectives for the business and then attempt to get as near to this list as possible. In so doing, it has raised its own expectations of what it can do, and has produced goods that are a byword in terms of value for money.

Schools, it could be argued, have gone through a tortuous process in this respect. The notion of aims and objectives has always been adhered to, if only in the sense that teachers can usually verbalize what they were trying to do. On the other hand, it took the writing of individuals such as Bobbit, Tyler and Bloom to make this process, for many, a planned proactive one, to the extent that the specification of objectives has become fairly standard curricular policy. Whilst there are plenty of arguments against a too-rigid adherence to such a notion (see, for instance, Eisner, 1985), the approach does have the undoubted merit of forcing individuals to place an educational vision in front of themselves before they enter the classroom. There may now, however, be an increasing danger that schools under LMS will be resource-driven, with schools determining the budget for a particular year and then tailoring activities to this budget. The danger with schools being resource-driven is that aspirations may be limited by the size of the budget. The example of M&S should enable schools to move once again more towards an objectives-driven approach – to the description of those goals they wish to achieve in that particular year and the devising of the means whereby they can achieve such goals within their limited financial constraints. Whilst clearly over-optimistic beliefs are as dangerous as limited vision, M&S is a good example of a company which believes that expectations which are raised are usually met successfully – with benefits for company, customer and employee. Raising expectations by beginning with a plan of what the aims for the year are, rather than simply by planning from budget limitations, is an essential exercise if quality in its many facets is to be raised in the school.

### The elimination of the poor sellers

One of the key developments in M&S policy followed the return of Simon Marks from America: his understanding of the importance of making each area of counter footage sell, and the ruthless elimination of those products which did not 'earn' their right to remain. This, it will be remembered, led to the reduction of the variety of goods sold by Marks & Spencer but, in a very short time, to a large improvement in its profitability.

From an educational point of view, the first problem is identifying what are the products which must justify their worth. A knee-jerk reaction would be to suggest elements of the school curriculum, but it is also possible to regard pupils and teaching methods as occupying the same position. All three must be examined.

*Teaching methods*

The issue of the elimination of teaching methods is deceptively simple. What could be more straightforward, it might be argued, than not using certain methods of teaching once they cease to be effective? However, a first problem is to define the axis along which teaching methods are to be judged. Are we talking about a numerical axis – individual versus group versus whole-class teaching methods? Or are we perhaps talking about an axis of social relations – teaching methods which espouse co-operative methods of work versus those which espouse competitive methods versus those which espouse purely individualistic methods? Finally, are we talking about an axis of style – the manner in which lessons are conducted – formal versus informal? It would be possible to have a teaching method which combined these axes in different ways, and thus rather complicates any suggestion of simple elimination.

Nevertheless, if one could precisely specify the axes of a teaching method, and then suggest its elimination because it failed to justify its worth, the problem still would not be solved. The elimination of consumer products from a store is generally based upon objectively defined and agreed criteria – this product has not sold $x$ amount in $y$ amount of time, and therefore it must go. Teaching methods are not so easy to dismiss, simply because the evaluation of their effectiveness is based not on objectively defined criteria but on personally held values. Individual teaching methods may be trying to achieve different things from group methods, and so their effectiveness is difficult if not impossible to compare; co-operative methods may be employed as much for perceived social needs as for any academic purpose, and for some people it may be acceptable to see a slight decline in academic performance if other social targets are reached. This is not to say that agreed purposes for a school cannot be reached, and therefore that teaching methods cannot be introduced or eliminated to achieve them, but there must be a recognition that this is based upon an initial adoption of certain educational values, which may be contestable. This element of contestability would seem to be part of the lifeblood of the educational system of a pluralistic democracy which need not figure so highly in the workings of a centrally defined company policy such as that of M&S. Therefore, before one can decide upon whether a teaching method is a 'poor seller' or not, one needs initially to be aware of what it is trying to do. A 'poor seller' to one observer may be a genuine success to another.

*Pupils*

Pupils, in a certain sense, 'compete' with others for a place at the school, and if they fail to satisfy behavioural or academic criteria it might be argued that they should forfeit their places. On *behavioural* criteria, it could be argued that they should forfeit their places because they disturb the learning of other children, reduce the quality of teacher input through so much time spent dealing with them and reduce the reputation of the school with parents. Whilst the Special Needs legislation in existence in the UK goes some way to alleviating these problems, it is a tortuous and protracted process, and damage to other children's learning and behaviour, and to the school's reputation, may already have occurred before the procedures are implemented.

On *academic* criteria, it could be argued that if one student holds back another, then it does neither of them any good to be in the same class, or indeed perhaps in the same school. Thus, if children show an aptitude for a certain kind of learning, it makes sense for them to go to a school catering for that kind of learning, rather than to one which is not suited to them. Moreover, the school with an eye to the wishes of parents will be aware that a major parental criterion for a 'good' school is one that promotes an environment and atmosphere conducive to good learning. The power of schools to reject or eject pupils who do not match up will be prized by those parents who wish to maintain this attitude. This is, I would suggest, one of the reasons why private schools and, to some extent, grammar schools, have done so well in the past.

It will be apparent that there is a link-up here between business thinking and streaming in schools or selection for different schools. Little thought is normally given by retailers to the fate of the goods rejected by the stores, but this has to be a major concern for the managers of state schools if they consider themselves as part of a national system of educational provision. Rejecting children with no thought to their future development is clearly possible if your school has responsibilities only to those children selected: this is, I think it is fair to say, the case of the private school. Where, on the other hand, the school is part of a system whose explicit function is to cater for *all* the nation's children, irrespective of wealth or ability, then eliminating the 'poor seller' should not be a viable option, as, by definition, all of the 'products' are to be 'sold'. It will be clear, then, that legislative routes that take schools down a road to pupil ejection and selection lead inexorably away from societal policies which cater for all abilities and backgrounds. Where no overall plan is made but children are picked up by competing institutions – competing in the first instance to fulfil their quota, but after that to accept the best and reject the rest – then some (inevitably the most difficult cases) will slip through the net. The simple translation of business practice here, I suggest, is not a viable one if the policy is to cater for an entire nation of children and not just those which 'sell' well.

## Curriculum

When the product to be 'sold' is the curriculum, the issues appear at first glance to be less thorny and problematical. Certainly, you are not going to hurt any curricular area's feelings if it is removed from the school timetable (though those practising it may not be too happy). If your policy is consumer-driven you may well feel that, within legal requirements, a return to some form of 'basic education' is all that is needed if parents demand this for their children. This could lead to the elimination of the likes of media studies, personal and social education, environmental awareness and peace education, and a concentration on such things as basic number work, more teaching of reading, and better spelling. It may indeed lead to the increased popularity of the school with some parents.

There are, however, larger issues to be raised. Whilst some may see the curriculum as a consumer product, dependent for its existence upon the tastes of the consumer, such a conception does not begin to address the larger issues to which a national system of education must address itself. Such a system must not only cater to the short-term consumer needs of the parent (and of the child) but also look to the future needs of that society, both in terms of the transmission of that nation's culture and also in terms of equipping the next generation with the skills to safeguard their, their country's and the world's future. Within such a context, an understanding of how the media represents (and misrepresents) reality may be an essential skill in the development of tomorrow's citizen; the ability to communicate adequately, to express and assert oneself will be essential personal and social skills which cannot be left to chance; an understanding of the impact of humanity and its technology on the environment will almost certainly be even more important in twenty years' time than it is today; and an appreciation of how conflicts, at the personal, national and international levels arise and how they can be dealt with would seem again an essential part of personal, social and citizenship development.

The school curricula, then, are areas of discussion and contestability – and education. Rather than simply responding to consumer demands, it may well be the wider duty of the school to listen to parents, but also to engage in debate and attempt to explain why such seemingly esoteric subjects gain a place. Some of this appears to be happening in business practices as well. Thus whilst Marks & Spencer has responded to consumer taste, it has at the same time attempted to educate the public to appreciate that lowering the price is not the only way of offering value for money. Improving the quality of the product may have as great or greater benefit. Further, whilst many companies still act as if they exist in a world of inexhaustible resources, on a planet with an everlasting ability to absorb pollutants, others are increasingly aware that they, like schools, exist in a wider society which calls on them to exercise responsibility in this larger domain. As we shall see in Chapter 3, they are urgently concerned with equipping themselves with the credentials which will, in the public's eye, give them a 'licence to operate'. Some companies have approached this by realizing that it is good business, or ethically more acceptable, to advertise that their aerosols contain no CFCs which are alleged to damage the ozone layer, or that their bleaches contain no chlorides liable to pollute the atmosphere, or that their tuna is caught in 'dolphin-friendly' nets. As with the issue of the care of staff discussed above, there is every reason to believe that such decisions are motivated by a combination of both ethical and profit concerns. Development of such societally and environmentally responsible perspectives includes the discontinuation of products which harm the environment even if they still sell well. This is clearly elimination not because of poor sales but because of other (ethical) concerns and the substitution of brands which may be more expensive and therefore less consumer-driven. M&S has had a fairly slow start in this area, and is still debating the issues. On the one hand all new company cars take unleaded petrol, and existing ones have been converted to take it. Further, its moves to reduce energy use and packaging are environmentally friendly, whilst also aiding profits. On the other hand, M&S's renowned standards for unblemished foods and for perfect food shape have left it equivocal as to the use of agrochemicals. Again, whilst M&S has instructed its apple suppliers not to spray with alar, they discontinued selling organic foods (introduced in 1989) in 1990, because they were not selling well enough.

The fact remains, though, that both schools and businesses are becoming aware that they are participants in a larger picture, and their vision of the pupil, the curriculum and the product have had to be adjusted to this vision. In some respects, the concept of counter footage which Simon Marks brought back from America may need to be adjusted to meet future conditions – and schools may well be leading in this.

**Controlling product development**

One of the major reasons Marks & Spencer has been so successful is that it has not been content to receive products determined by the manufacturer but has reached back into the productive process and specified what end-product it requires. In this way, not only does M&S bring consumer and producer closer together, and thereby effect a much more accurate match between wants and finished goods, it also maintains a much closer surveillance on the quality of the product from first conception to final product.

Again, definition of the meaning of the term 'product' is necessary at this time, and it can be interpreted in terms of both the pupil and the curriculum. Both definitions have their use.

*Pupils*

Reaching back into the child's life can mean reaching back in depth at any particular period, or it can mean reaching earlier and earlier back. Reaching back in depth means establishing stronger and stronger links in terms of homework, school visits, parental help, parent–teacher associations, evening workshops, extended trips – anything and everything which increases the understanding and communication between teacher, parent and pupil. This increase in depth must be started as early as possible. This could mean the kind of selection procedures discussed above. The same kind of arguments against them – of the responsibilities of state schools for educational provision for all children – however, still hold good. Nor can schools reach back into the family life and specify what should be done to or for the child during the pre-school years. However, it is obviously hugely advantageous to all parties concerned if communication exists between homes and schools from the very earliest ages. Not only do parents become aware of the expectations of the school for the child when it first enters the institution, and thereby allows them to have some idea of what the teacher will deem necessary for the child's effective performance in school, but it could also provide the school with an opportunity to educate the parent in techniques which will further necessary concepts, attitudes and skills. There is a large gap for parents in such training between the antenatal lessons they receive and their child's first induction into the nursery school (if this happens). There is still much room in the early years for the involvement of teachers in the identification of those children within the school's catchment area; initial contacts with the parents; the offering of advice; and running of workshops and contact groups where problems can be identified and talked through, and basic skills be introduced. In this way, schools can not only reach back in time to the ultimate improvement of the child but can also promote their own image and establish links which will increase the chances of parents registering their child at the school when the time comes. There is already competition between schools in this respect, with schools without nurseries adopting a 'rising-fours' policy to enable them to compete for initial entrance: much more remains to be done. Similarly, secondary schools are increasingly establishing strong links with their 'feeder' primary schools, not only to ease the pupil's transition, but also to strengthen the possibility of parents of primary school children choosing them in the first place.

*Curriculum*

Whilst controlling product development in terms of pupils would mean reaching back to engineer stronger links with the home and other schools, in curricular terms this would mean reaching back to the 'deep structure' of a subject area. Whilst at Marks & Spencer this reaching back is largely performed by the research and technical laboratories, and then the finished product is passed on to the stores, whose part of the process is to sell the product, such a division of labour is not possible in education. Here, whilst there are some who would like to see philosophy, content and pedagogy determined by specialist groups appointed by the Secretary of State, this cannot logically occur if the object is to achieve a genuinely high-quality product, for 'selling' a curricular product to a pupil necessarily involves a teacher's understanding of such deep structure. It is easy to spot individuals who do not really understand their subject. They are unable either to manipulate concepts to bring them to bear upon the way a discussion is proceeding at any particular time or to reinterpret such concepts to be understood by pupils of different orientation. The notion of simple curricular dissemination may be appealing to the contralist-minded, but it contradicts any serious desire for high-quality education. Such a desire would seem to demand a degree-level competence in a subject area at the very least. Such reaching back would then necessarily demand teachers to be involved in a dialogue about the correct approach to the understanding of their subject area, its content and the most effective means of its teaching. Such teachers would be no mere technicians, implementing directives, but would need to be highly competent professionals who were at least equal partners in attempts at defining philosophy, content or pedagogy. If, as Marks & Spencer found out, reaching back into the production process increases the quality and 'saleability' of the product, then the reaching back into the curriculum product would do the same thing, but, and differently from M&S, would necessitate the involvement at the highest technical level of those 'selling' the 'product' on the 'shop floor'.

**The development of staff**

The continued, structured and in-depth development of staff is one of the key features of Marks & Spencer's success, and one of the things that could and should be borrowed by schools for both staff and pupils. M&S spends a quite remarkable proportion of its budget on developing what it regards as its most valuable asset – its people. This involves a considerable investment, not only in terms of simple hard cash but also in terms of time and personnel. The fact that there are as many people behind the scenes as there are on the shop floor serving customers, speaks volumes for the importance attached to this. The fact that 4 per cent of an individual's week (1.75 hours) is spent on such development also speaks volumes. Whilst the company has throughout the last ten years increasingly cut back in most areas, this area has suffered no more than others. There is still the commitment to attracting the best recruits by offering to pay a salary more competitive than most other companies offer. There is still the commitment to select the best in terms of costly and lengthy interview procedures. There is still the opportunity for employees to go on a variety of courses which will further their development. Similarly, appraisal interviews are performed at a time and in a manner which places no pressure on the individual to return to the shop floor and serve the customers. Work attachments are still regarded as a crucial way of developing the all-round expertise of staff. It is then no accident that staff development and staff care tend to go together. When development procedures are followed in a professional manner, staff feel cared for and motivated.

In terms of the professional development of teachers a first move would be to recognize that first-class work is produced by first-rate motivated individuals, who are attracted by salaries equivalent to those in industry. A next move would be to implement the interview techniques used in business to ensure that individuals embark on a career in teaching for the right reasons – not because they can't think of anything else to do or because unemployment on the High Street has reduced prospects elsewhere. The time and money such interview techniques demand must also be provided for their use in the interviewing of qualified candidates seeking a new post. When one realizes that the appointment of a new headteacher can take less than a day, but that this process for a senior manager in business would normally take a number of days, with a variety of methods used to find the right candidate, it can be of little surprise that businesses who spend time and money getting it right at the beginning of a process spend much less time unpicking problems later on.

A third move would be the recognition of the need for career-long education for teachers, for government to act upon the recommendations of the James Committee twenty years ago when it suggested that *all* teachers should have the chance to enjoy a sabbatical term every seven, and in due course every five, years. Such sabbaticals would necessarily be supplemented and co-ordinated with regular appraisal interviews. These would not concentrate upon aspects of accountability, as politicians of most persuasions seem to view them at present. They would instead act as structures for identifying strengths and weaknesses, for expanding capabilities and for improving on problem areas. Such appraisals would not just be linked to such sabbaticals but, in a more continuous manner, would be linked to clearly designated courses, or placement schemes. A huge increase in financing would stem from the employment of extra staff to take the place of those on sabbaticals and training courses, and those actually engaged in appraisals. Finance would also have to be guaranteed for appraisal outcomes. If an appraisal indicated that a certain course of action was necessary to improve an individual's performance, then, unless very good reasons were forth-coming, the finance would have to be found to act upon such recommendations. There is nothing so destructive of credibility as promises for the financing of personal development being reneged upon. Nor must developmental activities be squeezed into playtimes or dinner hours, or after school or at weekends. They need to be recognized as part of a professional's development, and should therefore be dealt with within the professional's normal time. I personally am not sanguine about the introduction of many of these changes, but until they are introduced, until society values and funds the quality of its people in education, as Marks & Spencer values and funds its people, society will get the schools it deserves.

### Striving for professionalism and total quality control

Much of the above would fit in here. Professionalism is the first step on the road to total quality control in education. Society must recognize that schools need the right calibre of people to perform a really professional job, and they need the money, the resources and the training to keep developing their professionalism. It follows then that the professionalism of teachers is as much the responsibility of government and society as it is of schools, for schools must work within the financial framework government places upon them, and must live with the importance they attach to the role of schools. Further, it is by developing the professionalism of teachers that other contributors can be drawn into the educational circle and the system as a whole be improved. This is the route to total quality control.

Total quality control does not come through a myopic concentration upon attainment targets at 7, 11, 14 and 16. These should be the products of the system, not its objectives. Instead it comes by setting up the conditions for a high-quality delivery such that the attainment of these targets is a natural product of the system initiated. It is when individuals (any individuals in the organization) tackle any job with the same degree of professional thoroughness – because (*a*) they were selected because they are predisposed to do it that way, (*b*) they have been trained to do it that way, and (*c*) the culture and ethos they work in makes it natural for them to work that way – that attainment targets are passed as a matter of course, as outcomes of the system. M&S has already gone a long way in achieving such goals. The conception of such a system in education can be greatly helped by the example of the organizational techniques and attitudes discussed above.

## The end result: an enviable reputation

Marks & Spencer as a company is in the business of taking manufactured goods and selling them to the public. In pursuit of this, it has taken the conscious decision to advertise itself not by glossy full-page adverts or by minute-long commercials on television but by establishing a reputation for producing high-quality goods at very reasonable prices. Once such a reputation is established, the company has then set itself a yardstick which it must keep up to.

Whilst schools aren't retailers, there are those who would argue that there is a crude similarity in that adults do shop between them. Undoubtedly Marks & Spencer has the harder competition. There are stores selling similar materials who are only a few yards away. Parents do not have such luxury in choice of school. Unless they have ample time, and enough transport, their *real* choice – unlike the open choice theoretically on offer – will be severely limited to two to three schools at best. Even so, when, in 1993, the financial contribution to the school budget from the admission of each child (described officially as an 'age-weighted pupil unit') was worth from just over £1000 at the primary level to nearly £2500 at the higher secondary level, there is no room for complacency. Establishing a reputation is a long-term goal which considerably reduces this pressure. Its establishment stems from the implementation of the factors discussed above.

This analogy may, however, be ultimately unhelpful, for it diverts attention from a school's primary objectives. These should not be primarily about increasing pupil numbers or passing examinations, and any government policies which reinforce this pressure on schools are doing the schools, their pupils and society at large a disservice. Instead, a school committed to quality and professionalism should establish a reputation in the same manner as it passes exams or attainment targets – as a natural consequence of the activities it initiates and practises. In this respect the example of Marks & Spencer can be very helpful, for it is strong proof that a commitment to the long-term goals of high-quality products and the expensive and time-consuming development of staff is ultimately a highly satisfactory one for all concerned. It is a lesson that those more concerned with the short term and with apparent 'business lessons' for schools would do well to heed.

# Chapter 2

# BP Chemicals: A Leopard of Quality

## THE ORGANIZATION

The chemical industry is probably second only to the nuclear industry in the United Kingdom in terms of public dislike. Initial reactions tend to be concentrated on the negative trio of dangers, pollution and smells. So it was when the senior environmental adviser from the BP Chemicals Saltend works on the Humber estuary gave a talk to a class of second-year comprehensive pupils at a nearby school. As he tells it, he was poised with his felt tip and flipchart and asked the group for their thoughts on the BP site. 'Eyesore' was the first contribution, followed closely by 'big and ugly', 'dirty', health hazard', and 'gives off pollution'. On his asking for something positive to be said about the site, one pupil rather reluctantly answered 'I suppose it creates jobs'. Indeed it does – 1400 at the Saltend site alone, over 100,000 with the parent company worldwide. Nevertheless, initial reactions are still generally negative, perhaps because of its size and an inability to identify with it. This anonymity and lack of positive response are things that individuals at BP are intensely conscious of, and which they attempt to counter on a large scale. The post of senior *environmental* adviser is, for example, one which might appear to contribute little tangible to the output of the firm, and yet the budget and staff are not negligible. Furthermore, rather than seeing himself as being a member of a force which is essentially there for PR reasons, the present adviser views himself – and believes he was appointed – as one of a series of 'internal pressure groups', whose job is not only to improve BP's relationship with the community but also to enable BP it exist in harmony with its environment in the wider sense.

In the same vein, the company created the post of a community and communications manager with the function of dealing with the media, schools, local politicians, indeed anyone likely to have an acquaintance with BP which could have benefits for the company. One of the buzzphrases of the company at present is 'licence to operate', a term which indicates its acute awareness that its existence at any particular site is dependent on the goodwill of the locals. Whilst the prospect of Saltend closing down, and 1400 joining the dole queue, is one which disposes the local population to listen to

BP, the fact remains that they are likely to place the blame for any pollution into the air or the river at BP's door, simply because it has such a high profile in the area. If there is too much unfavourable publicity, building permission could be withheld; and if this happens, BPCI London will look to one of its other sites for the development. If a site doesn't change and grow, it usually dies, for BP is quite large enough to switch its production elsewhere. Individual sites, then, face competition not only from other companies but probably even more intensely from other company locations. So maintaining good relations with the local population, not only in terms of good publicity and education, but in terms of preserving the local environment, is at a premium. Self-interest and concern for environment and community coincide.

Public perceptions make this an uphill struggle. Yet, as more than one employee was to point out, negative public views of BP can be very unfair: the company has the money and the commitment to make sure that the chances of a spillage are fairly minute. Whilst it is the respective line manager's responsibility to make sure this does not happen, BP employs an entire team of health and safety officers led by a former government inspector, whose job is to monitor, analyse and police this area. Moreover, this health and safety team is viewed by the works in general as part of an overall policy of achieving a 'licence to operate'. Not only that, but having the tightest safety regulations is not only good for the plant in terms of public image, and good for the morale of employees, but also fits in with the notion that if the health and safety team is proactive, and prevents or discovers problems before they become big, its operations can actually add to the profitability of the company. Self-interest and altruism again coincide.

In fact, the whole of the BP site at Saltend conforms to British safety standard BS 5750 – a not inconsiderable achievement. The kind of accidents which are sometimes attributed to BP are probably more likely to be found at one of the smaller concerns on their eastern edge which do not have the resources to enforce BP's standards but which don't attract such public attention either. Indeed, whilst I was visiting, the local paper and radio were full of reports of people feeling nauseous one hot Sunday afternoon from what was believed to be a discharge from BP. The wind was certainly blowing in the right direction, and there *was* a consignment of a mercaptan (a sulphurous compound) on the site which, if released, smells fairly revolting. However, there was a large area between Saltend and the distressed individuals where no reports were made, no one on site smelt anything, and individuals at a distance from Saltend and in the wrong wind direction reported the smell. The odds were, then, very much on a discharge coming from elsewhere. Nevertheless, this story went out two days running in the local paper as a lead story, with the suggestion that BP had admitted it was 'their' smell – something I know to be a complete untruth. However, by implication, BP were involved in chemical procedures malpractice; and mud sticks.

Indeed, the three things which struck me when I first arrived contradict much of the public perceptions described above. The first was the absence of smell: the air seemed to be no better and no worse than anywhere else in the surrounding area, and the occasional whiff of the plant's main product – acetic acid (vinegar to the layman) – was not unduly unpleasant. The second thing was the intense security. There was an impressive central gatehouse barring the way in; numerous security guards; metal ratchet doorways passed through by means of electronic cards; and notices specifying what could and could not be brought on to the site. This was not, as I at first thought, to prevent industrial spies taking off with BPs chemical secrets. It was, instead, standard security to prevent the stupid, the ignorant or the uninvited from wandering round a plant which does have dangerous chemicals on it, and in which turning on the wrong valve, or striking lights or electric sparks in the wrong areas, could have far-reaching consequences. Talk of safety and security was then not just talk.

My third impression was not one of bigness and ugliness but one of impressiveness through the site's size, which is surprising but real. I was not the only one to appreciate it. A couple of days later I sat in on a meeting with a local film company who wanted to film the plant by night for precisely these reasons. I wouldn't want to see such plants dominating the English landscape, but I came to believe that they have their own individual attractions.

## BP history

The Saltend site, on the Humber estuary, has a history beginning in 1912, when it was little more than a jetty for an oil storage terminal. However, in 1924, due to the availability of adjacent land, an American called Herbert Green built a distillery there using imported cane molasses. This was bought in 1925 by the Distillers Company, and in the late 1920s other plants were built to produce a wide range of chemicals. When the Second World War came, the Ministry of Supply took over the running of the works to produce acetone, used in the manufacture of cordite, and 2-ethyl hexanol, used in the manufacture of plasticizers for aircraft cabling. During the 1950s the site continued to expand, mainly through joint ventures undertaken between Distillers and other companies. BP became associated with Saltend in 1967 when they acquired the chemicals interests of Distillers to form the basis of the present BP Chemicals. At the present time the annual capacity of the site is approximately 1.5 million tonnes from approximately forty different products.

The site, then, is large, but only a small part of an enormous company, which contains four separate arms: BP Chemicals, BP Exploration, BP Oil and Gas, and BP Nutrition – though Nutrition is increasingly seen as the weakest partner and may be sold off completely if the senior management judges conditions to be right. Each has its own Central Office, board and chairperson in London, and each reports to the main BP Board, also in London. The company is Britain's largest company, and, the third largest oil company in the world, behind Exxon and Shell. It was started in 1909 as the Anglo-Persian Oil Company by William Knox D'Arcy to operate his Persion oil concession, following the discovery the previous year of the first oilfield of any commercial significance. In 1914, with the outbreak of the First World War, the company further increased its credibility when the British Admiralty negotiated a long-term contract with the company for fuel for the Royal Navy. The British government also invested £2 million in the company, gaining two-thirds of the equity, an involvement which was only finally relinquished in 1987. After the First World War, refining and marketing activities expanded throughout Europe and Australia, Africa and the Near East, whilst exploration took the company into places like Canada, South America, Papua, East Africa and Europe, though the next major oil strike did not occur until 1938 in Kuwait. The end of the Second World War saw a process of reconstruction and reorganization, along with the company's first involvement in petrochemicals through a joint venture with the Distillers Company in 1947 in the formation of a joint company. The first plant, which produced ethylene from naphtha, was built at Grangemouth in Scotland in 1951, whilst a second complex was built at Baglan Bay in South Wales in 1961. In 1967, BP became the second largest chemical organization in the UK when it acquired the chemical interests of Distillers, and, as noted above, Saltend thus became a BP Chemicals plant.

Crude oil, however, remained the company's main interest, following the coming on stream of oil in Qatar in 1949, the massive expansion of oilfields in Iraq in 1951, major oil discoveries in 1958 in Nigeria, and new production interests in Abu Dhabi in 1962 and in Libya in 1966. It was also BP who discovered the Forties oil field in 1970, having begun developing the first commercial source of natural gas in the West Sole field five years earlier. The company expanded its interests to the USA when in 1968 it acquired east coast refining and marketing operations from Atlantic Richfield, and in 1970 entered an agreement with the Standard Oil Company of Ohio under which BP exchanged its Alaskan interests for shares in Standard.

The 1970s was a decade of shocks, firstly when a large number of BP's operations – particularly in the Middle East – were nationalized by the producer states. The second shock consisted of the two large oil price rises by the producers in 1973, and again in 1979/80. These difficulties were to some extent offset by the North Sea Forties field coming on stream in 1975, as well as BP's continued interest in Alaskan oil, through its involvement in Standard Oil. In 1978, it gained the majority interest in this company. In the same year, it also acquired Union Carbide and Monsanto chemicals and plastics interests in Europe.

The 1980s was a period of acquisition, of diversification and, towards the end of the decade, of divestment. Among its acquisitions, in 1986 BP took over Purina, the largest animal feed supplier in the USA. In 1988, it acquired Britoil, the UK oil and gas exploration and production company, thereby doubling its exploration acreage in the North Sea, and reinforcing its position as the largest oil and gas producer in the region. However, perhaps the most significant acquisition was the absorption of Standard Oil in 1987, and the forming of BP America. By the end of 1990, approximately 35 per cent of BP's fixed assets were in the USA. Another development in the late 1980s and 1990s has been the move by BP, as with other multinationals, into partnerships with countries like Russia, China, Indonesia and Korea in the development of plants and exploitation of resources in those countries.

However, as well as simple acquisition, events in the Middle East in the 1970s had led the managements of the major oil companies to rethink their long-term strategies, and they came to the view that future development would be more successful through the evolution of more diversified companies with a wider geographical spread of interests. Thus, to BP's major activities of petroleum and chemicals were added coal, minerals, nutrition, detergents and computer systems. There also, however, developed a somewhat contradictory impulse to concentrate upon what are considered to be the company's 'core' activities, at present identified as petroleum and chemicals. This has meant that a number of interests have been acquired and then disposed of. Thus, whilst BP developed its minerals interests relatively successfully throughout the 1980s, it sold most of this business to RTZ in 1989. Coal, a business started in the mid-1970s, was sold in 1989 and 1990. And BP's interests in computing, managed by a subsidiary, Sicon, were divested in early 1988.

Further shifts also included the launching in 1989 of a new corporate identity which featured a revised BP shield, with a stronger emphasis on the colour green. Internally, there have been major changes in terms of a co-ordinated policy through the determination of desired employee characteristics, as well as, within BP Chemicals itself, the pursuit of quality through the ideas of the business writer Philip Crosby. Both of these will be examined shortly.

This very simplified history is still somewhat tortuous, and is not easily accessible to the public. It seems fair to say that anyone wishing to find out about BP will have a reasonably difficult time making sense and continuity of the company's development. Whereas with a company like Marks & Spencer there are standard books (Rees, 1969; Tse, 1985) and a variety of memoirs by past chairmen, there is not the same wealth of readily available information regarding BP. This is not through any company coyness or secrecy. Rather the difference seems to lie in their different sizes and the nature of the two companies' development. Marks & Spencer has a much more focused occupation, with a clear, solid and continuous development, starting with Michael Marks and moving through its various chairmen in a way which built up its reputation for paternalism towards its workforce and quality in its merchandise. Indeed, to read the history of Marks & Spencer is, in many ways, to know the company. It is no wonder that the Rees book was, and the Tse book is, required reading for Marks & Spencer's managers. They have been the means of induction into a philosophy of management, a training into a business culture. BP is a rather different phenomenon. Being so diversified, being in so many fields and having gone through so many amalgamations, sheddings, expansions and changes in order to survive in its business fields, the company is precisely that – a leopard which perforce has changed its spots to stay alive in the world in which it lives.

## Employees and O-P-E-N behaviours

This is a descriptive statement, not an evaluative one. It does not mean that BP lacks an identity: people who work at BP are BP men and women almost as much as people at M&S are M&S people. BP people take pride in the company's size and strength. They know that BP is in the big league of companies, and there is something personally expanding about being able to talk of your company having interests not only in London and Antwerp but in Jakarta and Alaska as well. BP employees are also well aware that the BP administration is attempting to gear an enormous company to a post-Fordist agenda, at least in part by gearing the company to being more adaptable. With tougher competition, the globalization of markets, increased technological innovation and rising customer expectations, the belief is that companies which refuse to adapt will be overtaken by their competitors. The managements both of the Chemicals division and of the group as a whole have therefore developed initiatives which they feel are essential to survival. In terms of external policy, this is partly the reason for the decision in the 1980s for movement from diversification to divestment of the company's assets. In terms of internal policy, there have also been major initiatives. The first came with the advent of Robert Horton, the former group chairman, who introduced a picture of the kind of people he felt BP would need if they were, as he wanted them to become, the number one company in the world, overtaking the likes of Shell and Exxon. Horton was ousted in a boardroom coup in 1992, and with it expired immediate aspirations to be in the Shell and Exxon league. Nevertheless, his vision of the necessity of adaptability, of a continued personal development and training, has become even more central to the game plan of the BP management. It is based in what are called the 'essential behaviours' of a company employee. These behaviours summarize what the management believes to be the required changes in the way in which BP employees need to think and behave if BP is to survive and prosper. These behaviours are expressed through the acronym O-P-E-N.

'O' stands for 'Open thinking'. 'Open thinkers' are seen as those who challenge traditional approaches within the company and who come up with new ideas. They must also have the ability to see the broad policy implications of an action or decision, rather than just seeing the details of immediate repercussions.

'P' stands for 'Personal impact'. Those with personal impact are skilled at an interpersonal level. They will know how others are likely to react to their suggestions, they will be concerned about their impact, but they will also show self-confidence and a bias for action.

'E' stands for 'Empowering'. The ability to empower is another interpersonal skill, for it helps others to develop and lead when those others are best placed to make the decisions. 'Empowering' is therefore concerned with motivating, with building success through teamwork, and with assigning authority to the right person.

'N' stands for 'Networking'. This again is seen as an interpersonal quality which is shown when someone displays skills in sharing ideas with others and influences them.

These behaviours are cultivated through a variety of means, but probably the most influential manner is through Performance Appraisal, a process which is carried out for all BP employees. This is a process whereby individuals within the company reflect on what they have done, evaluate this performance, and then plan what they can improve, what they can initiate, within their jobs in the next twelve months. Whilst some may see this as a covert form of accountability to the company (which it clearly can be used for), it can equally validly be a helpful and profitable means for individuals to talk of their aspirations, to improve communications between themselves and their superiors, to negotiate a more enjoyable and profitable relationship with the company. Whilst the first stage of this appraisal process is a joint agreement between appraisee and team leader concerning the individual's objectives and targets for the coming year, the appraisees are strongly encouraged to take the initiative in setting these objectives and assessing themselves. One of the appraisal forms is a specific checklist of essential behaviours, and the individual is asked to draw up a Personal Improvement and Development Plan (a PDP), which highlights these desired behaviours. The management at BP, then, is cultivating in a very specific and structured way the kinds of individuals it feels BP will need if it is to survive in the marketplace of tomorrow.

Part of this 'essential behaviours' initiative stems from the company's straightforward concern with staying competitive. Part of it also stems from finding out what employees want from the company, and what they think of it. These two reasons are to some extent connected. This stems from the belief that an energized and enthusiastic workforce is the foundation for a successful company, and that it is therefore essential that BP finds out what its workforce thinks of it as a company. To this end, in 1991, BP employed the Survey Unit of the London Business School Centre for Organisational Research. One in five employees was chosen at random from all parts of the company and asked to complete a questionnaire. The results suggested that most employees were proud to work for BP: they saw it as a company showing concern for suppliers, customers, shareholders, the community and the environment: in short, a company with integrity. BP was also seen as having a clear strategy, but as having major weaknesses in terms of (*a*) poor communication with employees, (*b*) complex, wasteful and bureaucratic internal organization and (*c*) poor morale through a neglect of individual career development. In terms used previously, BP was perceived as being more Fordist than post-Fordist.

These weaknesses were subsequently addressed. The first, poor communication, was tackled by a conscious management effort to convey to employees what its essential aims were. To this end, materials were displayed within the site indicating what the company objectives were, both in terms of type and quality of product, and quality of staff. The determination of desired 'essential behaviours' clearly comes into this strategy, as does the entire process of Performance Appraisal. The second weakness, wasteful bureaucracy, was attacked by a reduction in the layers of management, though clearly not all welcomed this process. Implementation of the 'quality' concept mentioned above also helped this process, for this emphasis urged staff to point out problems and suggest ways of dealing with them. More will be said on this later. The third complaint, the neglect of personal career development, was countered by such measures as the more open advertising of jobs within the company. Up until then, there had been a 'grapevine' of information about these, but not all had been privy to it. With more open advertising, and thus their greater awareness of what was on offer, it was hoped that individuals would now feel that they were more in control of their development. Further, the 'essential behaviours' approach – indeed the entire Performance Appraisal process – was designed to make employees more aware of what the company was looking for in them, and thereby provided them with information to plan their own development. This emphasis on individuals' responsibility for their development is a current policy in the company – fitting well with the kind of person described by the O-P-E-N categories of the essential behaviours.

Similar surveys were carried out in 1992 and 1993, and indicated, not surprisingly, that things had improved slightly, but there were still problems in much the same areas. One initially paradoxical finding was that employees wanted both greater delegation *and* better leadership. I say initially paradoxical, because there is in fact a synergy between the two: more delegation invites more people to take on leadership functions. In many ways, they are getting it, whether they like it or not. When I began this study in 1991, BP Saltend had 2000 employees: since then the workforce has been reduced by 30 per cent, and five out of nine tiers of management have been taken out. This has meant less bureaucracy, more hands-on management, more responsibility. It has also meant considerable redundancy, and the kinds of post-Fordist tensions and insecurities described in the M&S chapter.

BP's O-P-E-N categories sit well with these changes. BP employees, it is hoped, will not sit back and accept existing structures and practices but will increasingly question them and suggest better ways of dealing with situations. Hierarchies, then, can be impediments; effectiveness demands groups of people of different levels not afraid to voice their concerns. Ideas then must come from the ground floor up as much as from the top floor down. BP is therefore attempting to create a culture which, at all levels, develops the individual who can input meaningfully into the organization's working, and, because of the acceptance of lower levels' inputs, will want to do so.


### The 'quality' initiative

This culture, it is claimed, is further enriched by one more theoretical input – that of the 'quality' dimension, articulated for BP Chemicals originally by the American business thinker Philip Crosby. The concept of quality has become increasingly influential in business thinking over the last decade, and is invariably connected with the notion of satisfying the customer. If the customer is satisfied, he or she comes back, the company stays profitable, and individuals within the company retain their jobs. So the production of quality must involve understanding customer needs, and bringing about lasting improvements in the service and products provided to them – improving the quality of the company all round. However, as defined by Crosby (1979: 15), 'quality' does not refer to 'goodness', or some degree of excellence, for it is argued that such definitions are woolly and vague. Instead, 'quality' means *conformance to requirements* – giving the customers what they want. If a product satisfies the customer, then that is a quality product. Many may object to such a seeming restriction and possible diminution in the power of the word 'quality', but, Crosby argues, if the bottom line is continuing to sell goods and services, the only way of ensuring this is by providing customers with what they want. Thus quality is defined in such a way as best enhances the chances of the survival of the company. 'Quality' then entails:

- finding out what requirements the customer has, and meeting them exactly;
- keeping in close communication with the customer, so that desired changes can be acted upon quickly;
- in so doing, keeping one step ahead of the customer and the competition by anticipating future needs and requirements.

Such an approach might well point some to the belief that 'the customer knows best'. Yet, even at the business level, this is a dubious proposition. Is it *always* the case that the customer knows best? One of the principal developments at BP has been a movement beyond this piece of simplicity to an understanding that 'conformance to requirements' entails the development of relationships of trust and honesty in which it is not only possible but necessary for the company to educate the customer beyond what he or she wants to what he or she needs. This will entail in some cases selling a less expensive product, in other cases a more expensive one, in a very few none at all. But it is now generally accepted at BP that 'conformance to requirements' does not mean that the customer knows best; rather, it means that a relationship has to be developed, in which real understanding by both parties takes place. It is a concept which will be picked up again and again in this book.

The achievement of these quality products is not produced merely by an extremely efficient appraisal, inspection, or quality control method, for all this does is to sort out the acceptable from the non-acceptable after the event; and, by the time unacceptable production is detected, the process has already taken place. Much better, then, is a system geared to *prevention* of lapses in quality. In so doing, the company cuts down on wasted effort and money, and is then in a much better position to guarantee performance to the customer.

But then, one may ask, what is the acceptable performance standard? At what level can one say that performance has reached a satisfactory level? The answer is simple, but, for some, startling: the standard must be one of *zero defects* – of striving to get performance right first time and every time. The logic behind this is also simple, using a slippery slope kind of argument: the acceptance of anything less than zero defects inevitably leads to work, and attitudes to it, becoming sloppy. Only by adopting a 'zero defects' approach, it is argued, do individuals keep themselves up to the mark. It may be very difficult, even impossible to reach such standards, but it is only by striving for them that a company ensures that it provides a sufficiently acceptable service to keep its customers.

The final piece in this approach – what BP Chemicals calls the fourth absolute of quality – is how one measures this quality performance. This – and again startlingly for some – has nothing to do with indices of performance but is called *the price of non-conformance*. The logic again is fairly simple: rather than trying to calculate what it costs to do something right, calculate what it costs to do it wrong. Whilst this can be difficult to do, it is claimed that it is possible to gain a fair indicator of such costs in money terms. The example which is given in one BP training manual is that of an office with a photocopier but with no collator. Whilst it will clearly cost money to buy a collator (the 'price of conformance'), the hidden price – the price of non-conformance – will almost certainly turn out to be higher. This is because, whenever collated documents are required, someone will have to spend time doing this, and their time is money spent by the company. Further, it will delay and impede the work of other people in doing *their* work, and this is time and money again. If someone is paid £5 per hour, and they spend only two hours each week collating, that is £520 per year – *before* we start to calculate the cost of delaying work by others. The price of non-conformance might take us well into the thousands of pounds per year. On the other hand, once a collator is bought, the price of non-conformance disappears and the overall cost of quality falls.

The pursuit of quality is seen as necessarily being the concern of all levels within the company, and of all branches, not just the quality department or the senior management. The philosophy explicitly recognizes that the ability to spot a problem, and to solve it, is as likely to come from those actually doing the work as from those supervising or dictating policy. It recognizes the importance of motivating the shop floor worker. To this effect, BP has its own version of the Japanese quality circles – a structure specifically designed to use this shop floor expertise. Having said this, it was not clear that this philosophy had been entirely embraced by the rank and file at BP. It clearly behoves the management to take this philosophy on board, and in many cases this is done with enthusiasm. However, there were mutterings from the ranks of 'Why should I do the company a favour for nothing? If they want my ideas, they should pay me.' Further, there was something problematic about the glossy materials used by the company to describe and sell this venture to the workforce with 'key learning points' like 'A Quality company is a great company to be in – Quality is fun . . '. Appealing perhaps to self-interest – that a quality company is a profitable company, and a profitable company is one where you are more likely to keep your job – may well have some mileage, but BP is not alone in shedding jobs during recessions, in de-layering or in pursuing a policy of divestment when seen as strategically necessary by senior management. Such measures may be perceived as necessary by BP management, but they send shock waves through the workforce, and indicate to them that even the most quality-conscious workforce is not necessarily secure in its employment. In such circumstances, scepticism is understandable and perhaps even inevitable. Whilst employment is considerably more secure in a company which produces first-rate rather than second-rate goods, there is still no guarantee of employment. There is here a tension which will never go away, and this is another reason why BP is a leopard changing its spots – not only does it need to adapt to outside conditions, it also needs to motivate its workforce, and, like many others, it has over the years produced a variety of campaigns to do precisely this. Whilst one of the company's small booklets announced in 1991 that 'training in Total Quality will become a permanent part of BPCI', by 1993 the 'quality' campaign was already receiving a lower, if more effective, profile.

**The stakeholder concept**

The quality campaign, then, is a project by BP Chemicals, and is part of a larger vision for the company, but the same kinds of ideas underpin the workings of the other companies within the parent company, and of the parent company itself. Robert Horton, the previous company chairman, declared in a summary of his vision:

> BP is a family of businesses principally in oil and gas exploration and production, refining and marketing, chemicals and nutrition. In everything we do we are committed to creating wealth, always with integrity, to reward the stakeholders in BP – our shareholders, our employees, our customers and suppliers and the community.
>
> We believe in continually developing a style and climate which liberates the talents, enthusiasm and commitment of all our people. We can then respond positively to the increasing pace of change in a rapid and flexible way to achieve real competitive advantage.

Horton then went on to describe the values to which he feels BP needs to be committed and which underpin his vision. These have not changed with the advent of the new chairman, David Simon, and centrally revolve around commitment to the *stakeholders* in the company. As these indicate the major means and aims seen for the company, it is important to examine these in a little detail. One group of stakeholders are the *employees*, who, it is stated, should be dealt with on the basis of trust, non-discrimination, personal development, teamwork and a balance between work and home. Another group of stakeholders are the *customers* who, because they have a different relationship with the company, should be dealt with in terms of integrity, fairness, quality and customer satisfaction.

A third group, the *suppliers*, should be dealt with in terms of mutual benefit, and being provided with a service with which BP as a supplier itself would be pleased. A further, and particularly interesting, stakeholder group is seen as the *community*, who should be dealt with in terms of responsible citizenship, safety, environmental consciousness, community involvement and contribution, abiding by law and ethics.

Central to this vision are the *shareholders*, and, it is argued, it is only through the kind of ethical commitment to the other stakeholders described above that the shareholders will benefit financially.

'Stakeholder' management, then, explicitly recognizes that a business has a number of different bodies to answer to, that a pursuit of profit cannot be the sole value, that companies have responsibilities beyond simple economic considerations. Now it must be stated that the different stakeholders will not have equal influence or power; as Abrahamsson (1993: 203) points out, the 'mandators' (those who provide the capital) will almost inevitably have more say than any other interested parties. This will be recognized in law, if only because they take more of the financial risks. Nevertheless, by stating their commitment to stakeholder management, companies like BP are acknowledging the complexity of the world in which they operate, and also of the numerous obligations generated thereby. In so doing, then, the management at BP is claiming that BP is increasingly an organization that recognizes the interdependency of the company and its varied environments.

To these concepts Simon had added two more. One is the target of '1-2-5' – one billion in debt payed back per annum, 2 billion in profit and 5 billion capital investment. The other is what he calls the pre-eminence of 'PRT' – Profit, Reputation and Teamwork. The former concept says something about Simon's personal mark, which is for a greater concentration on the measurement, management and control of finance at all levels of the company. This is a reflection of the fact that BP had dropped from a middle-rank player on the *Financial Times* list of the top hundred companies to somewhere near the bottom before he took office: it is now back somewhere near the middle. The latter concept, though, re-states much of what has been said above regarding the need for profitability, the need for good practice, the need for a licence to operate. Many might say that such interdependency and multiple commitments bear a striking resemblance to the varied interested bodies who claim to be stakeholders in education. It therefore seems appropriate to move to an examination of possible transferabilities.

## LESSONS FOR SCHOOLS?

### 'Licence to operate'

It was noted that BP Chemicals has gone to great lengths to achieve a 'licence to operate'. Whilst this has no formal status, it has a value in that it directs attention towards the kinds of decisions, behaviours and actions which ensure that the local population finds the presence of a BP site acceptable. This, as indicated, is no simple matter. It may require a degree of public education in what the company is doing, but this is not nearly sufficient: education by companies can all too easily be perceived as a smokescreen and propaganda. To ensure the success of such messages, the company needs to be committed to a process of stringent self-examination, and then an openness to external examination – moves which, as we shall see in Chapter 4, Anglo Motors has tried to make. Only in these ways – by getting your house in order and then by allowing the public to see this – can you convince others of your intent and actions. BP Chemicals at Saltend does in fact get visits from other neighbouring companies, who have also felt this need to acquire a licence to operate but who are genuinely surprised when they find that the site really is as open as it says it is.

It is of interest and value to consider whether the pursuit of such a licence to operate is conditioned as much by other-directed values such as an ethical belief in giving good quality and service because the customer is paying for this, or by values of self-preservation: if we don't, we go out of business. As with M&S's commitment to staff care, it is probably a mixture of both self-interest and altruism. However, whichever reason is paramount amongst BP employees, the concept of a licence to operate is very clearly a lesson that schools could increasingly take on board. The notion of an operating licence needs to be writ large in any school, whether this is because of its commitment to professionalism and service or whether legislation has put schools into a competitive situation with other schools in which their existence will hang upon maintaining a stream of entrants, which will mean communicating with and educating parents in what the school is trying to do. For both professional and pragmatic reasons, a 'licence to operate' will need to become a key concept in the thinking of all teachers.

### Open personalities, appraisals and Personal Development Plans

It will be remembered that the idea of the 'O-P-E-N' personality was developed to conceptualize what kind of person BP would need in the twenty-first century. Individuals are to be selected and encouraged to develop a path which is self-directing and self-motivated. To this end, the company encourages the individual to develop a 'Personal Development Plan': the individual plans his or her own development and translates this into action.

Whilst an initial reaction is to say that BP is promoting a considerable degree of autonomy in its managers, it has to be said that this would appear to be only second-order autonomy, dictated by a post-Fordist agenda. Had a higher degree of direction been seen as necessary to the development of the company, then this would probably have been encouraged instead. Further, only part of the cluster of desired personality characteristics is necessarily to do with greater autonomy – certainly 'networking' could involve a considerable diminution in the ability to pursue purely personal goals. The tension, then, between the needs of individuals to determine their own development and the need for an organization to develop individuals who behave and perform in a way which benefits the organization, is a problem which will always exist. Having said this, it is virtually impossible to conceive of working within an organization which did *not* have an effect upon personality development in one way or another. Kohn's (1977) research, for instance, suggests that the very act of working within an organizational structure is a more influential determinant on male values than are race, region, religion and nationality *added together*. This is because the very nature of the work – whether it is directed or self-directed – deeply affects personal attitudes to conformity and non-conformity, not only in organizational but in family and societal contexts as well. As Kohn says (p. 190), 'Occupational experience helps structure men's view, not only of the occupational world, but of social reality in general'.

BP is moving beyond relying upon mere organizational effect, towards drawing up in a very proactive sense the company's 'desired behaviours' in its employees, then attempting to create organizational structures which facilitate the development of these personalities. Many will be happy with the development of behaviours described by BP – open thinking, personal impact, empowerment and an ability to network – and might think that such development is a laudable objective for education. However, it is possible to argue that whilst such characteristics are those most suitable for a company in business, this is not necessarily all that a school needs to do. Whilst a school will need to encourage some characteristics commensurate with an entrepreneurial personality, there will be others which are not strongly stressed within BP's O-P-E-N personality. These might include the development of such qualities as 'care', 'self-sacrifice', and 'charity' to a much greater extent than a market conception would want to allow.

Moreover, it is also a matter of debate whether encouraging the development of similar characteristics in individuals will succeed in making the company more successful. Certainly, the work of Belbin (1981), already described in Chapter 1, suggests (p. 77) that

> the useful people to have in teams are those who have strengths or characteristics which serve a need without duplicating those already there. Teams are a question of balance. What is needed is not well-balanced individuals, but individuals who balance well with one another.

Is, then, a school functionally better off with a variety of different personalities, or with similar ones? It is a matter of more empirical research into company cultures and personality styles as to whether groups of similar or of varied personalities make the more effective team.

Even more difficult is deciding what behaviours schools need to develop. How far should schools and their society desire to 'develop' individuals in particular directions? In an age where curriculum dissemination is seen increasingly to hold sway, it may seem a natural conclusion that one selects and trains personalities for more effective dissemination. Yet, if, as Webster (1982: 92) argues, one of the educational functions of the teacher is to be aware that 'they cannot climb the ladder for their children, but they can secure it, adjust it, and advise ways of ascending', then to what extent should schools be both constructing and climbing ladders for teachers and pupils? Schools must function, and they need individuals prepared to develop personal skills and expertise which help the school. Yet if variety and personal expression are still values in this society, there will be many valuable behaviours which should be encouraged, not just a few to effect particular desired results. To what extent, one might ask, do companies like BP need to ask the same question?

## Stakeholders

It was noted earlier that the concept of responsibility to company 'stakeholders' – employees, customers, suppliers, community and shareholders – has assumed some importance in the formulation of BP's objectives. Varying values attach to the different kinds of stakeholders, because the relationships between the company and the groups are different. Thus the values attached to *employees* (because the relationship is one of employer to employee) are described as those of trust, non-discrimination, personal development, teamwork and a balance between commitments to work and home. All of these would seem equally applicable to the relationship between teachers and *their* employers.

On the other hand, the values attached to *customers* (because the relationship is one of provider to buyer/consumer) are described as those of integrity, fairness, quality and customer satisfaction. In education, this form of relationship is currently attributed to that between teacher and parent, and yet, even if we accept the dubious proposition that education is a matter of simple 'consumption', it could still be argued that the 'consumer' is in most respects not the parent but the child. Such values might then better apply to the relationship between teacher and child. Only here there is the complication that children as customers do not always know what they *need* to buy. The assumption of such responsibilities is part of the teacher's role, though it is increasingly being assumed by bodies such as the School Curriculum and Assessment Authority in the UK. As for the relationship between teachers and parents, it could be argued that this should be envisaged as one of partnership in the child's education, rather than as one of parents simply buying a service. Viewing the relationship as one of partners, not customers, certainly suggests the values of integrity, fairness and quality, but also the further value of *shared responsibility*. This nowhere needs to figure in the list of values to do with relationships with customers.

Discussion of the concept of *suppliers* only goes to show how difficult a straight transference of business concepts to education can be, for an initial educational question, surely, is: who are the suppliers? Whilst the suppliers of educational hardware (books, equipment, etc.) would come directly into this category – and the same values as those for BP would seem to be equally appropriate – yet, in a more meaningful sense, the 'suppliers' could also be seen as the parents, the 'suppliers' of the children. But were not they the 'customers'? Or was it 'partners'? This is not a mere problem of definition – for different stakeholder relationships will result in different commitments and values. And if stakeholders cannot be defined in the same way in business and education, it would seem that one must also talk of different commitments and values.

A further category of stakeholders – *the community* – leads to a relationship with the company of mutual need, and institutional responsibility, as companies like BP increasingly recognize the interdependency of community and company. It comes as no surprise, then, to see that the values of responsible citizenship, strong safety concerns, a consciousness of the fragility of the environment, of community involvement and contribution, and of the necessity for abiding by current legal and ethical standards, are all proclaimed for this relationship. Indeed, they seem to be an admirable analysis, one that a school might well use, with some minor modifications, to develop a set of values for its relationship with the surrounding community. It also, and most interestingly, suggests responsibilities to community (and the environment of the community) which would necessarily restrict the choice of strategies by either schools or BP. The behaviour of both, if stakeholder management is taken seriously, would be defined partly by their responsibilities to others. In the school's case, the 'teacher's secret garden' is over. In BP's case, the leopard would not be able to change its spots quite as easily as in earlier times.

The final category – *the shareholders* – is declared by BP to be the most central – and therefore, one assumes, the most important group. A precise definition of a share is 'any of equal parts, usually of low par value, into which the capital stock of a company is divided', and a shareholder is simply an owner of shares who, by virtue of being such, has 'a right to receive a proportion of the company's profits' (Collins, 1986: 1403). So who are the shareholders in a school? Whilst there would seem to be no direct translation – a state school's capital stock is not divided or sold, so there are, strictly speaking, no shareholders – an analogy can be made between taxpayer and shareholder. Shareholders by their very status receive a share of the profits, and may question the board as to their conduct during that year. Equally taxpayers and parents should be able to ask similar questions of the school if they fail to deliver 'profits' – however each school decides to interpret and measure that phrase.

Nevertheless, there are problems of translation. The transferability of the notion of 'profit' is clearly laden with difficulties, as is the decision whether the parent is a customer, partner or shareholder. It may be concluded, I think, that the notion of 'stakeholder' is a useful one for those dealing with schools to recognize, but that there must be, for schools, a different list of stakeholders. These would seem to be:

- children
- parents
- teachers
- government
- the community
- the world of work
- future generations

In some respects, the relationships between schools and these stakeholders may be more complex than for an industrial company like BP and its stakeholders, and, following from this, the values which permeate these relationships may also be more complex. For example, there is not one relationship but five between the school and the child: those of provider–consumer, of carer–caree, of educator–educatee, of steward-ship, and of processor–product.

This multiplication of relationships and values is the result of an important difference between educational institutions and businesses. In the work condition, at least at the level of theory, it is the producer–consumer relationship which is normally called upon to predominate. The central purpose of a relationship within a business context is to sell a product to someone, and for that customer to be sufficiently satisfied to return for more. In terms of the full range of possible human behaviours, this is clearly a limited subset. In the real world, there is considerable blurring of such neat theoretical edges, as genuine friendships (and antipathies) develop, which may well facilitate or conflict with business principles. Nevertheless, within the business context, the limited range of producer–consumer relationships is expected to be given priority.

More than one commentator has remarked on the way in which economic-based conceptions of school similarly reduce the range of relationships open to participants. As Ball (1993: 64) says,

> The introduction of market forces into the relations between the schools and parents, and into the work of teaching means that teachers are now working within a new and different value context – a context in which presentation, image and impression management are as, or more, important than the educational process.

As he continues to argue (p. 65), this is a reduction of possibilities, a 'confusion of social relationships and exchange relationships'.

It surely can be argued that, in educational terms, the school (in the form of the teacher) and the child should view each other in a number of different ways. There is an element of producer–consumer, in the manner in which a teacher may 'produce' a curriculum, and a pupil may sample this. But there is also the increased pressure put on teachers to see that their charges are 'processed' in such a way as to fit the requirements of the world of work. Conversely, many would agree with John Macquarrie (1972) that a crucial function of schools is precisely not to 'process' children, but to act in a way 'in which one leaps ahead of the other so as to open his possibilities for him, but never leaps in for the other, for this would be really to deprive him of his possibilities'. Further, teachers are given a stewardship for the pupil during the period the individual is in their care, and they must ensure that no harm comes to the pupil, and that he or she develops emotionally, socially, intellectually and personally in a mature manner.

If there are possible differences between schools and businesses in the variety of roles and ranges of behaviours open to them, the notion of stakeholder management, if taken seriously, is one which brings the functioning of companies like BP and that of schools closer together, for its implementation acknowledges that both businesses and schools have many partners to respond to. By recognizing these as stakeholders, a company like BP must acknowledge that these stakeholders have rights, and it has responsibilities to them. As mentioned above, this means that its behaviour cannot be determined purely on a market basis but will be limited by the responsibilities it recognizes. This suggests (for some) a rather new concept of the commercial enterprise – one that accepts parameters defined by or with others (its stakeholders), and only within which entrepreneurial goals are pursued. This makes a company's flexibility of movement less, its acceptance of restrictions greater. An acceptance of stakeholder management means that there are certain standards to which a company must increasingly adhere; and like schools, it must grapple with the problem of determining the balance between that which can be dispensed with, and that which must be kept if it is to maintain an acceptable definition of itself and its activities.

### The concept of quality

Any assessment of the applicability of BPCI's quality initiative to schools needs to look at the transferability of four things:

- the definition of quality ('conformance to requirements')
- the achievement of quality (through prevention rather than inspection)
- the acceptable standard ('zero defects')
- the measurement of performance ('price of non-conformance')

### *The definition*

As defined by Crosby, quality as 'conformance to requirements' necessarily means that the concept has no static, permanent level: it will be as variable as the customers. Thus, if customers' requirements change from year to year, then so must the concept of quality. Similarly, not only must the concept change with time, it must change from customer to customer, for what satisfies one will not satisfy another. At bottom is an essentially commercial and utilitarian notion which looks for its definition in personal, relativistic wants and desires: there can be no accepted definition, because each customer defines the term individually.

One can see why such an understanding might be popular in certain circles *vis-à-vis* education. Free market thinkers have made a particular point of stressing that the root cause of problems with most activities like education and health, which they regard as service industries, over the past forty years has been that the producers have defined what is good for the consumers. What has tended to happen in education (so it is argued) is that 'quality' has been defined in terms of tradition, which may have little or no relevance to present needs (see for example, Peddiwell's (1939) humorous but very incisive tales of the 'Sabre-Tooth Curriculum'), in terms of 'expert' opinion, or that the producers have defined quality as something which suits them rather than the customers.

The answer, then, is to devise a system which is more responsive to the customer – both children and parents. In such a way are hidebound practices dispensed with, and so are those which accommodate the teacher rather than the child. Parents either affect school policy through being well represented on the governing body, or vote with their feet by moving their children to other schools, and in so doing take the money apportioned to the child away from that school.

Murgatroyd and Morgan (1993), in a description of quality in education argue (Chapter 3) that there are three basic definitions of quality:

- quality assurance (quality defined by the expert)
- contract conformance (quality defined by the provider)
- customer-driven quality (quality defined by the customer)

They go on to suggest that the better schools are moving away from a model which, in order of importance, has expert-defined quality first, provider-defined quality second, and customer-driven quality trailing behind. It is being replaced, they argue, by one which reverses the order of importance – customer-driven quality must be given priority, followed by provider-defined quality, and only then by expert-defined quality. Furthermore, they extend the notion of 'customer' to include those in the school who receive a service from anyone else. This is an extension to Crosby's more usual definition, and provides a framework within which schools can begin to see (as M&S, BP and many other companies have realized) that the delivery of a high-quality product depends on the contributions of all within the organization, even if it could be argued that it conflates provider-defined quality with customer-defined quality.

There is clear merit in calls by writers like Crosby and Murgatroyd and Morgan. It cannot be denied that schools, when not submitted to rigorous internal and external appraisal, may retain practices which should be eliminated. Neither may there be the same degree of proactivity in listening to children and parents which is an essential feature of an approach based on partnership. To this extent, then, the prosecution of such free-market, consumer-oriented approaches to quality have their appeal.

Nevertheless, if, as pointed out above, the philosophy of the 'customer knows best' (where we define 'customer' as the external recipient of services) has its problems in the business arena, it certainly has them in the school as well. Undoubtedly, there is much upon which a school 'customer' *can* form quality judgements. The parent knows the child at least as well as the teacher, and may have a better insight into the way it learns and reacts to different situations. Moreover, parents' concerns for their children are likely to be both more immediate and more sustained than the teachers'. Moreover, the customer will be an expert in quality terms of the milieu within which the services take place. This means not only the functioning of the organization itself but also the personal characteristics of the expert service itself. This element can be judged by the consumer because such behaviours are common to most human dealings. They will include:

- *responsiveness* – how quickly, appropriately and courteously do professionals respond to consumers' requests?
- *accessibility* – how approachable and easy to contact are professionals?
- *ability to involve* – how well are others communicated with, educated and encouraged to engage in the enterprise?

Other features of a school's performance will be partly judgeable by the layperson. These will include:
- their *conformance to external standards* at both national and local levels
- their *performance* – their description of the schools' objectives and then their record of meeting them
- their *reliability* – how consistent they are in the performance of their expertise
- their *value for money* – the degree to which the aims of the school are achieved in a cost-efficient way

These all involve the use of a degree of expert knowledge which may not be totally comprehensible to the layperson but which also contain elements that are perfectly understandable, and increasingly so as the school community is informed by the professionals of what they are trying to do.

Other aspects, however, such as subject depth and pedagogical expertise, depend rather more upon teacher expertise. These are similar to the expertise of the doctor and the solicitor, and are areas in which the layperson normally defers judgement to the expert. This in itself is no argument: professionals are adept at inventing esoteric terminology which serves no other function save that of preventing the layperson from understanding their areas too well. However, there are issues of professionalism which move beyond terminology. In education, a good example of this would be the expertise to implement a 'quality' curriculum. At the very least such expertise would have to demonstrate:

- an ability to differentiate the material to match a child's developing needs
- an ability to make the material relevant to the child, and therefore capable of motivating him or her
- an ability to enable the child to take the next step in consolidating his or her learning
- an ability to make the material contribute to earlier understanding in a coherent fashion and therefore to support other learning activities
- an ability to result in learning which can be used and applied in a variety of contexts
- a degree of expertise to be able to utilize the best available research in the subject area and the pedagogy

One cannot conclude that customers will be aware of the criteria above, or that, if aware of them, they would know how they could be achieved or even insist upon them.

Expertise will always make a difference, a fact which needs to be recognized by both schools and businesses.

### The achievement of quality

It will already have been noted that the route to quality achievement by BP bears striking resemblances to that of Marks & Spencer. Both see this achievement as being accomplished through the *prevention* of problems rather than from quality control and inspection after the event. Both are committed to the more proactive procedure of quality assurance, and of a committment to total quality control and company-wide quality control, in which all staff are seen – and see themselves – as responsible for maintaining the company's standards. The achievement of quality, then, is not seen as the sole responsibility of senior management. The health of the company should be the concern of all, for it is usually those actually performing the operation who will have the keenest insight into how a process could be improved. This makes good sense for schools, indeed for any organization. The only qualification which needs making, it would seem, is that commitment and enthusiasm from those 'at the bottom' is usually produced by care, concern and motivation from those 'at the top'. A commitment to keeping a company in good health usually stems from good feelings about the company. Those designing policies for schools should take note. Low morale is not a sound foundation upon which to build such a policy.

### The acceptable standard (zero defects)

It will be recalled that the standard of 'zero defects' was adopted primarily to prevent a 'slippery slope' attitude to defects becoming the norm. A commitment to this standard keeps individuals aware of this requirement at all times. Educationally speaking, the necessity of such an approach would seem to be dependent on the people being dealt with. Some will be capable of maintaining high standards without such (excessive?) commitment: indeed it might dispirit some who feel they have failed if they do not achieve this standard of zero defects. Others may well need such an external yardstick to keep them up to scratch. A standard policy of 'zero defects' may not be good for all: adapting the ruling to the individual may be the more productive course.

### The measurement of quality performance

'The price of non-conformance' is one of the most startling things to come out of the quality package at BP. Initial reactions to it by educationalists are likely to be sceptical at first, based primarily on the difficulty of measuring this price in an institution whose 'production' is more qualitative than quantitative. This, to an extent, is a valid objection: quantitative measurement is certainly more straightforward. But even where it is primarily qualitative, the approach does make one conscious of the enormous number of ways in which wasted time and effort are created, and therefore of a cost far beyond cursory estimation.

Take the example of a two-hour university education lecture, with twenty students (who are all practising teachers) attending. If this is of poor quality, the price of non-conformance is not simply the lecturer's wasted time. It will consist of the cost of delivering the lecture and its initial (if poor) preparation. Other costs to be included, however, would be:

- students' wasted time (20 x 2 hours + travelling time + travel costs)
- cost of work otherwise done by lecturer and students
- cost of hiring, heating and lighting room
- cost of photocopying etc.
- cost of wasted secretarial work
- cost of boredom, frustration, headaches etc., through effect on future work
- cost to university's reputation ('Don't go to any of his courses – they're awful!')

When looked at in this way, the financial calculations may never be exact but they will certainly be no less than several hundred pounds, and may amount to several thousand (particularly if the remark on the awfulness of the lecture leads to one or more people deciding not to enrol for a future course).

It might be said that it is even more difficult to cost the price of a poorly delivered lesson in school. Some of these costs will certainly be very long-term – teaching in a turgid style may put some children off school, and have a negative effect on their aspirations, and thereby on their long-term approach to education, and ultimately upon their economic productivity. Another criticism of this approach might be that calculating the price of non-conformance asks only for a hard-headed financial calculation and says nothing of the spiritual costs. This certainly indicates the approach's limitations, but it does suggest that such spiritual costs are *further* costs to be added to the financial costs of non-conformance. Total education costs, then, will probably be even higher. The value of calculating the cost of non-conformance to education is thereby increased, not decreased. It is a concept that all educational institutions could find useful, even if they decide to supplement it with approaches more positive and qualitative in orientation.

## CONCLUSION: BP, EDUCATION AND CHANGING VALUES

This chapter was entitled 'BP Chemicals: A Leopard of Quality' because perhaps *the* fundamental quality perceived was the need, and acceptance by management of the company, to change as society and market conditions dictated – from a Fordist to a post-Fordist agenda. There is, at higher managerial levels, an acute awareness of the need to understand the manner in which societies and markets are changing and tastes are developing; and of the need to foresee future changes and be ready for them. The result is a very large commitment to research and development, to the recognition of the need to re-shape the company (in terms of either diversification or divestment), and of the need to develop individuals within the company capable of adapting to new circumstances. The perceived importance of this attitude to the company's long-term health cannot be overstressed. Those within the company are being sent the clear message that there is no room for uncritical satisfaction with existing structures and behaviours – they may have worked satisfactorily in the past, but it is increasingly unlikely that they will do so in the future. For some, such change will prove stressful. This is the reason why BP has stipulated the kinds of people it needs – the O-P-E-N kind – not only because they will cope better but also because they are the kind who will actively *enjoy* such changes and challenges. Concomitant with such changes in personnel must go changes in organizational structure – hierarchical bureaucracy is clearly unsuitable, and more flexible groups of individuals, less wedded to position and more to expertise, must become the order of the day. Whilst many employees will be – very understandably – concerned about job security as de-layering takes place and job numbers are reduced, many are beginning to accept the management's view that this is the direction BP needs to go in if it is to survive in an increasingly competitive world. Should those working within schools do the same thing?

At the pragmatic level to disregard such an approach would be foolish, for present legislation in the UK places schools in the same kind of post-Fordist arena in which BP operates. Consideration of much of BP's strategy would then seem to make good sense. Should schools not constantly be examining external conditions and adapting according to how these change? Should they not look to the future and equip themselves to deal with it? And should they not develop individuals who find such change not only challenging but personally rewarding as well? Indeed, if schools are preparing the child for future participation in society and in the world of work, is it not part of their responsibility to equip young people for these tasks? Does this not necessitate schools to do precisely this?

A great deal of this must be answered in the affirmative. If schools want to survive, they must accept the responsibilities which devolvement gives them, they must be aware of what their stakeholders want and be able to respond accordingly. Further, schools must become even more thoroughly integrated with their community and society. This means being aware of, and adapting to changes in that society, and providing students with the skills to survive, adapt and prosper within it. The lessons from BP in this respect are valuable and instructive.

And yet, this is not *all* of a school's – or BP's – responsibility. A school also needs to be a guardian and transmitter of a cultural heritage, a conserver of values, a discriminator between changes that are fundamental and necessary and those that are peripheral and transient, and it must attempt a balance between the two. BP has increasingly to recognize its *ecological* role – that it exists and has considerable impact through an interdependency of relationships at personal, community and environmental levels. It has to continue to expand its concept of 'licence to operate' into a recognition of a permanent and increasing responsibility to the local, national and global environments, as natural resources are depleted, as pollution becomes a global problem.

Further, rather than being simple agents of change, both schools and BP need to be participants in dialogues on change. In the schools' case, this is because agendas for change must not be set by governments, and devolvement of implementation amounts to no more than power without responsibility for outcomes for governments, responsibility without power for schools. As Codd says (1993: 168), 'If there is to be education for democracy, there must be education in democracy.'

Schools can learn much from businesses like BP, yet they must not forget their crucial role as educators of future citizens, a role which demands that they should do more than work out tactics for the implementation of policy whilst the state determines the strategy.

If schools need to assert their right to participate on policy, through its increasing devolvement, BP needs to accept its duty to participate in dialogues on change with stakeholders, because it is integral to the conception of a company which accepts its responsibilities to the communities and environments it works within.

Both schools and businesses, then, share the tension of needing to change to keep pace with the society in which they partake, yet they both must take on the responsibility for discriminating between these societal changes and acting as responsible citizens. If BP's business is one of riding the sea of change and using it to advantage, it also needs to recognize that this sea of change imposes its own limits and responsibilities, and that these set limits to exploitation. Only by achieving this balance can they ultimately benefit themselves and their communities. Schools, precisely because they must enable their charges to function in the society of tomorrow, need to debate what constitutes 'good' change, what part they should play in it, what a society should be and what its future citizens need to understand. Both schools and BP, then, need to be leopards of quality, but need to balance carefully the arguments for the rate at which they change their spots.

# Chapter 3

# Fabricast: Small Means Different

## THE ORGANIZATION

You could easily miss Fabricast. I did. Looking for it on the first visit, I drove around that part of Kingston-upon-Hull which at one time was the very centre of the city – close to the River Hull, along which most of the trade went on its journey to the River Humber, the North Sea and places beyond. Now the commercial and shopping centre has moved a mile or so south and west, and what remains is still active and varied, but very much a cluster of small streets, with small businesses dotted along them. The name of Main Street, on which Fabricast is located, suggests its former glory but it is clearly no longer the main street of the city. Fabricast is about half the way down its length, a little newer looking than some of its neighbours, as it had extensive internal restructuring and a logo facelift a couple of years ago, enabling it to achieve the initial impression of being neat, ordered and professional.

The firm's premises are fairly long and narrow, with the office section facing out to the road and much of the actual works located behind. It can therefore seem smaller than it really is. The main entrance leads into a rather cramped reception area, with stairs leading to the newly built floor above taking up a fair amount of this space. Off to the left is the office where the non-ferrous-metal sales and purchasing takes place. To the right of the reception area is a door leading to the office where most of the technical work for the foundry and machine shop used to take place: it has now gone into a new office in the main workshop, the old office now being devoted to a section of sales. Going up the stairs you find an office shared between the managing director and the sales director, and another one shared between Denise and Pam, the women who deal with the computerization of accounts and constant running totals of work and money coming in and out.

First impressions, then, are of comparative smallness; and lack of size can generate assumptions. Marks & Spencer is a large national leader. BP is a very large international leader. Both have proved themselves in the most difficult circumstances and have grown to positions of formidable reputation. Few people outside of the immediate group of workers, customers and competitors in the Yorkshire region have heard of Fabricast. In comparison with these two giants, it is a minnow. Why bother with it? What can schools learn from a company of only thirty employees? Clearly this assumes that lessons can best be learnt by looking at successful firms, that successful necessarily means big, and that therefore we should confine our attention to the big firms. Certainly, to have grown big is usually an indication of success, but size in itself is no guarantee of present successful and professional practice; there are too many examples of firms that have grown big, and then their size and poor management of that size have led to their collapse. Indeed, the trend of the last decade or so has been for larger firms to devolve finance and management to lower tiers and cut out middle management: in effect to run large firms as lots of small ones. Further, large successful companies were once small. As instructive, then, as looking at the large companies would be a study or studies which examined good small companies which might be well on their way to Marks & Spencer's or BP's present status.

A further assumption, though, is that big means professional, whilst small necessarily means amateur. This is an assumption that small schools have laboured under for most of their existence: that small is a reduced-quality version of big, that big is what we should be aiming for if we want to improve the quality of our schools. What is not usually considered is that small schools may not be miniature large schools, doing less well what big schools do well, but may have advantages with which large schools cannot compete. Part of the latter half of this chapter will examine the validity of this thesis. But the first half will ask whether small companies have advantages which large firms don't, and whether schools (particularly, perhaps, small schools) can learn anything from them.

This chapter, then, will question these assumptions, and suggest that small doesn't mean amateur; small companies like Fabricast have much of a different, professional nature to offer schools.

## Company structure

Fabricast itself is really three companies in one, or at least has three complementary arms. The first arm of the company (and the earliest in terms of its development) is the *stockholding* side. This includes the buying and holding in stock of a variety of non-ferrous metals such as brass, copper, aluminium, stainless steel and phosphor bronze, as well as valves and associated fittings. The company has also expanded into the stockholding of plastics such as nylon, acetal and polypropylene. Whilst there are never huge amounts in stock, there is invariably enough for day-to-day demand (an amount based upon years of experience of this demand), and more can be brought in very quickly. By keeping sufficient but never excessive amounts in stock, Fabricast doesn't tie up capital which it could use profitably elsewhere. Nor does it try to compete with its bigger neighbours, who have the financial resources to stock much larger supplies. Instead, one of the strengths of the company lies in its willingness to cut materials to virtually any size, and supply them in a very short period of time. So, by keeping a small but varied choice in stock, and by offering to cut and supply amounts that larger companies might not be bothered with, it is able to maintain a quick and flexible response. The company has spotted a niche in the market and exploits it well.

Having said this, it does not take a great deal of expertise to buy in an assortment of metals, valves and assorted fittings and re-sell them. Many in the area can do – and do – precisely this. Further, major profits do not come from it: demand is fairly constant, but margins are not particularly high, owing to the expense of buying in and stocking the materials. The stockholding side, then, provides a regular and reliable source of income, but needs to be supplemented by other activities, supplied by the other arms of the company.

The second arm of the company is *coppersmithing*. This involves the manufacture, repair, maintenance and manipulation of tubes made of materials like copper or stainless steel which may be used in heating and cooling systems in large installations. Customers include hospitals, prisons, universities and marine industries. The work is specialized and tricky: copper tubing, in particular, has an awkward habit of 'pinching' when manipulated, and needs careful treatment if shapes are to be achieved without damage to the piping. This can in part be done through the use of a special resin which is heated up, poured into the tubes and allowed to cool, the tubes being manipulated into the desired shape before the resin is reheated, poured out and re-used. Again, the fact that the company is small allows a flexibility and speed which gives it an edge over most of its rivals. The fact that much of the work is of a specialist nature, requiring as much in expertise as in raw materials, also means that profit margins can be higher. Of course, it is also dependent on demand, and so work will fluctuate from month to month. Hence the need for the other arms of the company.

The third arm of the company is the *foundry service*, producing non-ferrous castings in copper-based and aluminium-based alloys. The foundry service is not just the use of two gas-fired open hearth and crucible furnaces, but is combined with an ability to design and pattern-make, to cast and mould and finally to machine and finish. There is then the ability to go from the beginning to the end of the process, and, as with the stockholding, one of the strengths of the foundry service is its ability to turn its hand to jobs large and small. While I was there I saw moulds and castings being made for British Steel, Trafalgar House, Reckitt & Colman and British Rail, but also blocks for an Alvis car club, commemorative plaques, and even a few Victorian airbricks for an individual improving his house who could find no other way of replacing those bricks damaged by the years. As with the coppersmithing, there are larger margins to be made here than with the stockholding, as there is more expertise involved.

Having three arms to the company is no chance happening but deliberate policy, the reasoning being that if one arm of the company gets into difficulties there are two others to keep it afloat. Having said this, none of the three seems to be in any immediate difficulty. In a period of fairly deep recession, Fabricast has managed to keep its head more than above water. Started in 1981, it, like most newborn companies, suffered problems. Unlike many others, it learnt from them. The company came fairly close in its first couple of years to going under: a number of customer bankruptcies nearly brought the company down. However, in discussion with its accountants, the owner and managing director, Dave Langton, learnt a hard lesson which has never left him, and which has stamped an indelible imprint on the character of the company, which in part explains its comparative success. Yearly audits, he was advised, and saw, did not give sufficient information to make decisions and act quickly with rapidly changing conditions, including those of the financial status of clients. If commercial decisions are to be made, you cannot afford to work off information which may be months out of date. Even the passage of weeks can indicate dramatic changes in fortune. Far better, then, is to have quarterly rather than yearly accounts, to have weekly balances and daily printoffs. Some may see this as excessive, in terms of both time and money: quarterly accounts, after all, cost two to three times as much as yearly ones. As far as Dave Langton is concerned, though, this is money well spent. He has seen too many examples of companies going under because of inattention to financial detail. His commitment to this area seems borne out by the health of the company. In 1984, the company had over £500,000 in turnover, which rose steadily until, by 1988, the £1,000,000 turnover target was achieved. Despite the recession of the early 1990s, this has continued on an upward climb – £1,041,000 in 1991, £1,220,000 in 1992, £1,450,000 in 1993.

### Growth: its problems and possibilities

Indeed, if Dave Langton is right, the temporary slowing in financial growth may be due to factors other than just recessional ones. He suggested that a company can be expected, all things considered, to grow, in a fairly predictable manner. A one-person business can, if time and effort are put into it, be expected to grow at a fairly rapid rate until a natural pause sets in. This is when the company has grown to a point that there are too many customers for one individual to deal with. When this happens, one of a number of things can happen. The individual either can continue trying to cope alone, in which case he or she is liable to lose a lot of customers simply through not servicing them properly, or will come to an understanding of what he or she *can* service properly, and then stick at this number. With the first path, such individuals may go out of business; with the second, they will probably stay in business until they meet the same problems as before, or their clients move elsewhere, or new technology or societal movements overtake their personal expertise. Whichever way you look at it, the one-person business is going to have a precarious existence.

If, on the other hand, the individual recognizes that further growth necessitates more staff, then there will be a period of company reorganization, while the single manager and staff negotiate workloads and transferences of responsibility and become used to working with one another. Assuming they do manage this (and an inability to do so may spell the collapse of the company, a return to the one-person business, or another attempt to build another team), then the company is now ready to begin growth once more. If the team works well together, other things like recessions being equal, there will probably be an expansion of business until there comes a time when the team finds itself in the position faced by the one-person business – an inability to deal satisfactorily with the increased number of customers. Then comes the problem of finding new staff, of inducting them, of training them, of learning to form and work as a new team.

As a company gets larger, so it takes on more and different problems. The one-person business does not have to bother with the problems of recruitment, of staff development, of team building, of communication. Small means greater ease of access to individuals, of flexibility in decision-making. Staff meetings can be more spontaneous, issues discussed as and when the need arises, rather than being formally timetabled, appraisals being performed when the situation is most appropriate to appraiser and appraisee, rather than being conducted according to a precise formula.

Of course, Fabricast does have structures which ensure that things *do* get done, but there is still a sense that actions are taken because of current demands rather than because rules and procedures demand them. The small company, after all, existed before the bigger company. The big company grew out of the smaller; and not only is the smaller company prior in time, it may also be prior in terms of desirability of size. Moreover, problems of staff development, team building and communication multiply exponentially as the team gets bigger. In a two-person business, there are only two possible forms of misunderstanding: if A misunderstands B, or if B misunderstands A. In a three-person business there are six possible ways, in a four-man band, twelve possible ways, and so on. It is an interesting thought that the structures of larger companies are not necessarily advantages but may rather be necessary encumbrances to help them alleviate the problems caused by simply growing too much.

Such problems usually reach a stage where simple face-to-face communication is no longer possible or effective, and it is during this period of growth that company rules and procedures are increasingly laid down; to ensure that the members of the team are pulling together, that a customer does not get a different answer from different members of the team, that communications are clear. It is at this stage, too, that two styles of management begin to clash. The first, the central feature of the small business, is that of paternalism: the image, structure, and modus vivendi of the company are determined largely by the personality of the owner/manager. As the company expands, this framing of company procedures on the personal strengths and weaknesses of one individual becomes increasingly less possible. It does not aid in communication (and, as the company expands, communication becomes increasingly important), and it can lead to uncertainty: assumptions about procedures are not enough, they need to be clear to all. Fabricast is not alone in undergoing the problems and tensions associated with this kind of movement, though the issue becomes more central to the future development of the company both as the company gets larger and changes its character, and as Dave Langton reaches an age where he has begun to consider if not relinquishing the reins then taking more of a strategic role, and tending the company's newer shoots. Indeed, as Dave increasingly releases his day-to-day control upon the company's main site, Steve Hilton, the sales director, begins to attempt the necessary changes in the company, one of which involves the implementation of procedures which make the company less the stamp of Dave's personality. And whilst Dave's brain accepts the benefits and inevitability of such moves, his heart may not be as enthusiastic.

Nevertheless, there are prices to be paid for the advent of rules and procedures. Whilst undoubtedly large institutions have their benefits, it might also be the case that one has to be guarded in evaluating them. What are the effects of large institutions on individuals, and therefore upon society? There is a huge library on the problems of bureaucracies, but it seems possible to suggest that there are five possible major negative effects.

The first, described by Merton (1952), is what he termed a 'ritualism' towards rules and the subsequent treatment of individuals. The rules define what should be done, and therefore little or no attempt is made to use personal initiative, to explore ways of delivering a better service. With such ritualism seems also to go a loss of morale and motivation in the job.

The second, described by Handy (1985), is that, whilst one of the supposed strengths of bureaucratic organizations is their predictability, this very quality becomes a liability when the environment is one of fast change and innovation – which is certainly a good description of modern society.

Thirdly, Selznick (1949) suggests that the creation of bureaucracies usually means a spate of empire-building, as those in charge of different sections try to enhance their own prestige and power. Such self-glorification can mean that the different parts develop aims and directions different from that of the centre.

Fourthly, if the control of such parts is perceived as necessary, this is normally done by yet another layer of bureaucracy, which becomes increasingly inquisitorial. This results in what Gouldner (1954) calls a 'punishment-centred' bureaucracy, with consequent demotivation, antipathy, evasion and covert sabotage.

Finally, bureaucracies generally demand that employees, whose ideal is to treat others on an individual basis, are forced to treat them in a routinized and dehumanized manner. This can lead to some employees leaving their jobs, others submitting to such standardization, or others developing coping strategies which see them concentrating on some clients, and finding personal reward in these encounters, but at the expense of a large number of other clients. These dilemmas, of what Lipsky (1980) calls the 'street-level bureaucrat', can become endemic in the large company.

It might also be that the company's culture has powerful effects upon the personalities of individuals working within them. It should not be too surprising to find, as much of the literature suggests, that bureaucracies can have a generally demotivating and de-energizing effect upon individuals, whilst the smaller firms may have a much more positive effect. Not only does the literature on bureaucracies quoted above suggest just this, but the work of Kohn (1977) indicates that the nature of individuals' work very largely determines whether they are more conformist and rigid in their thinking or whether they are more flexible and self-directive. If this is the case, then small firms may have beneficial effects not only upon an individual's attitude to work and his or her personality but also upon his or her contribution to the running of the society within which they live. It is an interesting speculation that the health of a society – the degree to which its members perform as citizens – may be critically affected by the number of people working in large or small organizations. It will not go unnoticed by the reader that writers of both left and right of the political spectrum have increasingly attacked large bureaucracies, the left because of their damaging effect upon the practice of citizenship, the right because of their negative effects on individual liberty.

The clear message is that as companies get bigger, they do not necessarily get better; they acquire different problems. This is a message which will be returned to throughout this chapter: a small company is rather more than a miniaturized version of a big company. In many ways, they are different animals, and need to be treated as such.

Fabricast has come through the one-person business stage, and has begun to move past what one might call stage two of its growth: where all of the company can be kept under one roof. Whilst a lot of business is done in the immediate vicinity, much on the stockholding side is done throughout Yorkshire and Humberside, the foundry attracts custom from all over the north of England, and the coppersmithing takes orders from all over the United Kingdom. A natural move, then, has been to increase the company's number of geographical locations; when good customers exist in other parts of the country, it makes sense to exploit that resource. The result has been the setting-up of a stockholding operation in Grimsby owing to a dramatic increase in demand for stainless steel on that side of the Humber (due in part to the appointment of a salesman to service that side of the Humber); the appointment of a woman working from Norwich to increase coppershop and foundry sales in the south of England; and, finally, the establishing of a sales office in Rotherham for stockholding and foundry services.

These moves mesh well with other factors which are increasingly being considered. One is that Dave, the managing director, lives in South Yorkshire, and two hours' travelling into Hull every day is neither pleasurable nor profitable. Moreover, his coming into work on a daily basis usually means an inability to distance himself from the day-to-day hurly-burly. Yet Dave's best value to the company now, arguably, is that of policy direction rather than day-to-day administration and selling. With Steve Hilton increasingly ready to take over the reins, the position is being reached where Steve runs the major operation in Hull, and Dave can spend more time nurturing the new developments in Grimsby and Rotherham. Indeed, Dave's game plan has changed a little over the last few years. Not so long ago, the plan was to wind down to retirement, relinquishing the reins gradually. Now the search for security for him and his wife is still a vital consideration, but the expansion of the company, and the increased demands from this, have made for a more open approach to the future. He sees expansion as meaning greater demands on personnel, and sees Fabricast, being small, as needing to be able to call on all its human reserves, including himself.

Indeed, an absence of slack can be a genuine problem for a small company. Whilst leanness and tightness are generally seen as virtues in company structure, they can be taken too far. One of the real problems which Fabricast and other small firms and schools face is the lack of personnel to do anything other than the job at hand. Hence the problems Dave Langton and Steve Hilton face in finding the time to step back and look at longer-term policy, rather than day-to-day running. One or two people off ill or on holiday is all that is normally needed to bring the senior management right back on to the sales desk. This is at best a mixed blessing: whilst Steve Hilton pointed out that it prevents senior managers from losing touch, it also can prevent them from using their greater expertise most profitably. It also means that things like in-service training tend to be done out of office hours, or when there is a slack moment, and not when the individual may really need it. Nor, it must be said, is in-service training likely to be performed in the systematic, progressive manner that a larger company can adopt, if only because the smaller company does not have the resources to research, produce and train according to its own training manual. The reader will remember that not only is nearly two hours of each working week spent by a Marks & Spencer employee on development, but also that M&S has a specific team at Central Office to develop materials for this, as well as, at the store level, a similar number of individuals off the shop floor as actually on it. This all gives the kind of scope necessary for proper, systematized and planned in-service training to take place. Furthermore, much out-of-house training is expensive, and not necessarily appropriate to the problems of the individual company. Research on in-service work in education by people like Williams (1990) strongly suggests that whilst some courses are beneficial purely for reflection and self-awareness, schools get as much, if not more, benefit from courses which are directed at the problems of their particular workplace. The same would seem to apply to business. Pressure of money, time and relevance all work against the small firm. The large firm then has a decided advantage in this area. Its in-house formulations and deliveries are not only good from the point of view of delivery at the time and place most needed; they are also good for morale as people do not feel they are having to sacrifice their spare time to do something which would be seen as an integral part of the working day in the larger company. Fabricast is not alone in recognizing the problem, but also in not feeling totally capable of solving it. With the best will in the world, there is a tendency for such training to be done when a problem occurs, the cause of which can be identified as inexperience or lack of training by one of the staff. Further, it may be given by those directly above the individual in need, and the deliverer may be experiencing the same kinds of problems as well. Too much slack in a company is never a good thing: it is wasteful of resources, and generally bad for morale, but too little slack is not much better as it reduces flexibility to a point where it can damage the company.

If smallness allows for flexibility of decision-making, but also may constrict that flexibility, another double-edged benefit of smallness is the highlighting of the lame duck. In a larger company, individuals may be able to 'hide', their contribution (or lack of it) being lost in the larger order of things. At the very least, their influence is lessened by the size of the company. The reverse, of course, happens with the smaller company, which is much less able to tolerate the poor performer. In a small company a particular individual may constitute an entire department. Everything that runs through this department, then, will bear their imprint. They cannot hide, their functions cannot be given to others, and consequently the company may be seriously damaged. Small companies, then, necessarily must be right with selection of staff and their develop-ment, and yet these call for abilities which small companies may find hard to muster – namely, sophisticated and lengthy interview techniques, and costly and time-consuming training. The small company has its advantages, but it also has prices to pay for its size.

### The creator of the small firm

The heavy influence of particular individuals of course works the other way – given an extremely talented and hardworking manager, who *is* that department, the benefits to the company can be enormous, for all actions and decisions will flow through him or her. Nowhere is this more obvious than with the individual who owns the company. If the small company is reasonably successful, this will invariably be due, initially at least, to the vision and commitment of its founder. He or she will have taken an original conception, and steered that company through financial and marketing teething troubles, will have seen it grow, will have gone through the troubling but exciting times of bringing in new plant, equipment and individuals. He or she will, necessarily, be in a position to know more about the company than anyone else. This, incidentally, can be a major cause of poor or non-existent in-service training: what you have learned by experience is learned almost by osmosis, and you may fail to realize that others have not had this opportunity, and need a considerable amount of structured training in a way you never needed yourself, simply because you lived rather than learnt the experience – a point which comes out very strongly in the next chapter as well.

Any individual in charge of a concern, whether it be industrial or educational, has to face squarely their degree of indispensability. This is not an easy task, and not necessarily for egotistical reasons. They probably will be the best person for most jobs, if only at first, because they have lived with the company as it has grown, and know its problems and possibilities inside out. But as the company expands, as it takes on board more individuals, so it faces different problems. Can one individual keep close enough to all aspects of the business? Is the boss giving sufficient space to those below for them to grow into the job when he or she wants to relinquish the reins? Would policy-making benefit from a number of points of view, rather than the one? Judgements must then be brought into play about the suitability and potentiality of individuals for such policy discussion. One difficulty here is that of the chicken and the egg: in some cases only by participating in policy-making do individuals gain the expertise to be able to contribute profitably to it.

Dave Langton's personal development explains much of Fabricast's development and structure. An initial career in football was cut short by injury, and he began work with the Ford motor company in the tool room at Doncaster. He gradually moved to being part of a troubleshooting team of engineers who would travel from plant to plant, both in the UK and in continental Europe, dealing with tooling problems that arose within each. Three things came out of this: one was the opportunity to gain valuable experience in engineering terms; another was to see the variety of good and bad management practices at the various plants, and begin to formulate how he would do it differently were he in charge; the third was to begin to realize that being on call to travel away from home for much of the week was not a lot of fun. Curiously, his next job, at age 30, involved the same kind of roving commission, and this deepened his resolve to make this the final time he would work in this manner. The company he was working for had expanded to what might be called stage three of a company's growth: the point at which there were a number of small plants with separate branch managers. The problem, then, how to keep an eye on what each branch was doing, is one not peculiar to this company. This was Dave's job. Rather than being a roving engineer, he was now a roving manager. After ten years with the company, Dave decided for a number of reasons that he was ready for his own business: the desire to spend more time at home; the perceived weakness of small branches, when it was possible to do the same thing under one roof, and so keep closer control; and the desire to be his own man and create something which was his rather than someone else's. On approaching the owner to inform him of his plans, not only did he get a friendly reception to his ideas, he was offered a chance to buy the Hull manufacturing base, on the condition that he did not try to woo away or compete for existing customers. In 1981 Fabricast was born.

These previous experiences, as well as Fabricast's early financial problems described above, have clearly affected the manner of growth of the company, and its management structure. Sloppy management or work is anathema to its boss: those who aren't prepared to put in the effort don't last long. Part of the philosophy is also the belief that success invariably comes from an acceptance of long hours. Twelve-hour days have been the norm, and one of Dave's reasons for choosing Steve Hilton as right-hand man is the same workaholic tendencies. Another part of understanding the company comes, as one might expect, from understanding its creator. Dave Langton is not only a hard worker and a man who learns from experience but an individual with a shrewd understanding of people. For him, the topic of motivation doesn't need fancy theories and elaborate plans. The motivation of people is simple: get to know your people, find what turns them on, and use that carrot. As people are all different, this will mean different carrots. The philosophy is simple and usually effective, though there are people in the company whose carrot he is still trying to identify. Dave also has the disquieting habit on occasions of saying, in true Yorkshire fashion, the wrong thing at the wrong time and upsetting even his most loyal workforce.

Perhaps, though, the most interesting thing is that he is an individual who, in a very real sense, identifies with the company. Not for him the philosophy that a company is there to be built up and then milked for the good life: he can reel off plenty of examples of individuals whose companies are not half as healthy as Fabricast and yet have yachts, villas in Spain and large overdrafts at the bank. Clearly, for them, owning a company is purely a means to an end, and if it goes under then they try again with another. However, for Dave, Fabricast is a reflection of his achievement as a human being. It is almost true to say that the company's survival is Dave's life, and explains why so little, comparatively speaking, is taken out of profits for personal benefit but ploughed back in. Treating the company well is almost synonymous with treating himself well. It also explains why pay rises and bonuses are negotiated with individuals not on the basis of inflation but on the twin bases of personal performance and company health: extra money is there when an individual deserves it, and the company can afford it. This is a message that some in the company find difficult to understand and accept, believing as they do that pay rises should be automatic. For Dave, an individual is thinking like a manager (and therefore can be entrusted with responsibilities, and rewarded as one) when that individual comes to realize that his or her fate is intimately bound up with the fate of the company. When this vision arrives, he believes, they will see that the work, the commitment, the improvement, necessarily come before the pay rise.

This, then, is the standard and the vision Fabricast's aspiring managers need to achieve before they will be classed as such. And when they achieve this, only then will Dave think of inviting them to discuss policy, for only then will they have the company's best interests at heart, and have achieved the outlook necessary to achieve these best interests. And they are then only one step away from the sort of commitment Dave has himself: where they may even refuse a bonus or a wage rise if this is in the interest of the long-term health of the company. And individuals who reach *that* stage are just about ready to take over the reins of the company, for then Dave knows that they will never willingly sacrifice the company to their personal short-term ends.

For those, then, who believe that business and industry is all about making a profit for the sake of making a profit, Fabricast is a cautionary tale. Here is a company owned by an individual who sees profit as being necessary to pay the bills and be comfortable, but, probably as importantly, as something which signals the health of the company and allows it to continue to exist and prosper. And if *it* exists and prospers, then Dave's estimation of himself is largely maintained. There is a personal investment here which has its positive and negative sides. It must be reassuring for any workforce to know that its owner is as committed as this to its existence, but hard for those who do not share his vision. It must also be slightly worrying for his wife, a woman who provides an extra layer of reassurance for Dave's approach to finance, coming from a devout Methodist background and firmly believing that you don't spend what you haven't got, but who must still be concerned at the level of commitment Fabricast has extracted from him. And finally, it must be a problem at times for the workforce to have an owner and managing director who so closely identifies with the company: it will inevitably reflect his idiosyncrasies. Nevertheless, if you place all the factors together, you understand how it is that the company, in the middle of a recession, could buy new equipment costing tens of thousands of pounds, and could afford to purchase greatly increased stocks of stainless steel to meet new demand, in both cases without having to go to the bank for a loan. Other companies may have grown more quickly: few can be so financially sound.

## The health of the company

The pursuit of company health is then the overriding importance of Fabricast's management. This is seen and achieved in three different ways. The first is a stress upon financial health, and has already been discussed at some length. Quarterly accounts, weekly balances, daily printoffs: a constant scrutiny, interpretation and evaluation of these provide the kind of information that allows Fabricast's management to be aware of trends and possible problems long before they may become more physically obvious.

Allied to this is the second way of ensuring company health: constant re-examination of the books which record the calls made, from whom they are made, the nature of the enquiry and then whether a sale is made – or not. If a sale is not made, then an examination will take place in most cases as to why this did not happen. By looking at failures, and trying to correct them, the company practises one of the qualities which Peters and Waterman (1981) suggested was crucial to a company's survival – staying close to the customer.

Closeness to the customer is pursued in other ways as well, such as the practice of using account records to look back over customers' accounts, and spotting the ones who have not ordered recently. It then takes a phone call to re-establish contact with this company, and find out reasons why custom has tailed off. This can obviously be a tricky and sensitive technique: too brash an approach may distance a customer even further. It would seem to need some form of training for it to be performed successfully: it is again one of the problems of the small company that it does not have the same degree of resources, the time, nor the range of personnel to choose from in the trainee or the trainer. However, there is an awareness of the problem, a desire to tackle it, and a sales team which has been chosen carefully and cleverly (how many metal companies have an extremely knowledgeable and extrovert female selling for them?); all are undoubtedly a sign of company health. More likely, in a situation where a customer has not re-ordered for some time, the sales staff will give that customer a visit. Technique, needless to say, varies with the customer, but the strength of using the salesperson is he or she provides personal contact, so much stronger than disembodied voices over a phone. Moreover, this salesperson is an individual specifically hired because he or she shows talents in the area of explaining, displaying and selling the company products.

This, then, is the third major way in which Fabricast attempts to remain healthy: by using the sales staff as the eyes and ears of the company. By sending them out to customers, potential customers and sometimes lost customers, Fabricast is able to stay in touch with the changing moods and trends of the business they are in, receive quick feedback on their own service and products, and thereby can rapidly readjust to new situations. Dave Langton tells of the occasion when he went to a directors' conference, and one manager was bemoaning the fact that he could not afford sale staff. Dave smiled, and remarked that Fabricast couldn't afford *not* to have sales staff. He goes on, with some satisfaction, to point out that the company without sales staff went bankrupt a short time later.

It will probably have been observed by the reader that much of what Fabricast does is a person-inspired development which has close parallels with the company-wide 'quality' initiative at BP chemicals. Indeed, much of what Dave said could be (and had been) said at BP: a 'quality product' at both meant 'conformance to requirements' – giving customers what they want, at the standard they want, in the time agreed – essentially the basis for acquiring the prestigious BS 5750, the 'kitemark' of quality in the industrial sector, which Fabricast is moving rapidly towards. Dave, however, made two further comments about the standard. One was that, whilst it undoubtedly gave the producer a degree of security and the customer a guarantee of quality, it was difficult to acquire as it was a lengthy and costly process, and therefore acquisition – and future profitability – favoured the large rather than the small company. The second point was that he saw conformance to requirements (as BP increasingly does) as rather more than being given an order and fulfilling it. To do a really good job, one had to be close enough to the customer, he argued, to know their requirements and then be in a position to advise on the suitability of a particular order. Only in this way could situations be avoided where an order may be perfectly executed yet not be suitable for the task at hand, and the very real possibility of the customer blaming the supplier rather than itself. Dave gives the example – and mistake – of a West Yorkshire customer who ordered mild steel calorifiers for its swimming pools, without informing Fabricast of their purpose. Within six months they had perished, and the customer was considering suing Fabricast for loss of earnings, as it looked as if the pool would need to be out of use for several weeks. As it was, Fabricast, as a goodwill gesture, produced the correct calorifier shells within a couple of weeks and fitted them the following weekend, and split the cost with the council. This tricky situation was diplomatically resolved, but points clearly to the need for any company to know its customers' needs intimately. In an age when schools are being urged to be close to their customers as well, this acts as a good cautionary tale.


LESSONS FOR SCHOOLS?

Whilst there are *direct* transferabilities from the practices of small businesses to schools, just as interesting and informative is the fact that there are also strong similarities. This section, then, will be divided into two sections, on transferabilities and similarities.

**Transferabilities**

*Staying alive*

Perhaps the clearest message that came across from my visits to Fabricast was the awareness by those in managerial positions of the fact that the world did not owe the company a living. They saw the existence of the company as depending completely upon the expertise and hard work of the individuals who comprised it. If they did not do their bit, there was no one to bale them out. The company would simply fold. Whilst shock waves were felt throughout Marks & Spencer in 1991, and at BP Chemicals in late 1991 and early 1992, as reorganization took effect to streamline the companies and individuals were made redundant, this never achieved the kind of frightening and exhilarating 'you're on your own' feeling which I felt at Fabricast, largely, I think, because no one at the present time seriously doubts that both these giants will continue to exist into the middle future. Fabricast, despite its generally healthy situation, has neither the size nor resources (and the two go together) to cushion large blows. This chapter could have been called 'Fabricast: The Existentialist Company' precisely because its management believes that it needs to be constantly concerned about its existence, and must direct all of its energies, must ensure that all of its practices focus, to that end if it is to survive. It is interesting to note that it was one of the frustrations of the senior management team that it believed that this message had not permeated down sufficiently to the lower ranks; too many seemed happy with doing the minimum required, and then drawing their wages, rather than identifying with the company and seeing that their efforts provided for their and everyone else's long-term security.

There are parallels here between Fabricast and schools, in that aspects of the 1988 Education Reform Act attempted to give to English state schools the kind of 'existential danger' described above, but the process will not happen overnight, and, for some employees, possibly never. There has for many years been a security of employment in state schools which has both positive and negative sides. On the positive side, the lack of need for preoccupation with simple existence has meant that thought could be given to longer-term aims, and that experimentation could be attempted which would not be possible in a harsher climate. On the negative side, it has been argued that such comfort has led to some teachers being less concerned with giving children survival skills for the real world, less concerned with the skills their parents feel they need to learn, and more concerned with pursuing their own individual interests which might be intellectually satisfying but have little relevance to the communities within which the schools are situated and may provide for little continuity between the classes and the schools through which the pupils pass. One of the fundamental aims of the 1988 Act, then, has been to add a little more danger to the teacher's life. By connecting the number of pupils in the school to formula-funding, and by devolving the payment of salaries down to schools, the employment of a teacher then becomes inexorably linked to the number of pupils in the school. The logic is clear: not enough pupils, and teachers have to go. So teachers, like businesses, must ask the question, what must we do to ensure that we stay in employment? Most schools, even most small schools, have not reached the small company stage yet. They still think along lines of losing staff, rather than of the school closing. This is still a giant step from seemingly guaranteed employment, if not at one school then, through redeployment, at another. Fabricast is a refreshing, for some chilling, example of the need to re-examine one's priorities, and to continue re-examining them, with the prospect that complacency almost certainly leads to the dole queue. Staying alive could become the number one item on the agenda, even if, as at Fabricast, many still do not see it as such. Whilst many might argue that that is too great a preoccupation for an institution which needs to be able to pursue ideals not necessarily tied to the immediate wishes of its consumers, others might equally argue that staying alive has been for too long too far down the agenda.

*Local financial management*

It will be apparent that Fabricast places great emphasis on financial health, but that financial health is but a means to an end, which is the existence of the company. As explained above, Dave Langton does not see profit as the end goal of running a company but rather as an indicator of health, the necessary means to reinvest in the company and to have the resources to reward and motivate himself and his staff. The financial position of the company then sets the parameters for future planning. It does not determine direction or creativity as much as it sets limits within which such direction and creativity are pursued. This approach to the role of finance is important, because it suggests that a company like Fabricast, and a school in either the state or private sector are not far apart. Three complaints were frequently heard by schools when LMS was initially mooted. The first was that headteachers did not have the expertise to carry out such operations. A second was that they did not have the time, and that, if they made time, such financial involvement would steer them away from their real concerns – the children, the staff and the curriculum. Finally, it has been argued that, if schools were underfunded, LMS would act as a clever political move to shift the blame from central to localized management.

Fabricast's approach to financial management helps to place these criticisms in context. The first – that headteachers did lack these skills when LMS was introduced – seems undoubtedly to be the case. Several years on, however, this is much less often expressed, and in fact the general mood is one of having taken on a new skill which has expanded headteachers' understanding of the schools they run.

Again, the complaint of lack of time is a perennial one, and is made not just by those in education. The management of time is primarily about the prioritization of tasks so that those which are considered most important are allocated a greater portion of this time. Increasingly, headteachers have come to see financial management as an essential function, and so have found the necessary time, delegating other areas and responsibilities they now regard as less essential (a perhaps unexpected but welcome boost to schoolwide participation). Further, it is now increasingly recognized, as it has been by Fabricast, that financial management is an essential aspect of overall school planning. Thus, in one of the seminal books in this area, Caldwell and Spink (1988) argued that devolved financial management should not be seen either as something separate from the rest of school planning or as an obstacle to the achievement of these other areas, but as a recognition of the parameters that limited finance sets. Initial reflections upon the financial situation leads, as it does at Fabricast, to an evaluation of problems and possibilities, effects of raising finance, virement (the movement of finance) between different areas of activity, and therefore of achieving a more comprehensive understanding and planning for the school's future. Financial health, then, becomes as much a core concern for the school as it does for the company. This ultimately can only be good for the school and its community – for any organization that constantly lives beyond its means, does not learn from its financial situation and does not plan in accordance with this financial situation cannot ensure its own survival.

The final criticism, that devolution of finances could act as a buffer for governments from complaints of underfunding, is rather harder to deal with. There would seem to be some truth in this. Whilst Caldwell and Spink's book has been widely praised for its picture of the way in which a school might use self-management to produce a more participative approach, it has also been criticized for failing to address such political questions. Indeed, a number of writers, in a variety of countries, have voiced this criticism (see Smyth, 1993 on this). Here the differences with Fabricast are marked: there is an extra political dimension for schools, and other institutions funded from above, which Fabricast does not have to deal with. The general principles of good financial housekeeping are undoubtedly the same; the wider picture is clearly not.

## Similarities

*Paternalism, delegation and responsibility*

The small firm, almost inevitably, is going to reflect the personality of its owner, particularly if he or she runs the firm as well. This, as we have seen, has within it great potential but also the possibility of a variety of problems. English schools, and in particular English primary schools, have been faced with much the same kind of situation since their inception. Whilst the individuals running such schools may not actually own them, there still exists a strong and perhaps unsurprising degree of identification between school and headteacher. To understand this more fully, one needs to go back to the early nineteenth century to examine the kind of school which then existed in England, for a number of its core values can still be seen in schools today. According to Bernbaum (1976), the early English primary school generally consisted of one professional teacher (the head) drumming a few facts into a hall full of unruly boys with the aid of a small number of assistants who would each take sixty or seventy boys in an alcove for the same business. Both boys and assistants could be beaten if results or behaviour were unsatisfactory. The one 'expert' was the head, who also doubled as 'frontman' for the school, selling its wares to enquiring parents. In mid-century, to this archetypal conception of the headteacher was added the fruits of a Victorian evangelical religious revival, epitomized in the personalities of headteachers like Arnold of Rugby, who saw themselves not only as academic and entrepreneurial leaders but as pastoral and spiritual leaders as well. When state schools were formally established in 1870, who would be the individuals who would apply to lead such institutions, and who would be appointed? When both appointer and appointee had been through the same system, the headteachers of state schools would clearly be such paternalistic despots. This tradition was continued into the present century, and particularly so in the primary school. Not only was the average member of staff female, with all that this implied in a culture still laden with notions of female sexual inferiority, but such patriarchal superiority was that much easier to assume in a school filled with little children, rather than strapping adolescents.

Such paternalism was also aided by schools organized on the bases of class teaching rather than subject teaching. Being an expert in the development of the child, rather than in a subject and in the development of a child's understanding of that particular subject area, has for many years been seen as the distinguishing feature of the primary school teacher. Yet as Alexander (1984) points out, such a philosophy was initially the product of circumstance rather than ideology, for class teaching was originally seen as all that the average elementary schoolchild needed. Child-centred developmentalism came later and fitted neatly into an existing state of affairs. Such class teaching has provided, as Coulson (1986) puts it, 'sharp existential boundaries' for the teacher – a clearly defined area of responsibility for the teacher (the classroom) and for the headteacher (the overall running of the school). It unintentionally provided for the development of the 'restricted' professional as opposed to the 'extended' one, for teachers could know precisely for what they were responsible, and what they could leave to the head. A cosy arrangement tended to be the result, one uncongenial only to those who saw their jobs as extending beyond the cares and concerns of practical classroom tuition.

The combination of paternalism and class teaching has therefore tended to threaten the development of staff in the primary school. Where a system encourages individuals either (*a*) to develop autocratic attitudes to management or (*b*) to develop a myopia to an overall functioning of the school, then individuals in (*a*) will never need to develop the skills of delegation and participative management, whilst individuals in (*b*) will be hindered in the taking of institutional responsibility, and will fail to see that participation in the running of such institutions is not only a right but also a duty.

Confirmation of such psychological and cultural restraints comes from a variety of sources. Whilst Bell and Sigsworth (1987) indicate that children are given more responsibilities in small schools, and that the meetings between headteachers and teachers are both more informal and more constant, there is also evidence from others like Galton and Patrick (1990) that small-school organizational policies are remarkably unremarkable in their similarity to larger schools, for the reasons listed above. These writers, as well as Waugh (1990), also note that whilst some small-school heads do delegate rather better than heads of larger schools, there is a stubborn and paradoxical desire by others to retain a larger slice of duties than they can effectively perform, as if they feel that, having to be class teachers as well as heads, they need to retain some duties specifically to reassert their paternalistic position within the school. There is also the interesting observation by Galton and Patrick (1990) that heads of small schools are less likely to collaborate with secondary schools than heads of large schools. Whilst they give no reason for this, it seems a good bet that status factors, bound up so closely with the cultural inheritance just described, have an effect here as well.

A final point is worth making here. This is that the problems of company growth described by Dave Langton of Fabricast (p. 54) seem also to have parallels in the school. The problems of paternalism grow as the size of the organization exceeds the grasp of one individual, and the more that those within the organization become more specialized in their areas of expertise. Both these factors seem to go together, for increased size usually allows for and encourages increased specialization (though Marks & Spencer, for instance, try to counteract this in their demand that management trainees have a protracted experience of all sides of the stores' work). Secondary schools are generally of large size (700 plus) with specialist staff, and the problem of paternalism would seem to be less here because of this. In terms of the primary school, whilst this problem has been a fertile one for the last hundred and fifty years, present tensions in the UK have come about with the HMI report of 1978, advocating a greater degree of subject specialism in the primary school, and with the introduction of the1988 Act, which in effect made this inevitable, as well as putting considerable pressure on schools to provide one subject specialist teacher in each major area of the National Curriculum. With the increase in such specialism, the traditional role of the head becomes increasingly untenable, and the kinds of problems described above – particularly in terms of personality stamp – appear in much clearer outline. No longer can the organization exist satisfactorily with quite the degree of emphasis on the expertise and the predilections of its leader: it must look increasingly to a more dispassionate and rational analysis of the needs it is trying to fulfil and the expertise it can deploy to meet them.

## Small schools and personal development

It will be clear that both large and small organizations have their benefits and their problems. Whilst working in a large organization can be a marvellously broadening experience, providing scope, a variety of contacts and a responsibility to and for large numbers of people, the small organization provides the opportunity to exercise a degree of responsibility within the overall framework which the larger cannot match. Whilst the large organization can split up its duties into small specialist departments, and the individual can become a real expert in one area, the danger is of failing to see the overall structure of the firm. In the small firm an individual can be delegated and given responsibility for an entire area, and begin to see how the entire structure fits together. Of course, such delegation and responsibility have their prices, in particular of spreading oneself too far and of insufficient specialist development. Ideally, it would seem, then, that the individual would benefit from experience in both.

Small organization benefits should be clear to those who work in the business and education sectors. Both are organized around a small workforce, and normally have limited resources and a paternalistic management style. This can mean tensions between delegation and paternalism, increased responsibility and individual overload, and opportunities for personal development decided by others rather than by oneself. Such issues have come centre stage in small schools in the last few years as the whole role of the teacher in such schools has had to be re-examined. That role has always been disputed, mainly in a number of official reports critical of the viability of the small school. The Hadow Report (1931), the Plowden Report (1967), the HMI report on Primary Schools in 1978 and the *Better Schools* report of 1985 have all tended towards the conclusion that a far greater degree of subject specialism is needed in primary schools. This has now become reality with the 1988 Act.

The small school, under such analysis, becomes an ineffective and endangered species. As Bell and Sigsworth (1987: 53) trenchantly put it:

> Education is defined in terms of a nationally agreed set of objectives surrounding a common curriculum; a satisfactory education is therefore reduced to the satisfactory

transmission of this formal curriculum; a pre-requisite for that is held to be a satisfactory pattern of staffing of each school whereby the constituent elements of that curriculum are matched against the subject knowledge of the teachers.

The conclusion from this is inevitable: 'Demonstrably, the small rural primary school cannot be educationally satisfactory because it cannot provide teacher experts in each area of the curriculum' (*ibid.*).

Whilst increased subject specialism probably decreases paternalistic influences, and breaks down the limited conception of teaching generally associated with pure class teaching, and therefore may be very beneficial in the long run to the professional development of the primary school teacher (see Campbell, 1985), there are other less beneficial effects. One is that the strengths of such schools will probably not be utilized: this could well have serious repercussions for the personal development of both the teachers and the pupils in such schools.

Some small-school benefits are seldom noticed because of the domination of the culture of large-school teaching. A first effect of such domination is the generally accepted division of schools into classes in terms of age rather than other criteria. Organizationally, this is attractive, in that chronological grouping requires only basic information to place a child with other children and with a particular teacher. Further, even when grouping by ability is performed, it is invariably done within a chronological framework, that is by either streaming or setting. Chronological grouping, a practice which goes hand in hand with large-school organization, has become for many teachers an unchallenged orthodoxy, an almost automatic assumption of local and central governments.

However, the assumption that children's optimum personal development is to be found within their year cohort is based not upon deduction but upon accumulated observations over the years in medium and large urban schools. In such environments, children play almost exclusively with children not only of their own age but also of their own sex. The conclusion drawn by adults from such arrangements is that this is a natural state of affairs, rather than one created by institutional arrangements. As Bell and Sigsworth (1987: 98) remark: 'To be seen playing with, or associating with, a younger or older child, could be good cause to be regarded as odd.'

Yet Meyenn's (1980) study clearly indicates that when one moves beyond the standard urban classroom and looks at the relationships existing between children in vertically grouped small rural schools, different attitudes are apparent. The child tends to look at the organization in terms of school rather than class; he or she tends to view children older, younger and of opposite gender as significant others, rather than as irrelevancies. The child views the school as much more like the outside world, and therefore identifies with and integrates better into the school, for in both he or she socializes with older and younger without the artificial constraints imposed by the age-graded school.

Brown and Solomon (1983) suggest that major factors in the personal and prosocial development of children are their involvement from about age 6 with responsibilities for caring for young children, under adult supervision, mixing the ages of students at various levels from 2 years, and using co-operative learning that requires children to work with others of different ages and abilities. Vertical grouping would seem to be an ideal vehicle for providing such situations.

The problems of vertical grouping in terms of organization and provision of the appropriate curricular opportunities may be many, but so are the benefits. Integration into such a school can be immensely eased for children if they enter a new school in groups of only two or three at a time, for they will move into a class where the majority know the rules, customs and appropriate attitudes, and can act as role models. Once incorporated into the school, they rapidly come to realize that, as in life, they find others older and younger, brighter and slower than themselves. There are valuable social lessons to be learned in terms of patience, tolerance, helping and understanding others, as well as intellectual lessons in adjusting explanations to individuals of differing abilities – an activity which increases not only one's own deeper understanding of the concept at hand but also one's empathic understanding of others.

## CONCLUSION – THE DEVELOPMENT OF COMMUNITY, THE DEVELOPMENT OF CITIZENS

There are, then, a number of factors which suggest that the small school has, like the small firm, a number of advantages over its larger counterpart. A final major advantage may come through the role it can play in developing the citizens of the future.

If schools are to play their part in the development of citizens in a democratic society, children from the earliest age need to see and participate in such a democracy. The first part of this – seeing – comes through members of that institution participating in decision-making, such that it is clearly communicated to the children that participation is not simply a right, or worse a luxury, to be picked up or dropped as one feels fit. It must also be seen as a duty if that form of government is to remain in a healthy condition. This kind of participation has been extended in the late 1970s to include more directly interested outsiders like parents and others in the community, but in the first instance it is the children's sight of teachers' involvement on a day-to-day basis which will have the most lasting impression. It is from this sight that children can begin to pick up the same behaviours and begin to perform them themselves.

In small schools, the opportunities for this kind of citizenship education are probably greater than they are in larger schools. At the pupils' level, they are closely involved with children who display a much wider spread of age and ability than in the 'normal' classroom, and yet something which is much more representative of society as a whole. Moreover, there are comparatively so few children in the school that each child can take responsibility for a variety of jobs, jobs that would be shared between a number of children at the larger school or which would be performed by the teachers themselves.

There are so many responsibilities – particularly after the 1988 Act – which need to be performed that, for practical reasons alone, it makes good sense to delegate a large number of these. What one should see, then, is a logical and systematic appraisal by headteacher and class teachers of the tasks that need to be performed, and of those that can be delegated to other competent individuals. The result could be that both teachers and children in small schools have the opportunity to participate in decision-making and perform a range of tasks which might not normally be thought their due in the larger establishment (even if, as I shall argue in the final chapter, it *should* be). It would also mean that the individual headteacher could perform his or her central role more satisfactorily.

Organizationally, the small school can provide the kind of workplace where professional and personal development is fostered, and where the individual teacher sees much better the overall purpose of the institution and, in so doing, directs attention to the ultimate purposes of the educational processes in society. In so doing, the school becomes a vehicle for citizenship, thought and participation, rather than merely an institution for curriculum technicians. If it accepted that all schools should aspire to this end, then small schools are better placed than most to make it happen.

Finally, one of the major benefits normally associated with small schools has little to do with education as such, but comes from their contributory effect to that small part of society of which they are a part. Much of this stems from Durkheim's insight that people can identify with the more personal institution. Schools – and particularly small schools – may therefore contribute to the creation of a general identity, providing a linkage within that community for people who would otherwise be no more than individuals living in geographical proximity. When one mother complains 'We never see each other now because I take John to [the new school] by car and therefore I go through the village by car. I drive through the village and drive back again' (quoted in Bell and Sigsworth, 1987: 210), she is making the same point put bluntly by another parent, three pages on in the same book: 'It's just as important to the village as it is to the children. That's what it comes down to in the end. It's just as important for the village.'

The continuity of life in a community is determined by a number of factors: the school is one of them. If this sense of belonging, of personal fulfilment and therefore of meaningful contribution to that society is to be effected, then the existence of community schools may be essential. It is interesting to speculate whether small firms might also act in this manner. If small schools can act as generators for the development of a more actively involved and participative citizenry, because they allow individuals within them to practise the kinds of roles needed in the larger society, do small firms have a similar kind of effect? If it is the case that small firms are healthier for a democracy than their larger counterparts – and common sense would tend to suggest this to be the case – then one has another strong reason for arguing that small organizations are not amateur versions of bigger ones but different organizations altogether. They have their strengths and weaknesses, as do their larger counterparts, but they have a strong claim for being not only economically viable and personally motivating but perhaps politically necessary as well.

# Chapter 4

# Anglo Motors : A Change for the Better?

## THE ORGANIZATION

This chapter is rather different from the previous three studies. When those started, the three companies involved were all encountering the need for change and were meeting some difficulties along the way, but still regarded themselves as fundamentally sound in the directions they were taking, and the philosophy they were adopting as the motor to that change. In such situations, it was very generous of the companies to invite an observer in, but not very threatening to have someone watching day-to-day activities. Anglo Motors was different. There was little doubt that I was initially invited in by certain people in the company as part of a process of change, to assert to other sections of the management, workforce and the outside world that Anglo was open, accessible and willing to explain why it was doing what it was doing.

Rather, than being merely an observer, I was, then, I think, in a very small way, a part of the process of change. As far as I was concerned, that was quite acceptable: I did nothing but my normal job, for my presence was sufficient. Anglo, then, had courage, because opening up to possible criticism as the first step to personal growth is not easy. It is important, therefore, at the outset to this chapter, to thank those who made it possible. Nevertheless, I came into the company during the severest economic recession of the last fifty years, and observed, even during my fairly brief stay, an attempt at a fairly radical change in management style to one which can only be called basic survival management – how to keep the company's head above water. Indeed, as the situation deteriorated, I found myself increasingly sidelined, as management decided that their time could be better spent than in dealing with me. They became increasingly edgy about having an external observer in to see such difficulties, and I was more and more excluded from meetings.

The end result was that late in the day I was asked to make this chapter unattributable, and this is what I have done. The company has been given a different name (one which I have attempted to ensure applies to no other motor company!), and every effort has been made to prevent its identification. I believe that my exclusion and the request for anonymity were as much the result of the decline in the general economic condition of the country as of Anglo's management culture, though the former certainly didn't help the openness of the latter. So, whilst I did observe a concerted attempt by a motor company at changing its philosophy and practices in difficult conditions, I did not observe the following stage – that of survival management. Clearly, this latter stage would have been valuable and fascinating (if very painful for the company); but the management of change in difficult times is one which faces most schools at the present time, and so I still believe this to be a very worthwhile chapter.

**Hard times in the motor trade**

During the late 1980s and early 1990s, Britain, like much of the rest of the world, went through a severe economic recession. As more people were made redundant, found it hard to make mortgage repayments, or, if in work, discovered that there was less and less demand for what they produced, they drew their horns in, spent less money, put what little they could away for a rainy day . . . and waited. On the High Street, sales became the order of the day – spring, summer, mid-season, there was no time which wasn't sale time. If a shop *didn't* have a sale, then it was an unusual shop, and probably an unvisited one as well. A minimum of 20 per cent off the normal retail price became the going rate. Shoppers became conditioned to expect a bargain, until the bargain became the norm. The trouble with this kind of thing, long-term, is that businesses cannot remain in business without some form of profit, and, as Britain moved through the early 1990s, more and more businesses simply disappeared. A vicious circle began to appear, for the more businesses ceased trading, the more people there were out of work, the fewer people there were to buy the goods, and the more businesses ceased trading.

As the potential market of buyers declined, so companies chased fewer and fewer customers. Any weaknesses in companies were brought to light in a painful manner, and they were forced to take a long hard look at structures, practices and personnel. Lean and efficient became the watchwords. Of course, this should always be an important consideration, but self-examination tends to be neglected when times are good. Companies take on layers of fat, surplus tiers of management are created, and individuals continue to be employed for work that no longer exists, or that can be more sensibly done by others. But more than this, a slightly self-satisfied outlook, which can result in reduced customer service, has to be turned around. The company must now even more urgently turn itself not only to attracting customers and selling them products but – crucially – to getting them to return. In terms of the car trade, this means not just selling the car but ensuring that the customer returns to have the car serviced at the place of purchase, and will return in two to three years' time to buy another one. You don't do that by fleecing the customer, by shoving him or her out of the front door as soon as he or she has signed on the dotted line, by delivering cars that have faults, or by poor after-sales service. You do it by showing an ability to listen to what customers want and need, by helping them make the right decision for their personal and financial situation and then ensuring that they feel cared for by specific individuals within the company all the way through to their next car. This can initially mean changing personal philosophies of salesmanship. It certainly also means ensuring that the entire company – from sales to pre-delivery and inspection, to servicing, parts and repairs – pulls together. It is a commonplace to say that a chain is only as strong as its weakest link, but it is a commonplace because it is invariably accurate: one bad experience in this chain of experience from buying one car to another could well mean the los of that customer, and that affects *all* jobs in the company. So an awareness of interdependency in the workplace is going to be an essential prerequisite of staying afloat.

It is not unfair to say that Anglo has faced many of these problems over the past few years, having to shed over a third of its workforce in the last few years, and has found it hard to adjust. It is a company which over a number of decades had built up a profitable operation, developing almost casually from interests in a very different area of the economy. Acquiring a franchise with a large car manufacturer some twenty years ago, and hence also acquiring a captive market, it came to find itself one of the most important centres of the motor trade in its area.

Not surprisingly, there are those within the company who speak with considerable affection of those days, who find present conditions a long way from the pre-eminence they once undoubtedly had. It can be very hard to be self-critical when you're at the top. Particularly when rivals don't seem to be serious competition, a franchise with a major producer ensures a steady stream of customers, for if customers want one of these cars – and they invariably do – then they have to come to you. On top of that, the economy looked fine, everyone seemed to have money to spend, so it really did not seem that necessary to some to try too hard. In such circumstances, it can be very tempting to sit back and indulge in some self-congratulation. Handy, in his book *The Age of Unreason* (1989), tells the tale of the two frogs: one who is put into a pan of boiling water, and immediately jumps out; the other who, by being placed in water which only gently warms up, fails to realize that the climate is changing, and is boiled to death. It is clear which frog Anglo more closely resembled.

Fairly easy success tends to hide other problems. A company that is set up on a small scale and finds a ready market doesn't tend to look too closely at its own structure. A centralized, paternalistic approach, which worked well enough in what we have called the Fordist era of business and industry, increasingly found as the company expanded that efficiency and productivity came from post-Fordist ideas of decentralization – from giving responsibility to the dealer principals (i.e. those in charge of the branches) and their staff to run their areas themselves, rather than for them to have to come back to the centre for every decision to be made. But change in these circumstances is not just a matter of delegating power and then assuming that everything will be fine. Centraliz-ation over a period of time can produce a mentality which conditions against the exercise of personal initiative and responsibility. In other words, there needed to be a change in culture. If a company has gone along very comfortably for a large number of years with one particular culture, many of those within it are going to find any proposed changes difficult to adjust to.

Other problems began to appear. The other major car manufacturers started to produce some very attractive cars, and to provide serious competition. Furthermore, previous customers began to say that some of the range was beginning to look a little dated, and the customer with a taste for the new started to look elsewhere. There also appeared a problem with the predominant selling technique – what is called the Pendle system – which certainly sold cars when it was introduced some years ago but which, in its pure form, depended on a mixture of customer bullying and obligation. It was not customer-friendly, and probably was a disincentive for the customer to return. So, with a decline in the total number of cars being sold because of the recession, Anglo, like many other companies, had to look long and hard at a large number of things – from its structures to its practices to its personnel. Some of those at Anglo realized that if it was to remain at the forefront, then like it or not, it was going to have to change. This chapter, then, begins to examine this process of change through looking at the trade of the car salesperson, before taking a wider view of change within the company.

## The art of selling

Is there a more maligned or distrusted beast than the car salesman? (This stereotypical figure is invariably male.) In the pantheon of public villains probably only politicians and Dr Crippen come higher. Everyone knows you can't trust what they say, that they'd cheat their own grandmother given half a chance. Not to put too fine a point on it, the paternity of all of them is universally known to be in doubt.

The reader might then be surprised to learn whom the car salesman distrusts. Without exception, every car salesman I talked to said it was members of the general public. They lie, they cheat, they say they can spend this amount, when they've really got another couple of thousand back in reserve, they say the car has done so many miles, when they have actually wound back the clock, they expect a Rolls Royce when they've got the money for a Lada. Every car salesman can tell you a horror story about how in their early days they were taken to the cleaners by one of the general public. But never again. They now assume that the individual entering the showroom is totally untrustworthy and they believe they won't be too far wrong. It's a surprise either side ever does any business.

Where is the truth? Probably somewhere in the middle. A team of car salespeople is normally a fascinating mix. There will probably be the out-and-out rogue, the Flash Harry. There will be the rough diamond, the individual with the local accent and the quirky sense of humour. Then there will be the gentle individual, who hardly raises his voice, and is attentive and considerate at all times. There will probably be the older member of the team, the man you can rely on because he gives the appearance of knowing his cars, and therefore of giving you the right advice. And, increasingly, there will be the attractive young lady who charms you efficiently round the car. Each is a different key, each is designed to fit a different customer's lock. What will work for one customer will not for another. Having said that, they all tend to have certain qualities in common. Firstly, they tend to be tough. They will probably be rejected on more occasions than they are accepted, and rejection hurts. To fail, and to fail again, and to know you have failed, needs a strong ego. Successful salespeople have one. Secondly, they tend to have personality, for before they sell the car they have to sell themselves. Thirdly, they tend to be someone you can trust, and this means selling themselves before they can sell the car – and to do that, they have to know what will sell themselves. Therefore, fourthly, they tend to be excellent practical psychologists. Fifthly, for the reasons given above, they tend to be wary – the public is out for a kill just as much as they are. And lastly, and probably most importantly, they tend to be hungry. On more than one occasion it was remarked to me that the car salesman who doesn't *need* to sell a car usually doesn't sell it. The best car salesperson, it was argued, is probably a man with a wife, two young children and a large mortgage.

However, the selling of cars doesn't stop there. Whilst each salesperson has his or her own techniques, these are normally contextualized within a particular house selling system. This may come as much of a surprise to the reader as it did to me when I first realized this: most car salespeople, save perhaps for the most amateur back-street operator, go on training courses, and these courses are normally run by companies who recommend their own individual approach. Perhaps the three most used over the last decade have been the Pendle, Edginton and Sewell control systems. They are termed 'control' systems because none allows the customer to choose between cars on the forecourt – the customer is controlled, directed and persuaded into looking at *a* particular car which the company wishes to sell them – and the salesperson is similarly controlled in what he or she may offer to the customer by the manager in a back room. Each of these systems harnesses (some would say stifles) the talents of individual salespeople and then structures the interaction between them and customers. To customers, all may look spontaneous and personalized, but they are actually the subject of a carefully worked-out and systematic selling process. Indeed, only whilst doing the research for this chapter did I realize that I had been 'Pendled' with the last car I bought! It might then be useful here to describe these three systems briefly.

The Pendle system – the predominant system used in Anglo Motors over the last few years – is now nearly a decade old. It requires the salesperson to work out what the customer can afford and assess with the customer what he or she wants – even before they look at a car. Even if they come in, having expressed an interest in a particular car, the salesperson will still ask the customer what kind of money they have, what sort of car they want, what kind of deal they want. All of this is carefully noted down, and then, while the customer is having a coffee, the salesperson will take the initial figures to the controller in the back, who will select the car the company would like the customer to take. On returning, the customer is persuaded to agree to an initial set of figures (indeed, asked to sign a form showing that they are happy with such figures), a car (pre-selected by the controller in the office) is then shown to the customer.

The customer may by now believe that a deal has just about been struck, and that closure is only a step away. However, the control system now comes into play, for when the salesperson takes the facts and figures backstage, he or she returns to say that the boss won't allow him to do the desired deal. The customer is disappointed, the salesperson acts similarly so, and through this he or she may develop a relationship with the customer which is almost conspiratorial, as the salesperson supposedly attempts to persuade the controller in the back room to agree to the deal he or she (the salesperson) has set up. In actual fact, in a true Pendle system the sales staff have no control over what goes on. They are there to act as little more than go-betweens. Then, through a process of pressure and obligation, the customers, having been drawn so far into a deal which they had agreed to but which now appears just out of reach, may eventually come to accept a deal which they would never have agreed to when they walked through the doorway.

The Edginton system is described by many in the trade as 'soft Pendle', in that it has many of the trademarks of Pendle but works less on the hard sell, and more on making the customer feel obligated to the dealer. It will usually include such lines as 'What is the most you would expect for your car?' which is never replied to negatively but left hanging as if this valuation is acceptable. Like Pendle, it uses the controller in the back, will involve taking the customer to the car the company wants to sell, and also a written proposal carefully drawn-up by the salesperson which the customer will be asked to sign as declaration of intent. This is a crucial move, as it effectively in most cases obligates the customer to buy the car at that price. Of course, the customer doesn't get that price – the controller in the back sees to that – because this is where the prior high valuation of the customer's car is now withdrawn, and protracted negotiations between customer and manager, through the intermediary of the salesperson, begin. If the first stage takes half an hour, these negotiations take anywhere up to two and a half hours, as the customer tries to get nearer and nearer the original agreement, which he or she by now probably thinks was a super deal.

The Sewell system differs from the two above in that more attention is given to the car the customer actually came in to look at. However, as in all control systems, the customer is not allowed to move from one car to another on the forecourt and to compare cars. Furthermore, the controller in the back, upon being given the information regarding the customer's car, will tell the salesperson to 'low-bowl' the customer – to undervalue the car, and to work from that base. So the 'hook' comes from allowing the customer to select the car of his or her choice, but the hard bargain is driven by offering a low price on the car to be exchanged. Of course, this whole process will take place in actuality between the customer and the sales manager in the back, with the salesperson acting as little more than the 'gopher' – though the customer almost certainly will not realize precisely what is going on.

All control systems, it will be apparent, have their good points and bad points. Firstly, they utilize the talents of the manager in the office to the full, and get the most out of the latter's knowledge of cars and prices. Managers are, after all, the individuals who have the most experience at selling cars. It might seem sensible to have such battle-hardened veterans handling the overall negotiations of each deal. In so doing, they prevent the mistakes of the beginner losing a sale, and at the same time supervise the training of this beginner.

Secondly, by distancing the dealer from the scene of battle, they are able to maintain a cold rationality, which a salesperson faced by a particularly determined and persuasive customer may not be able to do. In so doing, the dealer is more likely to achieve the kind of deal that the company wants.

Thirdly, by analysing the selling process, and by systematically introducing at various points in the selling procedure certain hooks to keep the customer interested, car dealerships are able to use a full array of psychological ploys to sell their cars. Rather than relying on the individual merits of particular car salespeople, the dealership knows that a systematization – and therefore professional coverage – of the selling process has been achieved.

However, control systems do have their problems. If they utilize the experience of the manager, they can under-utilize the capacities of the salesperson. If they draw upon the skills and capacities of the manager, they can prevent the salesperson from developing his or hers, for it is only through the use of such skills – and reflection upon their success and failure – that real development occurs. The short-term result of using a control system may be a degree of success in persuading customers to part with their money, but the long-term result may be to stunt the growth of the salesperson, and thereby to prevent the development of a new generation of managers.

Furthermore, many of the salespeople I talked to said how strenuous a control system was for them – a process of 'chewing you up and spitting you out' was how one described it. After all, the salespeople take all the flak from the customer when the controller in the back issues new harder bargaining offers, and must force the deal through, but are not allowed to use their judgement or initiative. For any with feelings or scruples, it can be a very hard system to live with.

Moreover, control systems were explicitly designed to sell cars, not to bring the customer back to the garage. In other words, they are sets of procedures, psychological ploys, points of pressure, to get customers to leave the showroom only when they have bought a car. So other considerations, such as commitment to after-sales service, or returning in two years' time for a new motor, do not enter into the calculations, and generally suffer. Customers, then, may leave the showroom having bought a car, and yet instead of feeling satisfied and excited (a car may be, after all, the second-largest purchase they make in their lives) may well have a feeling of having been manipulated, bullied, of having spent rather more than they wanted to, and wondering how they are going to make the payments without having to economize on something else. The result will probably be that servicing will take place elsewhere, and next time they want a car they will shop elsewhere.

Finally, one might question the very ethics of such control approaches within the car trade. Selling a product can be seen as part of a larger picture in which quality and relationships play the predominant part. As discussed in the BP chapter, true quality is achieved only when a relationship of trust and honesty is reached. Control systems are, in many ways, the antithesis of such relationships, concentrating as they do on psychological hooks, pressure and an undercurrent of misrepresentation. It might well be that Anglo's fortunes have suffered as much from their selling style as from their internal organization. Certainly, in the past, it has been no encouragement to the trust and the development of personal relationships of the kind integral to the achievement of total quality management. In this respect, it is interesting to note that even the degree of bargaining, normally such a part of car cultures, has been dropped by some car dealers. 'One price' car dealerships are becoming increasingly popular in the USA, and are just beginning in the UK, and this may be due in no small part to people's desire to enter into agreements where all the cards are on the table: where relationships of honesty and trust may develop.

My views on selling cars were, unsurprisingly, not shared by many at Anglo. Typical are the comments in a letter by one senior executive:

> I think you have been somewhat hard on the various 'selling systems'. One has to understand that car sales, just like property sales, are negotiated sales unlike the 'take it or leave it' un-negotiable price of Marks & Spencer. Both the public and the sales force know exactly what they want or more importantly what they can afford. The first task of the salesperson is, therefore, to find how much the customer can actually afford and then commence negotiations. It will in the end be a compromise solution. One of the prime aims within Anglo is never to let a customer pay more than he can afford for obvious reasons.

This, it seems to me, is a reflection of present policy rather than a description of the hard systems used in the past. Certainly, where companies like Anglo have realized that stability and long-term viability come from repeat customers and are not gained by a hard control system, other techniques have been sought. *Customizing* the individual entering your premises is the first step.

Imagine (said the manager of one branch of the company in explanation) that you want to buy a hi-fi set. You go to all the major retailers, and ask them what is the difference between various systems. They look at the shelves, and tell you the names, and the prices. A fat lot of good that is, you say to yourself, I can do that myself. No wiser, and rather disgruntled, you head off down the road to the specialist's shop. You announce to the owner you want to buy a hi-fi set. Now before he even shows you a set, he sits you down and asks you a variety of questions. What price did you want to pay? What sort of system have you got now? What kind of music do you play? How big is the room you want it in? What do you want from the set? Have you a family who will be doing other things whilst you're listening? What is your favourite piece of music? Now he gives you a cup of coffee, and asks to be excused for a few minutes. He returns shortly, and asks you to come with him. You enter a dimly lit room, he asks you to sit in a comfortable chair, and, when you do, suddenly you are surrounded by the sound of your favourite piece of music. You listen, enchanted, until the end, and then he carefully explains the system he has chosen, why he has chosen it, how it fits with your described needs. It may be slightly more then you intended to pay, but his reasons for choosing this set are clear. You remember that the same set cost £30 less at the major retailer down the road. What do you do?

Most people (suggested my manager) would be happy to buy this particular set, and buy it from him, because, firstly, he had listened to your needs, secondly, he clearly knew what he was talking about, and thirdly, you felt that his time and expertise was *worth* £30 – you could trust him. Moreover, given this help, you feel, at some future date, that here is the shop to return to. This is what customizing is about, a step not too far from the relationships of quality, honesty and trust mentioned above.

Customizing the buyer can be developed to some extent within a control system, but it would be virtually impossible within a rigid control system, firstly because such control systems prevent the development of the flexibility required for such customizing; and secondly because they run counter to the relationships of honesty and trust which a fully fledged total quality management approach requires.

Certain branches in the Anglo group still use a control system, but of a rather liberal variety. The man in the back *was* used, but more in an advisory capacity, and, moreover, aspects of all systems were used in an artistic manner, to fit the personalities of the sellers involved. In the two main branches, an even more liberated system was in the process of being installed. This involved the complete dropping of control systems, and the use of salespeople to take the sale through from beginning to end. Managers felt capable of delegating such duties because they knew the salespeople. After all, they had personally selected them (with well over half having been dismissed in the last couple of years, they were in the position to handpick their teams). Moreover, both branches were in the process of training up their salespeople. I listened in one morning while one salesman was questioned on his 'homework' – had he learnt the advantages that the company's cars had over their rivals from other producers in terms of performance and extras? Only by ensuring that the salesman could handle such questions – and use the information when it had not been asked – did the managers feel sure that their staff could be 'trusted' with the operation. Certainly, the effect upon the sales team was beneficial. Being credited with the intelligence to carry a sale all the way through brought a personal involvement to each deal which undoubtedly increased morale. Moreover, I did not see the salespeople *not* using the manager for advice – on the contrary, the trust vested in them by management was reciprocated.

Thus, there is movement in the selling techniques at Anglo, though some might look to further developments. Relationships of trust and honesty with customers were still in need of development. There was still variation in how far down the road the sales staff were in educating customers as to what they needed rather than what they wanted; there was still considerable variation in whether a car would be sold purely on whether it was the most immediately profitable for the sales staff to sell: would the sales staff, for instance, be honest enough to tell customers if a less expensive car was more suited to their requirements? Further, and most tellingly, will a situation ever be countenanced where it is seen as part of the relationship between seller and customer for the sales individual to inform the customer if a model produced by another company suits their requirements better? Anglo, like most car dealerships (and most firms for that matter) would not countenance such a move, and yet it might be argued that a relationship predicated on trust and honesty, which stressed the long-term nature of such relationships, would ultimately demand such honesty. This would dramatically alter the nature of companies, and provide selling techniques with a much greater ethical orientation, one which many in schools might find much easier to live with. Nevertheless, one of the really encouraging things at the two Anglo main branches was the employment of sales managers who believed in individual potential and its nurture. In many respects, the sales department struck me as the flagship for change in the company. Others, however, were not so keen to follow. Why was this so?

## Resistance to change

Change is seldom seen as pleasant, and certainly many of Anglo's employees are no different from most others. There are some who would locate the reason for this resistance in a belief that human beings are by nature deeply conservative, and that any change will be taken as threatening. As Marris (1975: 51) points out, what such beliefs fail to take into account is that individuals are members of social systems who have shared senses of meaning, and to disrupt that meaning is to disrupt the individual's understanding of his or her world.

More accurate, perhaps, is Drucker's assessment that, if change is done well, it is at least tolerable, and may even be welcomed. What is essential is that certain conditions need to be satisfied if employees are going to be psychologically ready. As he says (1968: 324–5):

> The change must appear rational . . . man always presents to himself as rational even his most irrational, even erratic changes. It must appear as an improvement. And it must not be so rapid nor so great as to obliterate the psychological landmarks which make a man feel at home: his understanding of his work, his relations to his fellow workers, his concepts of skill, prestige and social standing in certain jobs and so forth. Change will meet resistance unless it clearly and visibly strengthens man's psychological security; and man being mortal, frail and limited, his security is always precarious.

If this, more optimistic picture is true, where have the resistances to change at Anglo come from? I will suggest five possible areas.

*The culture of the company*

Two aspects of the culture deserve mention here. The first is that the company has tended to employ individuals from the locality rather than further afield, and there has therefore tended to grow up an inwardness which has not encouraged new ideas. Indeed, it is only of late that Anglo has made a conscious attempt to provide an injection of fresh ideas by the employment in key positions of individuals from outside the area. A second aspect has already been mentioned – management by centralized paternalism – and whilst this originally seemed to work, such a style is antithetical to that which was increasingly seen as necessary to give Anglo a new start – greater decentralization of decision-making to dealer-principalships, more flexibility, more team and multi-level responsibility. Resistance, then, could be expected from virtually all levels, for both management and employees had long been socialized into one style of working.

*Reaction from the top*

It has already been remarked that change is not only an intellectual but a psychological process. Whilst it may look sensible and necessary on paper, it will need a good deal to make it effective. One major hurdle Anglo has had to overcome has been to do with the process of decentralization. This has necessitated a change of roles between both non-active and active board members, and dealer principals and their departmental managers. In brief, one group has had to learn to take more responsibility, the other has had to learn to let go of the reins. Those *taking* more responsibility have found themselves, when the process has gone well, being given this responsibility, but also found themselves more accountable to those above and below. Questions then arise concerning the kinds of procedures to be put into place to ensure that they are carried out, and who is monitoring them. Then comes the question of whether such procedures have been put in place, and how they are to be revised. Further, those *devolving* responsibility may find it hard to accept that a particular issue in a branch is not their responsibility, that their presence is neither as necessary (nor as welcome!) as previously. They will, at best, have to recast their role to take account of these changes in structures and functions; at worst they may lose their job altogether. Clearly, neither group will welcome such uncertainty.

*Reaction from the middle*

It was remarked to me on more than one occasion that change was going to be hardest for those at the top; but it certainly can be hard for those in the middle who may have their job descriptions re-created, and have to adjust work practices accordingly. Not only that but if these changes are not fully explained they can be seen as arbitrary impositions rather than rational adjustments, amounting to change by experimentation, where change is seen as being made to find out what will happen, not seen as initiated in order that specific objectives will be achieved. This naturally leads to resentment as those implementing the change come to see themselves as guinea pigs who are considered expendable. Too often it is assumed that change is the same as progress, and yet the two are not the same at all. Full and considered communication of changes, with time for adjustment, are therefore essential preconditions for successful change. And yet, as each individual adjusts at a different rate, there can never be one successful rate of change within a company. Invariably, change will be too quick for some, too slow for others, just right for the lucky few. Resistance will most obviously come from the first group, but may still be seen from those who think that not enough is being done at a fast enough rate, or in the right way.

### Reaction from the bottom

Perhaps curiously, those at the bottom may have few of their actual practices changed at first. There may be only so many ways to service a car, but their change will be as fundamental in the long run as anyone else's. This is for two reasons. The first is the increased emphasis on customer service, for everyone in the company is going to have to be skilled at dealing with the public. If those at the bottom are the weakest link, then, to repeat the commonplace, the chain is broken just as surely as if it was the managing director. For many, this is difficult, even uncomfortable to comprehend. They may well believe that they were hired to service cars, not to be experts at public relations, but this will increasingly be an integral part of their job description. The company is putting time and money into this movement by employing a team of trainers to improve such qualities. Yet, it was clear to me, sitting in on a training session run by an organization which has intimate links with Marks & Spencer, that there were those in the company who found this process distinctly uncomfortable, embarrassing even. It is a road, though, which they are going to have to travel.

The second reason is one mentioned in previous chapters when referring to quality. Quality comes not just from the quality control department but from each individual reacting to practices or structures which inhibit the delivery of a quality service, and feeding these upwards. Whilst Anglo has a structure of 'consultative councils' which should in principle perform this function, the hierarchical structure which has existed at Anglo since its inception has prevented the full realization of their potential. Those at the bottom are going to have to be encouraged to feel that criticism of structures and practices will be seen not as negative criticism of those in authority but as a genuine attempt to improve the overall performance of the company. This is a long-term job, and one which will be integral to the successful implementation of a new company culture.

### Change by outsiders

The insularity of the company culture was mentioned above. Such an influence can and does socialize those who spend any length of time within such a climate, and it is therefore not too surprising to find that Anglo has brought in new blood to create a new urgency and new expectations. Nevertheless, there is understandably a measure of anxiety and miscommunication between the new and the old. Those who have been passed over in favour of newer appointments, or whose power has been redefined or curbed, or who feel that they have done a good job for the company for a long time and that the changes are an implicit criticism of work which used to be well received, would not be human if they did not feel some degree of resentment which can translate into resistance to change. It is also possible that those outside the company, whilst brought in to initiate change, may be encouraged to initiate change before they fully realize the physical and psychological territory they are working in. An initial prescription then might be to understand this psychological precariousness, and allow for it. This is easier said than done in a company which is having to change rapidly. Nevertheless, this very speed can be a major contributory factor to a lack of effectiveness in the change process. As Marris (1975: 166) says:

> however reasonable the proposed changes, the process of implementing them must still allow the impulse of rejection to play itself out. When those who have power to manipulate changes act as if they have only to explain, and when their explanations are not at once accepted, shrug off opposition as ignorance or prejudice, they express a profound contempt for the meaning of lives other than their own. For the reformers have already assimilated these changes to their purposes, and worked out a reformulation which makes sense to them, perhaps through months or years of analysis and debate.

If the reformers were to deny others the chance to go through this internal process of debate, it is small wonder if change is at best only half-hearted.

A further source of resistance may lie in the fact that those who have been around for a long time may not have initiated new practices *not* because they have been insufficiently innovatory but because they knew the local conditions well enough to know they would not work. And to be fair, it may be the case that *neither* side may know the full truth until it has been attempted – and we are back into the problems of change through experimentation. Whichever way you work it, newcomers and their ideas are going to encounter some resistance – and the more a company is peopled by individuals used to other ways, the more resistance is likely to be met.

**The management of change**

If these are the problems, how are changes being managed? I suggest that they can be divided into five main areas:

- a change in philosophy
- changes in structure
- changes in communication
- changes in personnel
- change in attitude

Each will be dealt with in turn.

*A change in philosophy*

Some of this has been discussed above, but rather more needs to be said. 'A change in philosophy' is rather simplistic: it tends to suggest a monolithic organization which simply faces in another direction. In actual fact, Anglo, like any other organization, is made up of individuals who are at different stages of a continuum between the older paternalistic, rather secretive, centralized style characteristic of the company a few years ago, and the decentralized, more open, customer-oriented style being ushered in. There are those who have worked for the company for a good many years who feel that they have always practised the tenets of the 'new philosophy' (indeed, this may be one of the reasons why they continue to be employed by the company after a massive shake-up which saw a third of the workforce disappearing). Nevertheless, it remains true that a company with any degree of hierarchy or leadership will derive most of its philosophy, and hence its structure, from the top. Anglo has still a way to go in totally effecting change. The change in philosophy can really only come about when practices characteristic of such a philosophy are widespread and habitual, and they will become so only when there are sufficient people practising them. Some of this comes about through a change in personnel; other aspects come about through a change in attitude of existing personnel. In other words, the process of change is a process of dialectic – the practice derives from the theory, but the theory also derives from the practice. They need each other for both to grow.

Let us take a number of examples of this process of change. Firstly, the use of the training organization mentioned above is a conscious attempt by the company to make the discussion – and responsible constructive criticism – of existing structures and practices (including their own) a part of each employee's approach to working for Anglo. This kind of thing is a part of the culture at somewhere like Marks & Spencer; it is just accepted as part of the job. It is clearly not that yet at Anglo, and may take some considerable time to implement. Many individuals need to be given the basic skills and confidence simply to talk about themselves and their jobs, to raise to consciousness precisely what they are doing and why they are doing it, to see that sessions on improving work practice are part of their self-development within the company. This clearly has to be linked with an appraisal system which is sold (and seen) as part of this attempt by the company to aid the development of individuals in the company, and not one of punitive accountability. When the employees see such sessions as a normal and helpful part of their working day, when they understand and accept the philosophy behind them, then Anglo will really be on the road to change. But this is a long process which takes both time and money, and it might be tempting for some at board level to think that paying staff (and the training organization) to (seemingly) sit round for an hour and talk, when they could be doing other apparently more productive things, is rather wasteful. Anglo is to be applauded for starting the process, but it will be a key test of its commitment to genuine change as to how much and for how long it funds ventures like this.

Secondly, and following from this, such training needs to be part of a process of change within the individuals in the company such that they are empowered to take charge of their own careers and feel responsible for what they do, rather than referring this to someone higher up. If they are best able to see needed changes, they should have enough trust in the company, their superiors and themselves to suggest such changes. Indeed, this climate of openness could, as remarked previously, be unsettling for all levels of the company. Those below must come to feel that their opinions are respected and listened to; those above must come to accept that criticism from below can be constructive and productive. Again, a crucial test of this philosophy will be the extent to which such beliefs actually come about.

Thirdly, this philosophy demands a reorientation by those within the company to the functioning and structure of the company. Instead of seeing it as separate branches competing against each other, they need to see it as interdependent branches working together to compete against other dealerships, and other makes of car. However, probably even more importantly than this, they need to see that their jobs and others on different parts of the same site are dependent on one another. In the past, understanding and communication between, for example, sales and service has been fairly limited. Yet a salesperson who sells a car but leaves the customer with a lingering feeling of having been pressured into the sale is doing the service or repair section no favours – the customer is hardly likely to patronize them after such initial treatment. The same goes for treatment by services or repairs. All sections of the workforce need to realize that their bread and butter actually comes from *repeat* customers, and that this can be achieved only if all work together. Managerially, this can be done by the appointment of sales managers who adopt 'customer-friendly' rather than the more 'controlled' approaches, and it seems significant that the most recent appointments at the main branches have consciously adopted this philosophy, and are encouraging their staff to do the same. Further, in those branches which I visited which did ostensibly employ a control approach, they used a very relaxed variant. The philosophy of the company increasingly encourages openness, flexibility, responsibility and customer friendliness, and the sales approach is beginning to harmonize with this.

Finally, decisions by Anglo to become involved with bodies like EATE (Economic Awareness in Teacher Education) signal both a looking outward to the community within which Anglo exists and an invitation for others to look in. This has involved governing body connections with a local primary school by the chairman of the company, as well as the personnel manager, and a move by the company to allow the entire staff of this school to visit the company and see what is going on. Similarly, the invitation by Anglo for an outsider like myself to observe the company was an expression of the new company approach.

Nevertheless, there were discussions and activities which I was not allowed to observe. Some, such as a board meeting, would probably be too sensitive for most companies to allow an outsider to witness, so it was not that surprising when a company going through difficult times was rather guarded. I had also to be aware that after so many redundancies over the last year, people were naturally jittery about the presence of a newcomer like myself – was he *really* just doing an independent study, or was he there to see whether *they* should be the next to go? Nevertheless, taking all this into account, there remains a reserve of secrecy which still needs to be broken down: a visit by myself to different branches produced very different outcomes: one where I was treated courteously and openly, and given full access to the works and the employers, and another where I was treated courteously and not allowed out of the dealer principal's office for the entire visit! Furthermore, whilst the desire for anonymity of this chapter is partly due to economic problems, part of it, I am sure, is due to an ingrained culture of concealment. I return to a point made above: that part of the change in philosophy will only come about through more practical changes. I therefore move on to these.

*Changes in structure*

There seem to be two major ways in which structural changes need to be introduced. Perhaps the most crucial change in structures will come through the increased decentralization of the company. This will probably have its most obvious effects upon the job definitions of dealer principals, and board members, for, if carried out to its logical conclusion, it will obviate the need for the day-to-day involvement in individual dealerships of board directors. Overall strategy may need to be discussed, but devolvement would seem, logically, to be just that – the independent day-to-day running of branches, with board directors becoming involved only when they can point to major problems which individual dealerships are not handling satisfactorily. This will mean autonomy, responsibility and accountability for the dealer principals, but will also mean a change of role for board members, which some may find difficult as they feel their presence may neither be as necessary, nor as welcome by dealer principals, as in the past. This, then, may be another test of the company's ability to change in the longer term.

The second major way has been discussed at some length in the section on changes in philosophy. This lies in the change of structures from ones where the business is conceptualized as individual empires of sales, service and parts to ones where these become integrated parts of a larger conception – an individual dealer principalship. The success of this will to a large extent depend upon how well the company philosophy is absorbed, and how well each dealer principal manages to translate this philosophy into practice. The key to this is the subject of the next area of change – that of communication.

*Changes in communication*

Changes in communication may be divided into two main areas, external communication changes and internal communications.

**External communication** At the most general level, the image of the company needs to be communicated to the world outside – as selling a good product, efficient, caring for its workforce and involved in its local community. This is increasingly a function in which board members, released from internal duties by the greater autonomy of dealer principals, can become involved. Nevertheless, personal recommendations based on experience, the word-of-mouth asides in the pub, are the most effective enhancers or destroyers of business reputations, and these, in the medium to long term, are gained only through what actually happens in the company.

The company image is communicated most visibly to customers by the way they are treated. The large things are clearly vital – is it a good car, is it worth the money, was it efficiently serviced or repaired? Nevertheless, small touches are equally important. Was all this done with a smile? Does the company let customers know if there is a delay in work, so they don't turn up and kick their heels? Certainly, the reception areas at Anglo are generally customer-friendly – comfortable seats, coffee on tap, usually a colour TV to watch. Another newly introduced way is the manner in which all phone calls are now answered. Previously, it was a greeting and the company. Now it is a greeting, the dealership, followed by the name of the individual answering the phone. Not only personalization to the customer but personalization of each site. It may only be a small move, but the customer now feels a little more that here is a firm with character, peopled by individuals, rather than that they are dealing with some faceless bureaucracy. Another touch is the manner in which Dennis, the overseas sales manager, hands over each car with a large bouquet of flowers – which is one of the reasons why he was top Saab salesman in the world not so long ago.

If customer treatment is vital, external visitor treatment is probably as much so. Visitors may not be there to buy, but the impression created may well lead them to consider this. Even if this is not the case, they take a story away to tell their colleagues, who are just as much potential buyers. What is needed is rather more than a helpful individual within the company. Instead, a formally developed structure needs to be instituted, so that, granted that each visit will be different, there is a system understood by all, with individuals given particular responsibility for structuring that visit. The manner and efficiency of that structuring gives a very clear message to the visitor as to the general efficiency of the company. The handling of visitors needs to be seen as another part of a job to be done professionally, rather than as an extra burden. This again, is achievable through philosophy, practice, and the right personnel.

**Internal communication**   Whilst it will be apparent from what has been said above that a key area in the development of effective internal communication will be the degree to which the different functions *across* a dealership (sales, after sales, parts, repairs, etc.) communicate and integrate, another crucial area will be the development of internal communication *upwards* and *downwards* within the company. Whilst the degree of communication across a dealership may say a lot about the desire for empire building, communication upwards and downwards says a lot about its openness. Whilst many at senior levels may wish to develop channels primarily for the dissemination of information relating to new structures and practices emanating from them, internal communication needs to be far more than this. Clearly, if a company wants its staff to understand what they are required to do, then the development of standardized channels is going to be essential, and this can be done without radically altering the philosophy of the company. If, however, it is serious about developing staff who accept autonomy, responsibility and accountability for their sphere of work, then it is going to need informed and educated staff, and the only way to do this is not only to commit the management to an openness about what it is doing but to encourage it to come to grips with how others see the situation – and be prepared to change in the light of such understanding. As Fullan (1991: 95) says: 'Innovators who are unable to alter their realities of change through exchange with would-be implementers can be as authoritarian as the staunchest defenders of the status quo.'

Instead of working on the principle of 'Is there a reason why they need to know this?' and if not, not telling, the company needs to move to the principle of 'Is there a good reason why they should *not* know ?' *and then* 'What can *we* learn from their understanding?' This breeds trust, honesty and commitment if done wholeheartedly, but is clearly incompatible with secrecy. Les, the dealer principal at one of the central branches, described his approach as asking people to change practices by explaining the need for change, but of encouraging the suggestion of alternatives. If, then, they can think of a better way, then all the better for him, because his principalship's practice is improved, for his workers, because they feel their ideas are respected and listened to, and they begin to identify with the company, and for the company, because it gets better practices run by better staff. However, whilst communication, to be really part of the change process at Anglo, needs to be more effective both downwards and upwards, change can start only by example from the top. This, then, will be another crucial area in assessing the degree of successful change at the company.

### Changes in personnel

As noted above, Anglo has lost over a third of its workforce in the last couple of years. This is a very large reduction in personnel by any standards, and happened for a number of reasons, but all to do, in one way or another, with the process of change. Some individuals went through early retirement or simply moved to a job elsewhere, and they were not replaced. Indeed, in at least one branch, reduction in personnel has been achieved totally on these terms. However, sometimes this has not been possible, and sometimes it has not been desirable. A company which is failing to hold its share of a (declining) market, which, in comparison with other same-make dealerships, is not making an acceptable return on its investment, has to look at a variety of areas. These must include whether areas are overstaffed, and whether personnel are capable of adapting to the proposed changes. It is sad but seen as necessary for the long-term health of the company – and therefore of the continuing employment of the remaining workforce – that where individuals are not willing to change, or capable of change, and may even be positively obstructive, they will not stay with the company. This drastic pruning also allows for the appointment of people who have not been socialized into a now outmoded way of working, who come already working with the newer approach. Managements of all companies necessarily have the problem of balancing the need for new blood against loyalty to individuals who have worked for the company for a long time. Whilst the long-term health of the company as a whole is normally seen as the overriding consideration, this does not necessarily mean firing people: issues of staff morale have to be taken into consideration. Nevertheless, Anglo has in general considered the necessity for implementing change the overriding priority: individuals have necessarily taken the brunt.

### Change in attitude

It would not be truthful to say that Anglo currently has a good reputation, either externally or, and crucially, in many cases internally. Indeed, the response of one individual to whom I mentioned that I was spending time with the company was to pull a face and say they were not a company they would use. They justified this by saying that on the occasions they had used them, they had the distinct impression that the employees didn't think much of the company either. This unsolicited comment may have put a finger on a really vital area of change: not only do the general public need to have their perceptions of Anglo altered, but the staff within Anglo also need to feel that working for the company is more than just a job. They need to feel proud that they work there, to feel loyalty and commitment. The problem is that if an employee says that Anglo is a poor performer enough times, this becomes a self-fulfilling prophecy; they *think* the company into that state. If, however, enough people begin to speak positively about the company, the effect is infectious and beneficial. Part of this needs to come from the example of management – they need to say it. They also need to install the kind of practices described above so that the rank and file come to believe it and practise it themselves. Anglo, then, would have a self-fulfilling prophecy on its hands of the most benign and profitable kind. This, I believe, is the kind of attitude change it needs to be – and is working towards.

## LESSONS FOR SCHOOLS?

There are lessons to be learnt from a company like Anglo: lessons about selling, and lessons about being in trouble. Both will be dealt with.

### Selling schools

It is probably experience or knowledge of the sharper end of selling practices from the commercial sector which makes many teachers recoil instinctively from the word 'selling'. Selling, it may be argued, is from a different conceptual universe, and the world of cars is the commercial world, whilst schools are from a world of profession-alism, of a calling. Teachers, some may continue, are there not to manipulate customers but to provide help to parents and children. Even if the brave new world ushered in by LMS, open enrolment and the publication of results means that schools are in competition with one another, tying the allocated budget to the number of children in a school, schools should not get into the business of the car salespeople. At bottom are probably a number of concerns, which might be expressed as:

- a belief that selling is about exaggerating the claims for your product, perhaps even lying about it; this may be acceptable in the rough world of the car manufacturer, but it is not good enough for education;
- a belief that selling necessarily involves the denigration of competing products or institutions; this runs totally counter to the idea of a national education service, which most teachers subscribe to;
- a belief that selling inevitably entails an adversarial relationship with customers because you are trying to sell them something, and in so doing preventing them from buying elsewhere; such a relationship should not be part of a teacher's style, which must be much more engaged in a partnership with parents;
- a belief that selling might mean the implementation of a philosophy that the customer is always right, which would mean the teaching profession surrendering their remaining autonomy and professionalism to the market and to customer preference.

Each of these concerns needs to be examined.

Firstly, the belief that selling is necessarily about exaggeration and lying is simply not true; the car trade *has* acquired a reputation in this area, but there are many in it who are saddened by this reputation and who have spent their careers attempting to give customers a square deal. Indeed, if success in the long term comes from cultivating the repeat customer, then such lying and exaggeration is counterproductive.

Secondly, whilst it would be foolish to deny that schools in the UK are in competition to the extent that their budgets are tied to the number of children who enrol, this does not entail the denigration of other schools. Selling can be purely about one's own 'product'. Indeed, it could be argued, as by Sullivan (1991), that not to advertise and sell yourself is actually doing the community a disservice: how can they choose the best for their children if you do not provide adequate information, and if you are a particularly 'good' school, are you not depriving children of the opportunity to benefit by not flying your own flag? Moreover, whilst there is no virtue in going over the top in selling one's school, a principal who adopts a shrinking violet approach does a disservice to all the hard work put in by those employed within the institution if the schools fail to recruit adequate numbers of pupils. Nevertheless, there is a tension between selling and school partnership. Whilst the need to sell one's school does not *prevent* co-operation, a co-operation vital to the provision of a nationally co-ordinated service, it can provide the conditions for poor relationships. Much depends upon what the selling is intended to achieve.

Thirdly, and similarly, there *is* a tension between selling and home–school partnerships. In a true partnership, one party succeeds or profits only when the others in the partnership do. In a selling relationship, it is quite possible for one to succeed or profit whilst the other loses; indeed one may profit principally through the other losing. Thus, a possible scenario would be one where the teacher persuaded the parent to enrol the child at their school, even though another school down the road was more suited to that child's interests and capabilities. Similarly, the fear that children may be moved to another school may prevent the development of genuinely open partnerships for fear by the teaching staff that full disclosures of problems may lead to the parents moving the child to another school.

These are, however, no more than possible: much more healthy is a scenario where the school is committed to total quality management and where selling is a natural outcome of a commitment to quality. In such a situation, honesty is no burden but a pleasure, for one is describing something of which one is justifiably confident and proud. Schools on this road can talk about the procedures they have installed and are installing in the achievement of total quality management and how the child will benefit by teacher and parent working towards these together. Selling is a problem only where it encourages teachers and schools to present to parents an unbalanced view of their performance, for this prevents entry into the kinds of mature and honest relationship which genuine partnerships are really about.

Lastly, there is no reason to believe that selling necessarily means a philosophy that the customer is always right. This was discussed at length in the chapter on BP Chemicals, where it was suggested that selling should be predicated on honest and educative relationships. It should encourage a more open and listening attitude; it should encourage, if expressed parental views are disagreed with, an entry into dialogue, and an education of parents regarding what the school is trying to do. But it also makes more probable the situation where parents are right and schools change their policies upon consideration of such views. Selling, then, entails not necessarily one-way implementation but rather the development of much healthier relationships between teacher and parent, and therefore a better education for the children.

Schools, then, do themselves no favours by not taking their own selling seriously. If only because taking it seriously, and doing it properly, actually makes the parent feel more informed, committed and enthusiastic, it is worth investing time and resources in it. How successful, one may ask, would a car salesperson be if he or she attempted to sell a car to fifteen different people at once? He or she would not make a sale, simply because he or she could not pay the individual attention needed to customize the client. Do schools need to become more aware of such needs? Certainly the teacher who leads a group of anxious parents round the institution cannot do this either. Schools need to continue to develop customized admission systems where the individual parent is given time to describe their child, to explain their hopes and fears, and what it is they want from the school, instead of being told that this is what the school will do. Where schools do this, they are still at the stage of Henry Ford's Model T car – customers can have any colour they want as long as it is black. Customizing the parent would also provide excellent feedback for the teaching profession on such parental wishes, providing information for developing partnerships, information for areas needing greater explanation, even information leading to a change in policy. From pragmatic, educational and ethical points of view, schools cannot afford not to follow this path.

Finally, the control systems used in selling cars provide yet another useful insight into the possibilities, limits and dangers of bureaucratizing action. They may be seen as providing a useful checklist of possible approaches to be used by salespeople, as well as assigning ultimate responsibility and control to those who have the most experience. In so doing, they provide guidance and tuition for those just beginning, and for those who do not feel confident to assert their own control. Nevertheless, it was instructive to note that in those branches of Anglo which did use control systems, the better operators used them in an artistic manner – as an aid to their job, not as a restriction. They used systems, rather than systems using them. Similarly, where there had been experience of a system's rigid use, the universal opinion of the salespeople was that it prevented them from growing in the job, and from developing relationships, rather than helping them further. It is then highly likely that those who began with a lack of confidence under its regime never developed the confidence to go further precisely because it prevented them from doing so. The warnings for a heavily prescribed National Curriculum, which obstructs rather than instructs, which hinders rather than encourages professional development, could not be clearer. At bottom, both, I argue, are based upon a lack of belief in the ability of the individual; and both, by employing the methods they do, may well become self-fulfilling prophecies.

## Being in trouble

There are lessons to be learnt from a company which is in trouble: areas in which it is achieving some success in negotiating the process, and areas where it is less successful and which can act as cautionary lessons for schools travelling the same road.

Many in Anglo's management are forthright about the situation, accepting that it would be easy to blame all of its problems on the recession but recognizing that, whilst some are attributable to national economic difficulties, these have only highlighted and exacerbated the internal problems. The recognition of this is a sign of health, and something from which schools can learn: the first step to recovery is to recognize that there is something wrong.

Further, Anglo is a company which has realized that authoritarian, secretive and non-delegative management is no longer viable. Not only does it result in lowered commitment, morale and effort by those lower in the hierarchy; it also impairs the ability of those at the top to do their job effectively, because it prevents upward communication which can be a source of helpful constructive criticism. Both the management of schools and their political masters can learn from that. Very often, reasons for a move from such structures are predicated on the improvement of the performance of the rank and file. One lesson from Anglo is that there might well be more emphasis on the potential improvement in the performance of those at the top – with due recognition that such changes will probably be harder for them than for the rank and file!

A further point worth mentioning is that change must necessarily *start* from the top if it is to be successful. Not only must it be seen to have official approval, it must be seen to be an integral part of management thinking and action. 'Do as I say but not as I do' is probably the best way of consigning institutional change to the dustbin. Change, then, cannot be something which management does to others: managers must embody it themselves. For those brought into a company or school already well down the change road, this may not be a problem; for those who have worked within a different culture, it can be enormously difficult. This clearly indicates that change agents must be aware of this learning process, and have sympathy and give time to those who are only just beginning the learning curve.

Such a point emphasizes that change *is* a process, not an event; passing a policy on change is not the hard work, it is only the beginning, for a change in philosophy does not happen overnight but over a process of years. It takes time for individuals, at whatever level of a company or school, to become open, self-critical or communicative; they need reassurance, help and occasional prodding. This is an intangible yet vital role of in-service training. There are those who feel that, unless something specific and identifiable comes out of a course, it has been a waste of time; yet much of development in learning curves comes from involved conversation or quiet contemplation, which in many cases may be unquantifiable, about one's general approach.

This leads directly on to the next point: that fundamental change is accomplished not by simple changes in materials or practices but in beliefs by those at all levels of the company or school. An in-service course, then, may be useful for handy tips for a particular lesson, perhaps an idea for an entire lesson, but the course which allows those to reflect upon their general philosophy of the job, and how this affects their general approach, and through this the kinds of materials and lessons they run, is probably more important in the long run. Sadly, this kind of course has received rather less attention of late in the UK through preoccupation with National Curriculum implementation, but this is a mistake, if an understandable one: implementation may be better achieved precisely through reflection upon general philosophy. Indeed it could be argued that one of the principal reasons for current legislation was precisely to achieve a different approach. Clearly, discussing personal philosophies is, contrary to some opinions, one of the most intensely practical things one can do.

## CONCLUSION – LESSONS FROM SCHOOLS?

Finally, both companies and schools need to come to grips with the fact that change is a messy business, which has to be tackled by all types of procedures, from all kinds of angles and by all sorts of people. There is probably a tendency in all of us – what one might call the rationist tendency – to believe that change can be structured, planned and implemented by a simple, linear plan, deriving essentially from one understanding and one perspective. It does not happen like that: it is inevitably, incurably, ineradicably *messy*. If different subjectivities are the order of the day, then the acceptance and success of management initiatives on the direction and success of organizational change are going to be conditioned by the degree to which other subjectivities are given chance to understand these reasons. The management of change then becomes much less the rational drive towards one purpose, and much more the acceptance of the need to understand and accommodate a variety of subjectivities. Now, whilst educators are probably no better and no worse than anyone else in the management field, they have the advantage of a masterly summary of the successes and failures of attempts at change (Fullan, 1991: 105–7). This chapter therefore concludes with his ten essential understandings for a successful approach to change. Whilst they are the distillation of his voluminous research into educational change, they look remarkably good as recommendations for the wider management community, and they are quoted virtually in their entirety.

### Ten Understandings for Successful Change

1  Do not assume that your version of what the change should be is the one that should be or could be implemented. On the contrary, assume that one of the main purposes of the process of implementation is to *exchange your reality* of what should be through interaction with implementers and others concerned. Stated another way, assume that successful implementation consists of some transformation or continual development of initial ideas . . .

2  Assume that any significant innovation, if it is to result in change, requires individual implementers to work out their own meaning. Significant change involves a certain amount of ambiguity, ambivalence, and uncertainty for the individual about the meaning of the change. Thus, effective implementation is a *process of clarification* . . .

3  Assume that conflict and disagreement are not only inevitable but fundamental to successful change. Since any group of people possess multiple realities, any collective change attempt will necessarily involve conflict . . .

4  Assume that people need pressure to change (even in directions which they desire), but it will only be effective under conditions which allow them to react, to form their own position, to interact with other implementers, to obtain technical assistance, etc. Unless people are going to be replaced with others who have different desired characteristics, relearning is at the heart of change.

5  Assume that effective change takes time. It is a process of 'development in use'. Unrealistic or undefined time lines fail to recognize that implementation occurs developmentally. Significant change in the form of implementing specific innovations can be expected to take a minimum of two to three years . . .

6  Do not assume that the reason for lack of implementation is outright rejection of the values embodied in the change, or hard-core resistance to change. Assume that there are a number of possible reasons: value rejection, inadequate resources to support implementation, insufficient time elapsed.

7 Do not expect all or even most people or groups to change. The complexity of change is such that it is totally impossible to bring about widespread reform in any large social system. Progress occurs when we take steps . . . that *increase* the number of people affected. Our reach should exceed our grasp, but not by such a margin that we fall flat on our face. Instead of being discouraged by all that remains to be done, be encouraged by what has been accomplished by way of improvement resulting from your actions.

8 Assume that you will need a *plan* that is based on the above assumptions and that addresses the factors known to affect implementation . . . Evolutionary planning and problem-coping models based on knowledge of the change process are essential . . .

9 Assume that no amount of knowledge will ever make it totally clear what action should be taken. Action decisions are a combination of valid knowledge, political considerations, on-the-spot decisions, and intuition. Better knowledge of the change process will improve the mix of resources on which we draw, but it will never and should never represent the sole basis for decisions.

10 Assume that changing the culture of institutions is the real agenda, not implementing single innovations. Put another way, when implementing particular innovations, we should always pay attention to whether the institution is developing or not.

## POSTSCRIPT

Six months after this case study took place, the managing director of Anglo Motors 'resigned', the major locations of the firm were sold off, and the business was reduced to approximately one-fifth of its previous size.

*Chapter 5*

# East Yorkshire Hospitals NHS Trust: The Merging of the Public and the Private?

## INTRODUCTION

The previous chapters have all focused primarily upon particular organizations and their individual practices. This chapter is rather different. It seemed to me that the East Yorkshire Hospitals NHS Trust experience could only be fully understood by some detailed research into the organization of which it is a constituent part, the UK National Health Service; and the more that I performed this research, the more it became clear that this chapter needed to describe similarities with education as much at a national as at an institutional level. This means that the view in this chapter tends on the whole to be taken from further back. Nevertheless, as schools are increasingly coming to recognize that they cannot understand themselves without understanding the national agenda for education, this was a perspective that I felt was needed, and proved to be fascinating in its own right. I hope the reader finds the same.

Having said this, it would be wrong to ignore the particular. The NHS may be the largest employer in Europe, with some 850,000 people on roll, but one's immediate feeling for Castle Hill, the main site of the Trust, is not as part of some massive monolith. Arrival is attractive from whichever direction you approach. A gentle climb up Castle Hill Road to the hospital gives one a panoramic view of the city of Hull. Arrivals from the other roads are through rolling countryside. Initial impressions of the site are similarly favourable: originally an isolation and TB hospital, Castle Hill has developed into an attractive landscaped facility of one- or two-storey buildings, a legacy of the time when virtually the only treatment for TB was an extended period of rest and fresh air. Wards were therefore designed as single-storey buildings with verandahs, and infectious wards were buildings of separated rooms opening out to the outside. The whole complex gives the impression of space, of rest, of tranquillity, particularly with the ubiquitous grey squirrels playing on the grassy areas and scampering up the trees. It is paired with the Beverley Westwood hospital, which has a similarly fortunate situation, overlooking a large public area of grassland and trees, which bears the same name as the hospital.

The workforce of the two branches of the Trust amounts, all told, to just over 1500 staff. The Trust is one of the third wave of trust hospitals, set up under the 1989 Act but which came into being in April 1993. The creation of East Yorkshire Hospitals NHS Trust, like that of other trusts, derived from a number of sources. Many of the general principles of its functioning, particularly the devolution to the Trust of much finance and responsibility, the cutting-out of middle tiers of management within the NHS itself, with the retention of a strong central hold, can be traced back to the post-Fordist trends first seen in business and industry, and mentioned in a number of places earlier in this book. Structural ideas for the whole scheme were based largely on the work of Alain Enthoven (1985), who proposed the development of a health system of 'market socialism', which would create a competitive internal market within the National Health Service, where purchaser and provider functions were clearly split, and where providers (i.e. hospitals) competed for patients. In this way, it was hoped or believed, the NHS would become a more responsive and more cost-efficient service. More immediately, and yet not very obviously, the creation of trust hospitals was part of a governmental response to a perceived crisis of funding in the NHS in the late 1980s.

The foundation of trust hospitals like East Yorkshire can also be seen as similar in intention to much of the 1988 Act in education. Both health and education services can be seen as being driven by post-Fordist ideas. As key players in businesses and industries have tried to come to terms with changes in technology and society, so they, when asked for thoughts on the running of other organizations, have tended to suggest the kinds of solutions which they have found useful in their own areas of expertise. Thus both schools and the NHS have found themselves the subject of new forms of reorganization, derived largely from the commercial sector.

Further, one might ask whether the introduction of LMS, open enrolment and opting out was designed to provide greater quality and accountability to customers by stimulating competition between suppliers, or whether it was a means of emasculating the power of teachers and of local education authorities. The answer is probably that both were intended, for an increase in the power of the client normally implies some diminution in the powers of the providers. Similarly, was the setting up of trust hospitals part of a plan to create an 'internal market' within the National Health Service, where quality and accountability were improved by the clear split between purchaser and provider functions, and where providers (i.e. hospitals) competed for patients, or was it a way of restricting the power of doctors and of district health authorities? The answer is probably both again. Free marketeers in successive Conservative governments have long had a suspicion of provider monopolies in education and health, and the reforms engineered in both have almost certainly been designed to improve the quality of service to clients and at the same time reduce the power of providers.

Indeed, the NHS and its hospitals like Castle Hill have been the subject of almost constant reorganization since their inception, which is not necessarily a bad thing if structure and practices *need* changing. The NHS itself has developed into one of the nodal points of party political controversy. Its aims and objectives are now hotly debated, its very existence in certain quarters questioned. These debates, and the changes taking place at the East Yorkshire Trust, can be fully understood only in the light of a fairly detailed description of the evolution of the service. This chapter, then, begins by outlining these debates, before moving on to a description of the development of current practices and structures at national and institutional levels, and a discussion of transferabilities.


## THE CREATION OF THE NHS

Medical provision, prior to the setting-up of the NHS on 5 July 1948 had been both inadequate and irrational. It had been inadequate in that the voluntary hospital system could not cope with national health demands; it had been inadequate in that the medical insurance legislation in existence provided cover only for general practitioner services, and then only and exclusively to manual workers (excluding even their families); it had been inadequate in that in many cases only those who could pay could afford treatment. It had been irrational in that clinicians were to be found in the more prosperous parts of the country, and in the leafier suburbs of those parts, where those who could afford medical treatment lived. In other words, the medical profession was concentrated precisely in those areas where it was least needed. Many today might also say that it was irrational in that it was left almost exclusively to the professionals to plan and run the nation's health. But more of that later.

Conditions after 1945 were as propitious as they probably could be for the founding of an NHS which would be free and comprehensive, and based upon general taxation. The experience of coming out of a damaging and destructive war had had a strong unifying effect. It had generated a vision of a nation as a community, where the provision of services like education and health could be seen as a public good, based on the needs of the nation as a whole, rather than on a belief in a country as merely a collection of self-interested individuals. Whilst the BMA Medical Planning Commission in 1942 had advocated the extension of state involvement through health insurance, such voices were in the end defeated.

There was also surprisingly little resistance once the Bill actually came to Parliament, this being as much because of the behind-the-scenes negotiations between the various interested parties as because of all-party agreement. Thus, the passage of the Bill may have been fairly smooth, but it had been preceded by some weighty concessions, in particular to the medical profession. The concept of an NHS was counter to the medical profession's whole tradition, training and ethos, for almost unanimously they held that no layperson could or should dictate to them over what they did. Whilst arguments like that by Bevan that 'we cannot perform a second-class operation on a patient if he is not quite paid up' (Klein, 1989: 38) might hold the moral high ground, he was still forced to admit that he had 'stuffed' the mouths of the medical profession 'with gold', such were the concessions he had had to make. These included retention of the independent contractor system for GPs, the continuation of pay beds in NHS hospitals, the option of private practice, the loss by local authorities of their hospitals, and a major role for doctors in administrative control at all levels. The agreement reached, which put the NHS on the statute books, was one which, as Strong and Robinson (1990: 4) put it, became a 'system for servicing individual clinicians'. Each doctor was to treat his or her patients as he or she saw fit, with little regard to cost, or to the overall financing of the system, thus pursuing a perfectionist policy of giving the best treatment (as they saw it) to the patients they were treating at the time. Problems with administering and financing the system were not to be their concern. Yet clearly, whilst such goals were pursued, managing the system was going to prove extremely problematical.

## INHERITANCES AND DEVELOPMENTS

Whilst it is clear that what came into existence was more a case of what was possible than what was desirable, it has to be re-stated that for the system to come into existence in the first place was a substantial achievement in itself. Moreover, compared with many other systems, expert opinion seems to be that it has done rather well, particularly in terms of equity of access, and in terms of administration costs. Butler (1992: 89), for instance, suggests that administrative costs in the NHS amount to only 5 per cent of the total expenditure, as compared to the 20 per cent under a variety of insurance plans in the USA. Yet, through both an inheritance of problems and the development of others, the history of the management of the NHS has been one of almost constant change as it has tried to deal with these inheritances and developments. It is important then to dwell on these for a little while.

The *inheritances* have already been largely pointed out. These were, firstly, the geographical distribution of resources, both material and human, which led to an inequitable pattern of quantity and quality of treatment. Secondly, and consequent upon this, there were variations in local practice, which made national measurement and co-ordination of services extraordinarily difficult. Finally, the individualistic approach by members of the medical profession to their jobs compounded these problems of measurement and co-ordination, as well as making almost impossible the rational financial planning of the system.

The *development* of problems was invariably tied up with finance. One of the assumptions behind the creation of the NHS is rather neatly put by Ham (1992: 17). It was assumed, he argues,

> that there was a fixed quantity of illness in the community which the introduction of a health service, free at the point of consumption, would gradually reduce. It was therefore expected that expenditure would soon level off and even decline as people became healthier.

It was a cruel realization to many that what had been created instead was a gigantic Topsy. Rather than expenditure being reduced, demand for services dramatically increased. Those individuals who in the past had had to put up with illnesses, from the unpleasant to the incapacitating, were for the first time in a position to get such problems sorted out. Similarly, the medical profession, unconcerned with financial constraints, and given a free hand to treat as and how they saw fit, gave little if any thought to individual treatment expenditures. Furthermore, when in the next couple of decades new technology – kidney dialysis machines and hip replacement surgery, for example – clearly and dramatically improved the quality of life in a manner not possible before, it also placed dramatic new costs upon the NHS budget. And finally, whilst in one way the creators did seem to be right – the population as a whole was healthier and did live longer – this also meant that other diseases, the diseases of middle and old age, now presented themselves, and had to be treated, to a much greater extent than they had before.

What quickly became apparent was that there was no necessary ceiling to the NHS budget. Further, by solving one set of problems – particularly to do with the equity of medical care for the majority of the population – another set had been instituted. These were now to do with even more intractable problems:

- What is an adequate level of health care provision?
- What should be the balance between health care provision and other public goods like education?
- Which areas of health care should get the lion's share of resources?
- Who should decide upon these issues?

The history of the NHS is in many ways a history of the working-out of such issues, and the practical problems of implementation once a decision was made. At the heart of such issues throughout has been the role of the doctor in the system. It became increasingly clear to politicians that allowing doctors exclusively to determine treatments and levels of treatment was not viable if questions of equity, effectiveness and efficiency were to be resolved.

Questions of *equity* could not be resolved because the debate could not move from the question of individual treatments to the questions of institutional responsibility and the treatments of populations while doctors had a stranglehold over policy.

Similarly, questions of *effectiveness* could not be resolved because, despite claims to professional expertise, the medical profession had produced an astonishingly small amount of data on comparative effectiveness of treatments. In 1863 Florence Nightingale had commented: 'In attempting at the truth, I have applied everywhere for information, but in scarcely an instance have I been able to obtain hospital records fit for any purpose of comparison.' The situation has hardly improved in well over a hundred years. Maynard, in 1992 (p.2), is cutting:

> It is commonplace for health care policy to be formulated and executed in a data-free environment. The information needed to inform resource allocation decisions in health care markets is largely absent. There is a dearth of data about costs (inputs), process (activities) and outcome (health gains).

Most judgements were based on intuition, and on past experience. As one regional general manager put it:

> there was a study in our region of cataract surgery. The variation in length of in-patient stay for the operation was between three and twelve days, with a mean of four days. Yet for private patients, the mean was just two days. When we challenged the twelve-days man, he said it was to ensure high quality of care – yet his private patients were only staying two days.
> (Strong and Robinson, 1990: 32)

Some of this lack of data stemmed from problems of definition: while a broken leg is clearly 'unhealthy', other issues are not so easy. Who, after all, is to say what constitutes 'adequate' good health, a 'healthy' lifestyle, a 'healthy' diet? Much of this is bound up with personal viewpoints and cultural background, making for much ambiguity and disagreement. Moreover, even where more scientific rigour is possible, it is not always possible to say from where the causation for such good health derives: health care is only one of several causes, which could include lifestyle, housing, nutrition, education, public health and heredity. Further, some of this lack of information stemmed from the medical profession's syndicalist approach, from the lack of structures to pursue such research. Some sadly also stemmed from personal pride and professional rivalry. Whilst the vast majority of doctors worked in the interests of patients, it has to be said that they have always been astonishingly effective at pursuing their own interests as well. One district general manager put it very pithily: 'there's not much difference between the professions and the trade unions. The BMA is just the most successful trade union of them all' (Strong and Robinson, 1990: 86).

Finally, if the data are not available, questions of *efficiency* cannot be resolved. One manager at Castle Hill remarked to me that, when he arrived there from a commercial company, he was astonished to find a 'desert' in terms of data to do with the comparative costs of different activities – and this is not confined to Castle Hill. Further, efficiency is not a neutral issue. As Williams (1989: 9) points out, being efficient is a moral obligation: 'for not to be efficient means imposing avoidable death and unnecessary suffering on people who might have benefited from the resources which are being used wastefully'.

The history of the NHS, then, can be seen as revolving around many of the same kind of issues as have concentrated minds in the education sector. Around issues of *equity*, the NHS has tried to devise means of achieving fairness of access and treatment, while education has wrestled with the respective merits of tripartite and comprehensive systems. Around issues of *effectiveness*, the NHS has seen an increasing effort to provide the facts and figures to assess the efficacy of treatments, while education has debated whether standards have declined, and how such an issue is to be tested. Around issues of *efficiency*, both have been concerned with prior questions of effectiveness but also with the question of whether the best way to finance the system is centrally, regionally or institutionally. Both have increasingly been concerned with the issue of the *accountability* of the producers in their respective systems to their clients, while, finally, both have been concerned with the degree of *professional involvement* in the determination of national and local policies.

Like education, the NHS has had its fair share of attempts at resolution of such issues. Realization of what a gobbler of resources it was led in the 1950s to a policy of 'make do and mend', and, as Klein (1989: 40) points out, to the NHS evolving from being 'an instrument for meeting needs' to one of being an 'institutional device for rationing scarce resources', with central government imposing cash limits and expecting the periphery to work within them. At the same time, because of the absence of generally accepted measures of performance, and the dependence on professional judgements, there could be no uniform national standards imposed from the centre.

Partly because of this perceived necessary lack of central directive, but also because of growth in the economy that characterized Britain in the 1960s and early 1970s, there was still little disagreement between the two major parties over NHS purposes, but rather an increasing concern with the cost of the technology needed to run the system, and a desire to squeeze the most out of limited resources.

The 1970s saw the advent of oil shortages, balance of payments crises and problems with sharing out a diminishing revenue among increasingly vocal sectors of the public domain. This state of affairs polarized political viewpoints, though both ends of the spectrum became ever more disenchanted with producer-dominated systems, and large bureaucracies, one end because of free-market individualism, the other because of a belief in participatory democracy. Nevertheless, politicians had to recognize the inevitable – that the experts still had to be consulted and utilized. The result in 1974 was a reorganization which tried to satisfy everyone: to promote managerial efficiency, but to accommodate the professions, to create a hierarchy for transmitting central policy, whilst also allowing room for initiative at the periphery. The result was an elaborate set of structures for incorporating just about all interested parties into a teamwork approach, what Strong and Robinson (1990: 18) have termed 'the apotheosis of health service syndicalism'.


## THE ADVENT OF GRIFFITHS

Sadly, when you try to please everyone, you usually end up pleasing no one. By having each craft managing itself, with co-ordinating committees at the different levels of the organization, what in fact tended to result was massively increased bureaucracy and little sense of direction. Whilst the 1982 reorganization redirected the organization back to the values of localism and small size, more fundamental changes yet were to be initiated by the inquiry, chaired significantly by Roy Griffiths, the deputy chairman and managing director of a leading example of good business practice, the supermarket chain Sainsbury's. His key concern is epigrammatically expressed in a phrase in the report (DHSS 1983: 12): 'If Florence Nightingale were carrying her lamp through the corridors of the NHS today she would almost certainly be searching for the people in charge'.

The choice of Griffiths *was* significant, for it was a clear declaration of the belief that the principles of good management applied to any form of institution, public or private. In many ways it is from here that much of the current structure and recommended practice takes its cue, against the background of totally different (syndicalist) structure and (individualist) practice. In effect, the appointment of Griffiths, and the ensuing Act of 1984, stated that good management requires:

- a clear line of command from the top to the bottom of the organization, with those in command at one level directly responsible to those in command of the level above
- clear and firm leadership within that structure at all levels, to monitor, control and integrate those within the tier
- the systematic specification of goals for all within that level
- the devolution of responsibility for devising the means for running that level to each individual manager
- the detailed measurement of individual and group performance to facilitate this monitoring, control and integration
- the use of a system of rewards and punishments as inducements to the achievement of these goals

Such a post-Fordist view of management was, if not anti-professional, then certainly of the view that, whilst essential to any organization, the professionals within the organization were not the people to run it. Theirs, it was held, was a parochial perspective. Only the professional manager, hired to take a global view, and dedicated to the interests of the whole organization, could do this job satisfactorily.

## THE REFORMS OF 1989: PRACTICE AND PRINCIPLES

Here we have then a sea change in the management of the NHS, but more was yet to come, for the reforms of 1984 still allowed for considerable central intervention in tactics as well as strategy. The result was that managers tended to be preoccupied with keeping within budget, balancing the books, and responding to centralist agendas. They were much less concerned with the kind of experimentation and innovation associated with consumer responsiveness and issues of quality. The reforms of 1989 were originally intended to extend the reforms of 1984 by giving the freedom to hospitals to opt for self-governing status as NHS hospital trusts. Following the principle of devolving implementation to the lowest effective level, under this plan hospital managers would be given greater responsibility and power to run their own affairs. Trust hospitals would thus provide health services through contracts with providers, set local pay and conditions for staff, be able to acquire and dispose of land and property, generate income and be able to borrow money subject to certain financing limits.

The reforms of 1989 were clearly informed as much by a free-market agenda (with each trust acting as a separate actor in the marketplace) as by a post-Fordist agenda (with each trust acting as a tactically free but strategically subordinate unit of the larger organization). Events since 1989 have tended to follow the post-Fordist agenda, not only with central government keeping a strong grip upon operations, but, in late 1993, with proposals for the excising of more layers of management – this time the regional health authorities. The parallels with education are interesting if not identical: the emasculation of intermediate bodies like local education authorities is clearly post-Fordist, as have been attempts to undermine higher education involvement in teacher training. However, the use of LMS to create devolved responsibilities is both post-Fordist and free-market, and the continued push for City Technology Colleges and grant-maintained schools is very clearly free-market-oriented, as they are both intended to give greater choice to parents. In some respects, the experiences are very similar: both areas have suffered legislation, with a significant lack of trialling and testing, with little consultation, all leading to a devolvement of responsibilities. Both find themselves in a fragmented situation, which could, if the political will were there, be fairly quickly turned into either a fully post-Fordist scenario or fully privatized systems.

Underlying such proposals, however, were a number of other principles which it is important to bring to the surface.

### Purchaser/provider split

Firstly, the 1989 reforms developed the thinking of 1984 by clearly separating the functions of purchaser and provider. The purchasers would be the district health authorities, and fundholding GPs (originally those with 11,000 clients or more, but now substantially reduced). District health authorities would determine referrals on the basis of government policy, on communication with providers, on GP feedback, by consultation with other interested bodies, by the type and quality of service offered, the waiting time for patients, and by hospitals' comparative prices. Fundholder GPs would determine referrals on the basis of immediate presenting cases, within a climate of limited finance and an understanding of population needs, as well as comparison of quality, waiting time and price. It may be significant that more than one person at Castle Hill saw the GPs as the real drive towards better care in the system. One senior manager described them to me as the 'wild card' in the system, though this was not meant in any pejorative sense. Situations where district health authorities purchase treatments or operations from hospitals in bulk may well lack a sense of individuality. GP referrals, on the other hand, are based on one-to-one contact between GP and patient, and then GP and consultant, and feedback to GP by patient is also more immediate and effective. In this situation, comments about lack of quality are more likely to come from GPs, and therefore the drive towards better-quality care appears to be being driven more by these GPs at present than by the district health authorities.

The providers, then, would be the hospitals, whether of trust status or not, and in theory they would stay in operation by attracting sufficient contracts from purchasers to finance their operations. Provider planning thus becomes much simpler than in the past, for now they do not plan for a balanced intake but plan predominantly on the basis of purchasers' requirements. They are driven by the need to attract and retain contracts, for they are now, in many cases, in open competition with other hospitals for these contracts. One can see the influence of free-market thinking, and the parallel with schools, here: the need to please the customer, the need to maintain and improve quality of service, the need to advertise and sell oneself. One can also see the whip hand moving from provider to the purchaser, though curiously, as we shall see shortly, it is debatable whether in the NHS the whip has passed to the clients being treated, or to their 'representatives', the purchasing authorities. Indeed, it was the dramatic transfer of power from hospital consultants to GPs that was remarked on to me more than once, as consultants become the deliverer in competition with others, while the GPs increasingly control which consultant is to be used.

### The search for greater efficiency

Secondly, like the NHS reforms of 1984, and the educational reforms of 1988 and 1993, the NHS reforms of 1989 were clearly not about the kind of funding to be used within the NHS, nor about increasing existing levels of funding, even if the perceived crisis which sparked them *was* about the level of funding. As Culyer (1989) points out, they were rather about the most efficient and effective ways of using present levels. Thus, since 1984/5, health authorities had been required to prepare annual cost improvement programmes, as part of this efficiency drive. Nevertheless, and despite the fact that there was a cumulative shortfall in hospital and community health services funding between 1981/2 and 1987/8 of £1.8 billion, government ministers were still not convinced that the slack had been taken up. Implicit in the Act, then, was the belief that there was still waste within the NHS, and only when more effective accounting, auditing, co-ordination and management had been given time to make better use of what was available would any extra funding be provided.

Certainly, the information systems being instituted at the East Yorkshire Trust should make this easier to demonstrate, as we shall see shortly. Nevertheless, it seems clear already that the issue will not be easily resolved. Late in 1992 a number of reports started to come through (e.g. *Guardian*, 14 December 1992, Channel 4 News, 16 December 1992) that hospitals nationwide were no longer taking in patients from purchasing authorities because their quotas had been filled, and the purchasing authorities lacked the finance to contract any more treatments until the next financial year. Similarly, a television programme (*The Troubleshooter*, 15 December 1992) indicated that at least one trust had reached a situation by mid-1992 where, with improved efficiency, it was treating previous annual totals of patients in a much shorter time, but was unable to take on more patients because the purchasing authorities had no further finance. Increasing efficiency in effect meant skilled staff remaining idle for considerable periods until more money could be found to purchase treatments. Such reports have continued throughout 1993 and into 1994. All of these could be due to underfunding, over-pricing by hospitals for their services, or mismanagement of the purchasing district health authorities. And even when the drive to facts and figures so evident in the NHS at present comes to fruition, the situation is unlikely to be resolved. Value judgements determine to a considerable extent the facts and figures asked for, and used in evidence, and there are sufficiently diverse competing interests in the NHS to make this issue probably unresolvable for the general public.

Thus, for the professional staff of hospitals, this drive for efficiency has become an increasingly sensitive issue. I have listened to a number of doctors who feel that their Hippocratic oath is compromised if they stand by while patients whom they regard as urgent cases are placed on waiting lists which will only be addressed in a new financial year. Moreover, the attempt by hospital management to involve doctors in the decision-making process regarding the prioritization of treatment for different kinds of illness has also met with a mixed response. Some doctors accept the need for an integration of managerial and medical responsibility, if only because they recognize that they are best qualified to make decisions which in many cases are primarily medical. Some, however, state bluntly that they are paid to be doctors not managers, whilst others will have no truck with problems of allocating a limited budget to ever-increased demands, feeling that their medical ethic does not allow such prioritization, and further suspect that they are being used as footsoldiers to make workable an underfunded organization.

Finally, a twist in the tale of efficiency came to light in November 1993, when it was reported in a number of newspapers (e.g. *Guardian*, *Independent*, *Today*, 18 November 1993) that the number of managers in the NHS had increased between 1989 and 1992 from 4610 to 16,690, administrative staff had increased during this time from 116,900 to 134,900, while the number of nurses during this period had decreased from 398,050 to 378,790. Part of this can be explained by the re-classification of some nursing sisters as managers; but it still illustrates that devolvement of responsibilities doesn't necessarily reduce administration costs. Rather, because of the drive for facts and figures (see below), and because of the institution of more managerial responsibilities at lower levels, there seems to be good reason to believe that such ranks are bound to swell in numbers. Indeed, it is of interest to note in this regard that a study on the progress of grant-maintained schools (Bush *et al.*, 1993) showed that the increased initial financing that was made available to these schools was predominantly spent, at least according to the perceptions of teachers in these schools, on administrative staff and their information technology equipment. Whether the cost of the increase in administrative numbers in the NHS – and education – will be compensated by the increased efficiencies and quality of service it is believed will be generated by such moves, is something that only time will tell.

Financing the NHS then continues to be, as it increasingly has become, a political football, in danger of becoming as much a matter of scoring points as of serious debate about adequate financing of a national health care system. Nevertheless, and while this goes on, those within the system, either in purchaser or provider function, have to make the best of what is there – a situation not good for morale if you have achieved greater efficiency, and see no *quid pro quo* in terms of extra resourcing.

### A restatement of original principles

If a second principle was one of improved efficiency, a third is a restatement of a core proposal of the 1944 White Paper – that the service should be freely available to all regardless of income. This commitment is spelt out very clearly in the foreword of *Working for Patients* (the White Paper (Department of Health 1989) which contains the core proposals for internal markets and trust hospitals). This may come as something of a surprise to those observers of Tory policy through the 1980s which had increasingly adopted the principle of individual choice before that of equality. Nevertheless, even if this principle is upheld in theory, it is doubtful whether future administrations will be any more successful in implementing it than their predecessors. Whilst the record shows (see Klein, 1989: 147–51) that there has been a good degree of equity in terms of the first point of access, it is also very clear that the middle classes have been much more successful than their working-class counterparts in manipulating the system to their advantage, because of factors such as better social skills, more time and greater mobility. Nevertheless, comparatively speaking, the NHS has done rather better than most other countries in this respect. Exploitation of providing institutions by the middle classes appears to be a given of societal functioning.

### The curtailment of professional power

It isn't hard to change a system where the public feels a poor job is being done: the constant reorganization of the education sector, and the impotence of teachers facing it throughout most of the 1980s and early 1990s, is testimony to that. It is considerably more difficult when there has been, and continues to be, overwhelming public support for a system, as in the case of the NHS. Indeed, many of the complaints about the NHS have come from the professionals themselves. Some might say that this has been as much self-interested as altruistic – better resourcing usually derives from making enough noise. Nevertheless, the fact remains that governments tread very warily when the public stubbornly refuses to change its opinion about a national institution.

So, allying public trust in the NHS to a belief in medical competence, and to an acknowledged and irreplaceable expertise, it has been much easier for the medical profession to view itself, and to behave, as if the hospital is there to serve it, rather than the profession being there to serve the hospital. Legislation, in such circumstances, will not be impositional. Other methods have to be used. Three in particular have been used: the purchaser/provider split; financial targets; and peer review.

The first method, the purchaser/provider split, as in education, in theory made adequate finance for individual hospitals contingent on the retention of existing patients, and the attraction of more. The move passed the whip hand to purchasers, the district health authorities and the GPs; but as the GPs were dependent for their salary on retaining and attracting more patients, they occupy the position of being purchaser to hospital but supplier to patients, and therefore face many of the same pressures. As in schools, doing your own thing, if it is not perceived as being as good as the next supplier, loses clients, and loses money.

The second method is tied up with the first. Financial targets, again in theory, make clear to those in hospitals that there is a limited budget, and it behoves all practitioners to make the best use of limited resources. Waste means less for other patients. Added to this, the allocation of individual budgets to trusts has meant the renegotiation of doctors' contracts, such that they are much more clearly tied to individual hospitals. So while doctors still retain considerably more financial independence than do teachers, they are increasingly being roped in.

A third tactic of curtailment, clearly allied to the others, is that of peer review. Unlike in education – where the public seems reasonably unworried, with formerly 'professional' decisions increasingly being taken outside of a school and professional context – in the NHS, rather than non-specialists attempting to tell specialists what to do, a far less controversial tack was seen as getting specialists to deal with each other. As we have seen, the lack of comparative evidence on the efficacy of medical practices continues to be an Achilles' heel of the medical profession. It may be difficult for governments to convince the public that they know better how to run the NHS than doctors do, but it is hard to argue with a government which says: we need to know whether one treatment is better than another, whether a more expensive treatment gives as good value as a less expensive, and doctors should be able to justify what they do. So why not get them to justify this to their colleagues? Neatly sidestepping the issue of professional judgement, they tie doctors into an organizational design which leaves them room for individual judgements *if* they can be medically justified to peers, and financially justified to peers and managers.

There seems, then, good reason to believe that doctors' thoughts and actions are being directed beyond the individual diagnosis, towards a more institutionally managed setting, where the method of performance has to be justified against another method, where, within a given financial framework, the performance of one operation has to be balanced against the non-performance of another. This, it could plausibly be argued, is not a denial of medical freedom as such, but rather the integration of medical judgement into a wider scenario, which transcends pure medical judgement, to include social, ethical and political considerations which others are capable of making, and in which the medical profession should be included. It has already been noted above that there are doctors who have genuine reservations about a process which, they believe, compromises their Hippocratic oath and which seems to put them in the front line of cost-cutting implementation. Moreover, it could also be plausibly argued that such a process is a path towards deprofessionalization, as decisions and procedures are standardized to such an extent that individual judgement is curtailed, a course which is of benefit to no one. These matters will be given further consideration in the next chapter.

**Extending choice**

A fifth principle, and a continuing aim of recent Tory governments, has been the development of extending patient/client/customer choice. The logic is the same as that in education and in other areas of public services: by instituting structures so that finance follows the customer, the provider will be motivated to provide a better service in order to retain present finance, and to improve it by attracting others. In this way the service as a whole is improved. However, and again as in education, while it is certainly the case that finance will follow the client, it is equally certain that this will not usually be on the choice of the clients themselves. In the case of education, and as pointed out above, this is because of the problem of defining who is the client – parent, child, business, or society as a whole? In the case of the NHS, the issue revolves instead around the problem of internal markets. As Mullen (1991) points out, internal markets can be of two very different varieties. The first is the kind which has underlain some of the government publicity on trusts – patients selecting their hospitals for treatment, and health authorities being sent the bill at the end of their stay. In practice, this is simply not happening. A second model, which gives much less consideration to customers, is being instituted. This assumes (rightly in most cases) that the general public cannot make sensible choices between different types of treatment for an ailment – it needs a professional to assess the effectiveness of the treatment and the comparative costs. This being the case, it will be either fundholding general practitioners or purchasing authorities who will seek this information and make the contracts with the suppliers. The patients are of course under no duress to accept such decisions, but they will find it difficult to secure treatment if they refuse.

If one defect in the application of market theory to both education and the NHS is that the customer will not actually make the selection, another is that provision will not be driven by the customer. In classical market theory, provision will be driven on the basis of individual want – bananas will sell well in the marketplace because and only because customers want to buy bananas. In the form of internal market proposed for education and the NHS, there will be a heavy degree of post-Fordist planning and co-ordination, with a great deal of power still held at the centre. Thus in education the demands of the National Curriculum, the extremely limited finances actually available to schools for creative virement, as well as the hugely increased power of the Secretary of State for Education will severely constrain parental and governing body choices. In the case of the NHS, central government will specify a minimum number of certain kinds of operation which purchasing authorities must contract with supplying hospitals. Further, and contrary to earlier intentions, planning by NHS trusts will be constrained by the fact that they are not to be allowed to employ junior staff on locally negotiated terms; nor have they been given greater access to funds for capital development to the extent they originally thought they would be. Finally, assurances to non-fundholding GPs that they would continue to be free to refer to hospitals of their choice have been steadily withdrawn as the exercise of such freedoms has begun to conflict with the contractual obligations of their district health authorities. There is still, then, a centralized grip on the system, one which will remain there while politicians believe that autonomy must be tempered by the need for co-ordination and planning.

Further planning can also be seen in the case of the purchasing authorities themselves, for, in consultation with a variety of interested bodies, they will draw up a list of priority treatments over and above central government specifications. In the case of the East Yorkshire Purchasing Authority, for example, there was a priority in 1992/3 on operations which cost relatively little yet provided immediate, significant and lasting benefit to the patient, cataracts and hip replacements being quoted to me as examples of such.

A further defect in classical application with regard to the NHS is that whilst the role of the hospitals is to supply, and that of providers is to provide, neither will do just that. The hospitals, like virtually all businesses, will have their own ideas of how they wish to develop, and will attempt to move into closer consultation with purchasing authorities to ensure that investments will result in contracts. The purchasers, as we saw with Marks & Spencer, will want to ensure that certain standards are maintained by their providers, and will increasingly attempt to reach back to specify standards which providers must attain if they are to be used.

Moreover, whilst competition will probably increase as any existing personal relationships within purchasing and provider institutions slacken, there is in the Humberside Region, perhaps surprisingly, a considerable degree of collaboration going on between the two trusts, Hull Acute and East Yorkshire. This, I was assured, is a regional accident, in that a plan to rationalize resources in the area between the Department of Health and the Regional Health Authority coincided with the introduction of the internal market. Thus at present agreements have been reached whereby some specialisms will be left to one (cardiothoracic, for instance to East Yorkshire, gastrointestinal to Hull), while other areas (geriatrics, gynaecology, general medicine and obstetrics) will be in direct competition as they are seen as being core areas of hospital functioning. This may be in the best interests of the patient, but it is certainly not a fully-fledged free market, and it is not extended choice by the customer. At the end of the day, free-market operations and system-wide control may both be necessary features of an efficient and effective service – a point which will not be lost on many educationalists.

**The drive for quality**

Much of this fifth principle is bound up with the last, that of ensuring better-quality patient care. The problem of 'quality' is, however, one which is not easily resolved. A first issue, as we have already seen, lies with questions of definition. If it means, as Crosby (1979: 15) has defined it, 'conformance to requirements', then it is problematical mostly at the implementation level. There are many issues within the NHS which come under this description of quality – things like the courtesy of staff, the information patients are given before and during their stay, the time they are kept waiting for an appointment, the facilities provided whilst they wait, the time they are woken up for breakfast in the morning (*if* they are woken up, or allowed to wake naturally!). Most of these, it could be argued, are relatively simple matters of improving or changing existing practice, and the task of training, recruiting and motivating personnel to perform these functions is in principle relatively straight-forward. More difficult, but certainly a key issue within *Working for Patients* and certainly central to questions of quality of care, is the length of waiting lists. Yet this, as we have already seen, is not quite so simple to solve. Long waiting lists can certainly be due to simple inefficiency, and would then come in for the kinds of treatments required for the services above. However, they could also be due to lack of suitable equipment, specialists or finance, and we now begin to tread in the much murkier areas of quality to do with professional judgement. This split between the service and the professional areas of quality would again seem in many ways to be directly applicable to education, and will be taken up in the next chapter.

**The drive for accountability**

We have already seen the lack of data on the comparative efficacy of treatments, on the way in which a considerable amount of professional clinical judgement is still based upon personal experience and intuition. In this kind of situation, the provision of better-quality care is bound to founder upon a lack of objectively verifiable evidence. From a practical point of view, it is therefore vital, if improved quality is to be achieved, that a variety of mechanisms are put into place to achieve this aim.

Nevertheless, there are other reasons, equally convincing, for instituting information mechanisms. Both the NHS and schools are, after all, financed by public money, by people's taxes. It is clearly an important ethical point – though one sometimes missed by providers – that they should therefore be accountable for what they do. This means that those outside of the service should be able to see that the money given is being used wisely and that practice is as efficient and effective as it could be. If not, resources will be wasted, and children will not receive the education they could, patients who could be treated will remain on waiting lists. The accountability of providers, therefore, is a matter of fairness, the recognition of a contractual obligation. Clearly, there is going to be a need for some form of assessment of practice, for facts and figures from both practical and accountability points of view. This is the subject of the next section.

## THE DRIVE FOR FACTS AND FIGURES

It is a cardinal assumption of post-Fordist management that units with devolved responsibilities are made accountable by means of the centre making increased use of data supplied by information technology systems. Similarly, the management approach in the new NHS is that a system cannot be managed without information from which to make decisions. No longer will it be permissible to let doctors 'do their own thing'. The hospital is now an organization in a competitive environment, and strategic decisions have to be made about the kind of shape it will need in the future if it is to survive and be a success. It is therefore essential, it is argued, that people within the organization have facts and figures to bite on. Five developments in this area at East Yorkshire Trust will be described. An underlying theme within this, though, is the problematical nature of 'objective' knowledge, as we shall see.

**Medical and clinical audit**

As quality can be seen to be necessary at the level of patient satisfaction, and at the level of treatment efficacy, so audit is divided into medical and clinical audit. Audit performs a number of functions. In essence, it is a form of peer review in which individuals make plain their reasons for a particular course of action. A first function, then, is to communicate – to let other people involved in your sphere of work know what you are doing. But importantly, it is also an exercise in justification, in explaining to people why you are doing what you are doing. This can be seen as threatening, and undoubtedly is by some, but ideally it should be seen as educative, both for the individual explaining (for they improve their practice by thinking it through) and for those listening (by learning about how another performs their job). And as those listening will in some way be involved in the process of care, audit should also be seen as integrative – as encouraging people to see how their different actions fit together, and how one person's actions affect another. The result should be an improvement in individual performance, and in overall total quality care.

**Weekly audits**

Closely allied to the clinical and medical audits, nursing staff also perform weekly audits against defined performance indicators. At Castle Hill Hospital, most wards have now developed specific 'standards of care' for their areas, together with the monitoring procedures to assess whether these standards are being attained.

Clearly, for some people, audit is going to be a threat. For those who have never had a spotlight put on their practice, whose performance may leave things to be desired, it may well be. For some consultants, used to being the nearest thing in the hospital to God, the whole process might be seen as a threat to their status. And for those who have never been asked to work as part of a team, this could be a painful transition. Nevertheless, audit is an important exercise in the move to bring into the open the nature and reason for individual practices, and thereby to submit them to scrutiny and, if necessary, change. Again, the parallels with education are clear: the teacher should be able to justify his or her practice and integrate it in a coherent and consistent manner into that of a team. Anything less is providing a sub-quality service to clients. But it also means that the teachers can no longer act as individualists, for they must submit not only to the discipline of outside accountability but to the discipline of the school team as well. For both professions, doctors and teachers, this change can be hard to adjust to.

Having said this, audit does have its problems. It is dangerous to assign it a status of objective accuracy, when in fact it is a process of interpersonal debate. It is part of a process of searching for clinical and medical 'protocols' – agreed standards and methods of treatment and patient care. In many cases both audit and protocols lack a credible research base, which gives the procedure a limited scientific value, if little can be appealed to in terms of justification save the individual experiences of people in the group. Moreover, even where a research base is available, every scientist is aware of the fallibility of such findings, of their challengeability. Having said this, and accepting that audit will probably never give definitive final answers, it is still a considerable step forward from practices which hid from scrutiny.

**Case mix**

Case mix is basically the provision of a research data base for people who need information on which to base medical and clinical protocols. At Castle Hill, this provision was still in its early stages, and there were questions raised about what its precise function would be, who would use it and how they would get to know how to use it. Clearly, the provision of such a data base and the development of a protocol base at Leeds are going to be essential if strategic decisions and case judgements are to be based on more than intuition and individual experience. It remains to be seen how quickly this gets off the ground, how rapidly it is integrated into a decision-making network and how it is actually used in practice. Different interest groups within the NHS would probably use it for different purposes, and would extract different data from it for their purposes.

**Job analysis**

This procedure was the least developed of all the procedures described, and after my initial visit the decision was taken not to implement it because of a lack of resources. Nevertheless, it is worth mentioning as it indicates the essential aim of the other procedures: attempting to open up the structure and practices of an organization and make them more 'rational' – a move away from the 'intuitive' to the researched and argued. The kind of job analysis being discussed at Castle Hill was developed by a Manchester team of consultants to enable organizations to define more clearly the location of a job in the spine of an organization. To do this, individuals were invited to give scores to fifteen different dimensions of the job. Because, it was argued, some jobs require a greater range or depth over a larger number of dimensions, it is possible to score such jobs as higher than others. This information can then be fed into issues of organization hierarchy, responsibility, salaries and work appropriateness.

What, of course, such analysis cannot escape is the need for a prior set of underlying criteria and values regarding what are believed to be more important work assets than others. This issue of the drive for facts and figures being underpinned by values is also raised in the final example.

**Skill mix**

In the drive to develop the most appropriate and cost-efficient procedures in hospitals, the Department of Health earmarked funds which had been channelled by the Regional Health Authority into an exercise which investigated the matching of the skills of staff to particular wards. Hospitals were invited to bid for funding for such research, and Castle Hill was successful. The exercise began with an invitation to wards, and the shifts on those wards, to participate. Some were more eager than others, probably for the same kinds of reasons that resistance has been shown by some to the practice of audit.

An analysis of ward activities was first undertaken by all those working on the consenting wards through the identification of one of ninety possible activities performed during their period of work. The research has so far thrown up some interesting variations, not only between wards but between shifts on the same wards. Some variation is to be expected: the activities of a geriatric ward nurse, for example, are going to be rather different from those of a nurse on an intensive care unit. If, then, different areas were found to demand different types of care, one might well expect the employment of different categories of carers, or at the least of a different balance in the numbers of different categories of carers. Similarly, if an analysis of the jobs performed on a ward indicated that highly qualified nurses were spending time doing work that an auxiliary nurse was quite capable of doing (e.g. making beds), then a conclusion might be validly reached that money could be saved if more auxiliary nurses were used. Of course, the reverse would have to apply – if the results indicated a lack of specialized help, then more money would have to be put into hiring such individuals. At present, the policy is one of providing the information to the wards themselves in order for decisions to be reached: senior management is presented with this information only six months later. This seems to be a clear signal for lower levels to become actively involved in management decisions, rather than the information being used as part of a top-down exercise (which *is* happening at some hospitals in other areas). It will be interesting to see whether this commitment is maintained, if the exercise is not reduced to little more than a cost-cutting operation. Certainly, at this early stage, there are those at the lower levels of the Trust hierarchy who do see it as little more than this, and considerable energy needs to be, and is being, used in communicating the reasons for such research, and the possibility of their involvement in the use of its findings.

## RATIONALITY AND VALUES

It would seem clearly advantageous to have such information available to hand, and very much in line with this drive for a data base from which strategic decisions can be made. Nevertheless, as we have seen, the existence of such a data base does not exclude the problem of having to make value judgements which no data base can ever ultimately resolve. For instance, lowering the skill base on a ward because of an assessment of current work practices says nothing about what optimum work practices might look like. Nor does it address the fact that lowering a skill base on a ward may become a self-fulfilling prophecy: placing more unskilled individuals on a ward may lower the chances of problems or patient needs being spotted, ones which more skilled helpers might see. Indeed, providing a higher skill level than is indicated by this procedure could detect further needs which less skilled carers could not detect. It does not, then, necessarily follow that an analysis of current work practices provides accurate recommendations for an appropriate skill mix on a ward – it tells you only what is appropriate for the behaviours you have observed (and even this involves some value judgement). There might well be here, unless researchers and managers are not very careful, a commission of what philosophers call the 'naturalistic fallacy' – the assumption that what *is* the case *ought* to be the case. At the end of the day, what is the appropriate skill mix for a ward is a matter of value judgement. Facts and figures give one only raw data: they cannot decide how or where they should be used.

This point has been made at some length because it points up substantial matters of perspective in the study of organizations. A long-running battle in administrative theory has been between writers like Simon (1957), Griffiths (1964) and Willower (1980) who attempt on the one hand to create a 'value-free' 'rational' administrative theory, which attempts to discover 'scientifically' and describe certain universally applicable management principles, and writers like Hodgkinson (1978) and Greenfield (in Greenfield and Ribbins, 1993), who argue on the other hand that such study is castrated without the initial understanding of the different subjectivities within organisations, of how different perceptions necessarily attach different values to different approaches. Not only would this latter approach argue that the former systems approach ultimately makes academics little more than the hand-servants of management, in that it provides this particular group with a set of tools believed to make their job (i.e. pursuing the implementation of their point of view) easier; it may also be pragmatically incoherent, at best assuming a concordance of different viewpoints within an organization, at worst ignoring their diversity. In so doing, it necessarily stores up troubles for the future. A better strategy would then be one of an appreciation of different subjectivities, and then a movement by management to communicate and address others with their understanding. This kind of insight, it will be remembered, was explored at some length in the chapter on Anglo Motors. 'Macho' management in any form of organization fails in the long run precisely because of its lack of appreciation of different subjectivities, different value bases. The call, then, in the new NHS management philosophy, for facts and for evidence cannot be value-free, and it cannot be separated from the judgements of individuals.

Not only may the new philosophy fail to listen to individuals, it may offer a totally different conception of the role of hospitals and of individuals within them. Both free-market and post-Fordist approaches suggest a role for the individual which may be antithetical to currently held conceptions. The danger with the new 'managerialism' in both the NHS and education is precisely that it may fail to listen to other points of view. Examples of this have already been seen, as in the description by John Patten, a Secretary of State for Education in the UK, of parent–teacher association representatives as 'Neanderthals', and his similar description of Tim Brighouse, a highly respected professor and chief education officer of a large local education authority, as a 'nutter'. Some business commentators may see such failures as little more than a failure of tactics: in post-Fordist management, decision-making remains with management, and consultation is no more than one means of gaining the workforce's consent. Others may argue that this approach is inappropriate for the education and health services, and that genuine participation and responsibility constitute the road to improved organization, because both education and health contain a considerable number of professionals who have real expertise and a commitment to the service. Perhaps a complementary demand for justification of practice, for self-examination, by their respective managements could usher in these different perceptions and would be a sign of health for the future.

The history of the NHS, then, like the history of any organization, including education, has been a history of the working-out of a series of, at times, conflicting perceptions, conflicting values. These have included the values of clinical autonomy versus system-wide strategic planning, of individual choice versus bureaucratic state provision, and of perfectionist treatment of the few versus adequate treatment of the many. A drive for facts and figures cannot eradicate such conflicts, but a greater appreciation of different standpoints, of different subjectivities, can reduce the number of misunderstandings. This it can do, firstly by making one viewpoint appreciate another, but secondly, and just as importantly, by making this first viewpoint examine itself again with this heightened appreciation of others. It is with such an approach that the next chapter considers the subjectivity of one particular group common to both the NHS and the education service – the professionals.

# Chapter 6

# The Future of the Professional in a Bureaucratized World

## INTRODUCTION

One of the paradoxes of both schools and hospitals is that those within them, who regard themselves as professionals, find their autonomy circumscribed not only from above, by senior management and central government, but also from below, by increased consumer power. Government legislation on schools, for instance, has been characterized by central government directive (most notably through the National Curriculum) but also by an appeal to free-market forces (through opting out, open enrolment and LMS). I have argued elsewhere (Bottery, 1992) that there is within this a strong element of contradiction, for it would seem that if successive governments in the UK were true believers in the free market, the logical thing to do would have been to devolve responsibility for the curriculum down to schools, rather than imposing a national system upon them.

Yet, reflection upon previous chapters in this book suggests that not only is a free-market ideology at work in schools and hospitals but so also is a post-Fordist agenda. In such circumstances, the devolution of responsibility and of tactics to schools, accompanied by the retention by central government of a considerable degree of power and strategy, is rather more understandable. Similarly, the restrictions placed upon the implementation of an 'internal market' in the NHS suggest that free-market thinking may be pursued only as far as is consonant with other post-Fordist aspirations. Within such a rationale, one major plank of policy will be a drive to greater accountability. Whilst a public justification will be that when public money is used, the public should be able to see that such money is spent efficiently and effectively, another reason will also be that by this means any devolution of responsibility is effectively monitored and controlled. As part of this policy, there will be major attempts to curtail the autonomy of individuals and groups within such devolved units so that the units implement policy more uniformly, and so that the units themselves are more easily monitored. This is the subject of this chapter – the use of both centralist imposition and consumer aspirations as tools for the prosecution of corporatist policy aimed at roping in the autonomy of the professionals in state bureaucracies.

## THE CURTAILMENT OF DIONYSIANS

Both teachers and doctors have in the past liked to think of themselves, in organizational terms, as what Handy (1985) calls 'Dionysians' – professionals working in organizations, but in organizations built for the autonomous display of individual expertise, accountable to no one, because no one is capable of judging their practice. It will not be surprising, then, if managers (and behind them, administrators and politicians) differ quite radically from professionals as to the form and function of accountability. Professionals will tend to feel their toes are being trodden on, that they are being prevented by red tape and managerialism from carrying out their work most effectively. Such individuals will clearly be galling to those who wish to develop post-Fordist corporate aims, and will do their best to turn such egocentric self-conceptions (as they see it) into something much more amenable to organizational (and managerial) imperatives, based upon wider strategies of political and economic development.

One striking similarity, then, between schools and hospitals has been the struggle in both for supremacy between professionals and managers, as professionals struggle to maintain their autonomy and managers attempt to convert them into team-players for the benefit of the organizational plan, which itself is part of a larger agenda. This in fact is the classic antagonism between bureaucracy and the professional, and one which teachers in particular have constantly to deal with. After all, as Leggatt (1970: 174) points out, schools are bureaucratic in a classically Weberian way:

> there is a functional division of labour; the authority structure is hierarchical, disputes being settled by reference to superiors, and each employee derives his or her authority in the first instance from the office rather than from any personal qualities; great importance is attached to rules and to formal records; each client or pupil is treated impartially according to universalistic criteria; there are clear qualifications for recruitment and promotion.

Indeed, one might go further and suggest that such moves are what Lawn and Ozga (1987: 52) call the 'proletarianization' of occupations, a process, rooted in the scientific management of Frederick Taylor, whereby formerly skilled occupations are analysed, systematized and routinized to such a degree that the autonomous and non-standard application of expertise is seen as neither desirable nor necessary. In education, under such a system, suggest Lawn and Ozga (p. 55), 'Headteachers moved from being primus inter pares and the trainers of the inexperienced, to become managers of human and technical resources.'

This road of de-skilling and straitjackets is already well travelled in schools. There has been a virtual dismissal by Conservative governments in the UK of areas of academic research (notably in the philosophy and sociology of education), and deliberate attempts at the sidelining of teacher-based testing. With this has gone the systematic isolation of schools from each other, of local education authorities and of universities, with a consequent attempt at the elimination of alternative explanatory codes. In their place has come the employment of advisory groups hand-picked for their sympathies to government views, the institution of simplistic and misguided testing, the recourse by schools to direct government advice and funding. Research is increasingly driven and controlled by a desire to support and extend managerial imperatives, not by a desire to support and extend professional practice. The results in terms of lowered professional morale are evident.

However, whilst one striking similarity between the educational system and the NHS has been the struggle for supremacy between Dionysians and managers, their manner of treatment has been rather different. Teachers are currently controlled mostly from outside of the school by legislative imposition and administrative fiat. Doctors, as noted in the previous chapter, are treated rather more circumspectly, with legislation taking a backdoor approach, using purchaser/provider splits, financial targets and peer review to divide and rule, though with a consequent increased tendency for managers to tread on previously sacrosanct 'medical' ground in the attempt to tell doctors what or how to do things. Much of this difference in treatment, I suggest, stems from differences between the two professions in terms of their perceived degree of 'professionalism'. Whilst teachers may have liked to think of themselves as Dionysians, it is doubtful if they qualify. Dionysians are true professionals. Are teachers? Clearly, before proceeding any further, a definition of 'professional' is needed.

## PROFESSIONAL CRITERIA

There have been a number of attempts at definition of the word (see, for instance, Becker, 1962; Goode, 1969; Hoyle, 1980; Perkins, 1983 and Sockett, 1983), and an examination of these suggests that there are at least seventeen criteria which have been considered in decisions on whether to accredit an occupation as a 'profession' or not. These criteria can be summarized as follows:

- A body of systematic knowledge is needed to exercise the occupation's functions.
- It requires considerable technical skill to exercise this function.
- The acquisition of this knowledge requires a lengthy period of training.
- There is a requirement for the practitioner to reflect on and improve current expertise.
- Notwithstanding the need for systematic knowledge and training, situations are constantly arising which require these skills to be applied in a non-routine way.
- Because of these non-routine situations, the occupation requires a considerable degree of autonomy as to appropriate judgements and practices.
- The occupation controls selection, training and qualification into its ranks.
- It should be represented by one authoritative body.
- There is a need for a monopoly of service by this body.
- Because of the above need for expertise, disciplinary matters must be decided by members of the occupation, rather than by external authorities.
- The occupation in question performs a crucial social function.
- Because of both the high level of skill and its crucial social function, the occupation should have high prestige.
- Because of all of the above, the occupation should have a comparatively high level of financial remuneration.

- The occupation should have a large say and influence in the formulation of institutional and public policy.
- The occupation is underpinned by an ethic of service to the community.
- The occupation's values are usually explicitly stated in a code of ethics.
- During the period of training, a process of socialization into occupational values takes place.

It will be clear from this that 'professionalism' is not an easy concept to define and apply. It is not apparent either that the criteria all have the same degree of importance in an occupation's achievement of professionalism; nor is it clear that an occupation needs to conform to all of these criteria to be deemed a 'profession'. Much more likely than all seventeen being essential is that there are certain core criteria around which the rest cluster. So, whilst the number of possible professional criteria may go into double figures, I will suggest that there are actually only three necessary and sufficient criteria, under which the rest may be subsumed:

### The occupation possesses a specialized and systematic knowledge base

All professions must have a specialized and systematic knowledge base which is known in its entirety only to them, and which they draw on to perform their occupation. In the case of doctors, this would be a factual knowledge of biology, epidemiology, etc., and a technical knowledge of surgery, etc. In the case of teachers, it would be the factual knowledge of a particular subject area, the technical knowledge of how to apply this through disciplinary strategies, classroom management techniques, and the (contested) knowledge of the philosophy, psychology, sociology and history of education. This knowledge provides them with a base to exercise *considerable skill*, and necessitates a *lengthy period of training*. The nature of such work will almost certainly require them to *apply this knowledge base non-routinely*.

### The occupation performs a crucial social function

No matter how expert an occupation may claim to be, it will fail to qualify as a profession if it does not perform a function perceived by the majority of society as crucial to its running. Both of these together – the knowledge base and crucial social function – will then give the occupation considerable *prestige*, large *financial remuneration*, and considerable *influence* in matters relating to their field in the society at large.

### The occupation possesses the prestige and power to maintain occupational autonomy

As knowledge of the information base is essential for correct practice, and as through it and its social function the profession acquires prestige, so it becomes perceived as necessary for the occupation to be given a high degree of power and *autonomy*: that it *controls entry* into the profession, that it should be allowed to exert a *monopoly* over

**Table 6.1**   *Teachers' and doctors' professionalism compared*

| Criterion | Teachers | Doctors |
|---|---|---|
| Body of systematic knowledge | contested | yes |
| considerable skill | contested | uncontested |
| lengthy period of training | contested | uncontested |
| non-routine application | limited | yes |
| | | |
| Crucial social function | yes | yes |
| large influence on policy | rapid decline | relative decline |
| high prestige | relative/rapid decline | yes |
| high financial remuneration | no | yes |
| | | |
| Prestige and power | relative/rapid decline | relative decline |
| control of entry | no | yes |
| monopoly position | no | yes |
| represented by one body | no | yes |
| internal discipline | no | yes |
| high degree of autonomy | rapid decline | relative decline |
| socialization into values | unclear | yes |
| explicit statement of ethical code | no | yes |

the service involved, that it is united in its aims, and so is *represented by one body*, and that it therefore maintains an *internal discipline* by its own *code of ethics*, as opposed to an externally imposed one. Entrants are then *socialized into the values* of that profession.

This categorization is illustrated in Table 6.1, which also compares the claims for professional status of doctors and teachers. Perhaps the most interesting part of Table 6.1, in the light of the post-Fordist hypothesis running through this book, is the manner in which teachers, as compared with doctors, have failed to maintain the prestige and power necessary for genuine autonomy. The power and prestige of an occupation will be reduced precisely to the extent that doubts are cast upon the other prerequisites of a profession, namely that it possesses a specialized and systematic knowledge base, and can be entrusted with the autonomous control of its crucial social function. It will be of use then to examine the criteria in more detail with specific reference to teaching.

## A specialized and systematic knowledge base

There can be little doubt as to the sophisticated factual and technical knowledge base which the public accepts that the medical profession possesses. Much is driven by the acceptance that only they are sufficiently knowledgeable and have the skill to be allowed non-routine application and a considerable degree of autonomy in terms of things like entry into the profession, the need for a lengthy period of training and the ability and wisdom to judge disciplinary matters.

The public are not nearly so sure of the expertise of teachers. Like doctors they have a factual knowledge base – the subject matter they teach. Yet, unlike doctors, they seldom move beyond transmission of this knowledge into its application or the creation of new knowledge. Further, the public have a very variable perception as to the quality and depth of that knowledge base. Some teachers, like those of science and language, are probably perceived as drawing on a body of knowledge which expresses a genuine expertise which the general public do not possess. Other teachers, however, like those in the primary schools, and in arts subjects, are probably perceived as doing something which most of the general public believe *they* could do given the time and inclination. It is from such perceptions that ministers like John Patten in 1993 could suggest that there was little objectionable to a 'Mum's Army' for the teaching of infants.

In terms of technical knowledge, this would normally be described as the art of teaching itself. If doctors inject and cut and sew, teachers organize classrooms, explain and keep discipline. Paradoxically, however, the technical expertise of teachers is diminished the greater the expertise shown, for the essence of good teaching is to make clear and accessible the difficult or unintelligible; and to the extent that the teachers make it look easy, so the public may believe that there is little expertise involved. Non-teachers, after all, have all been through the educational process themselves. What would we think of doctors if each member of the public, compulsorily, had to undergo 15,000 hours of medical training until the age of sixteen? I suggest that in that situation there would be considerably less mystique attached to doctors' practice.

Moreover, where professionals like doctors enhance their mystique by the use of esoteric terminology, teachers tend to do precisely the reverse – and need to, because of the nature of their occupation. Lortie (1969: 52), for instance, quotes research by Haller who found that 90 per cent of vocabulary used by elementary teachers in ordinary conversation with non-teachers consisted of the two-thousand-odd most commonly used words in the English language.

So if teachers' knowledge base is perceived as variable, and their technical expertise is viewed as non-technical, what else can they offer to make them 'professionals'? One thing which has been claimed as essential to good teaching over the last few decades, and indeed has been the staple diet of trainee teachers, is the need for a science of pedagogy, mostly composed of the philosophy, psychology, sociology and history of education. From such a base, it was claimed, teachers were privy to concepts, research and pedagogic material of which the general public were not aware. Thus, the philosophy sharpened their understanding of the general purpose of education, the psychology gave them an understanding of children's capabilities in a systematically researched rather than experience-driven (and therefore extremely limited) information base, while the sociology and history of education enabled them to place and understand the role of education within its societal constraints and possibilities. Such understanding would inform their technical base in a rich and grounded manner. Further, it was argued, the establishment of such a base provided the theoretical foundations for a unified profession, for even if primary teachers did not have a subject base to match that of the sixth-form teacher, they needed, it was argued, the same understanding of the philosophy, psychology, sociology and history. One could then contemplate the creation of something like a general teaching council, rather than the present array of disparate bodies haggling over hegemony – hardly a good advertisement to the general public.

So far, perhaps, so good. Unfortunately, there is far from unanimous agreement on such an argument. Many teachers may not be particularly perturbed if a body like the right-wing Hillgate Group (1986) suggests that 'Teaching, like business, is a form of practical knowledge and may be as much destroyed as enhanced by the attempt to impart it as a theoretical discipline'. Such pressure groups, it might be argued, have always had a jaundiced eye towards teachers, and deserve little actual intellectual consideration. However, if the holding of professionalism is at least in part the development of prestige and autonomy, and the prevention of its erosion, then teachers would be well advised to recognize that such pressure groups provide the kind of ammunition that committed politicians search for to bolster their arguments. Their arguments need to be combated just as much as any others.

It is also troubling when writers like Halmos (1971) or Reiff (1971) argue that the approach needed in the actual practice of teaching is antithetical to that taken with academic knowledge, for the former requires subjectivity, personal commitment, and trust, while the latter requires objectivity, neutrality and scepticism. Whilst academic knowledge is not totally discounted, it is given a much lower status than the quality of relationships the practitioner develops with students. Both – echoing the kind of approach taken by Perkins (1983) – argue that such academic knowledge is little more than a ploy by an occupational group to launch itself into the professional ranks, but which adds little to the quality of teaching, and may actually damage it.

Furthermore, anyone who has supervised trainee teachers will know that remarkably few find this science of pedagogy of great use to them when starting out. They are, perhaps not surprisingly, much more concerned with sheer survival skills – with classroom organization, the most appropriate teaching techniques for a particular subject and class, and with the best disciplinary strategies to undergird all of this (see Wragg, 1984). And so, the argument goes, whilst some of this can be learnt in college or a university department of education, the most appropriate place to learn it is where it is happening – in the classroom.

Most opinion, then, seems to be shifting to the need for greater concentration of teachers' time at the start of their careers in the classroom rather than the lecture theatre. This will probably help teachers' claim to professionalism in the long run, in that they will be perceived as more competent. Nevertheless, any movement to make teachers' training totally classroom-based would have a similarly wounding effect, for now the charge would be that because teachers have so little theoretical knowledge of the purpose and place of education, and of children's capabilities, they can only be seen and treated as little more than technicians. Add a twist of Taylorian scientific management, and one has a truly de-professionalized occupation, with the important questions then being decided by external bodies of 'experts' – by a National Curriculum Council, a National Body for Pedagogic Techniques, or what have you.

Where Halmos and Reiff go wrong, I believe, and what I suspect that bodies like the Hillgate Group are trying to do, is to suggest that education can be treated in a value-free manner. Whilst the quality of personal relationships in a classroom cannot be underestimated, and the organizational strategies employed may be vital for good learning and discipline, one cannot escape the fact that there are debates about what *are* the proper kinds of relationships to be fostered, and debates about what is good learning and discipline, and so what kinds of organizational strategies should be employed. This, after all, is the nub of most so-called 'traditional versus progressive' debates: both have conceptions of the kind of person and society they wish to see, the kind of learning which is necessary for their definition of an 'educated' person. All of these then go to determine the kinds of teaching methods to be used in the classroom.

Inevitably, then, educators must have their relationships and teaching styles informed by reflection on what these styles and relationships are trying to do.

Moreover, education must transcend the classroom. As part of its function is in dealing with the values and attitudes of the next generation, so it is inescapably bound up with debates about the values a society holds, with the conflict within society between competing values. It is clear from the writings of the Hillgate Group that they would be happy to see schools espouse their set of values exclusively. However, if one believes that schools should not restrict choice to one ideology, this means that they must not prevent recognition and debate of other ideologies. Reducing teaching to subject matter and teaching technique does precisely this because it prevents reflection upon the current status quo, and so asserts one ideology by the omission of debate over others. Only with a carefully thought through philosophy for education can teachers decide on why they are doing what they are doing, only through a sociology and history of education can they understand previous and present competing forces over the role of education within society. Only with a psychology of education can they know what children can understand. Without these tools, teachers cease to determine direction, but have their direction determined for them.

In similar vein, a too-rigid National Curriculum and associated assessment procedures – carefully sculpted to be understandable and assessed by the layperson – would hasten the view that assessment is value-free, rather than being something which *is* contestable. After all, what you test usually says that you value these things more than those things you aren't going to test.

It is therefore vital that the public should not see a government making all the running, and the teaching profession apparently either simply reacting or meekly complying. When this happens – when a government's ideology (of any political hue) isn't proactively contested – then the public cannot be blamed for believing that perhaps the government has got it right after all, and that there is only one way of seeing and doing things, the government's way.

In the light of the above, four suggestions to enhance teachers' professional status are made.

Firstly, a sufficient degree of teacher training needs to be located in schools so that trainees are able not only to survive but very quickly to show skill in the basic techniques of organization and control. This will not only make the novice teacher more effective, but it will also upgrade the quality of the teaching profession as a whole, *and* it will contribute to a better perception of teachers by the public. However, from the beginning, this emphasis on the *how* of teaching must be tempered with sufficient discussion on the *why*, for this will clearly inform the *what*, and the *how* as well. Teachers, from the beginning, must be able to articulate why they are doing what they are doing – not only for better-informed practice but to inform the public better. For these reasons, Hoyle's ( 1983: 52) suggestions of a much more stratified profession, with an elite having an academic pedagogic background and the rest trained only in survival and organizational competencies, would simply accentuate present problems. Here we have shades of Patten's 'Mum's Army' again. A high-quality profession means having a universally well-educated body, not having a few leaders and the rest led.

A second proposal, then, is that teachers should be encouraged to expand this theoretical pedagogic base as they develop their careers. Such a base is not a discouragement to the public's trust in teachers. It is so only when it is not backed up by a visible display of practical competence. What would you think of doctors who 'talked a good operation' but killed most of their patients? This theoretical background – if clearly worked into existing practice, and articulated as such – *does* raise the profession of teaching above the mundane, for it locates it within an important and defensible base – as a practice crucial to society and needing to be discussed within this wider context. Again, those in higher education must look closely at their own practice in this quest for relevance. They cannot, as has happened too often in the past, leave teachers to make the connections.

My third prescription is closely linked to much of the above. If, as I am suggesting, there is a move within most state organizations for the centre to control more, and to limit the professionals to decisions as to the tactics of implementation, then these same professionals will need to ally themselves with a powerful group prepared to support them. This group must be the parents. Teachers have done themselves no real favours in the past by their self-imposed distance. Such a policy *might* for some occupations increase the degree of mystery and hence strengthen claims to professionalism, but it will not work for teachers, and for the reasons given above. Their subject knowledge base is sometimes little higher than that of parents, and their (perceived) inability to explain the need for a theoretical pedagogic knowledge base has provided governments with too-easily-obtained ammunition when they wish to denigrate teachers. Only by developing an increasingly informed parent population – by teachers educating them as to what they are doing – can teachers hope to re-establish a widespread trust and belief in their expertise. Teachers need to demonstrate their willingness to be publicly accountable, and direct communication with their parents is an excellent way of achieving this.

Schools, then, must become politically active. If they believe, as most do, that they have been systematically misrepresented by politicians and media, and their functions undermined and trivialized, they must just as systematically prepare agendas for the education of their parents in what they are trying to do, to apprise parents of the complexity and depth of the issues involved. If a Secretary of State for Education argues that primary schools must return to setting and streaming, primary schools must not react in a knee-jerk manner either for or against such proposals but must coolly and professionally survey the evidence, evaluate the evidence, and develop channels of communication through which they help parents to understand the complex social and intellectual implications of such organizational issues.

Such a move would mean that teachers would be perceived by the general public as capable of arguing their case, as being competent in their occupation, as being willing to be accountable. Far too many teachers, however, have little or no experience of the justification of their practice to those outside the profession, except for the lame didactic presentation at a parents' evening. Yet if the teaching occupation is to be regarded as a profession, this they must be able to do. And those who can't do it need to be helped to do so. This is a role that those in teacher training institutions could occupy rather well, more experienced as they are at educating adults. The teaching profession as a whole needs to develop a wider concept of what good practice involves, and this involves the education of parents. Without parents, they lose a vital arm of educational persuasion to children. They also fail to enlist the help of parents in creating a more decentralized, more responsive system, as well as failing to create a pressure group for a more professional body of teaching.

Only if teachers can convincingly persuade parents that they actually know as well or better than politicians and the media what education is for, and how it can be achieved, will the general public be convinced that teachers are competent in what they do. Only then will the general public come to trust teachers, and accept that such a theoretical base is necessary. On such a foundation will the public accept, and pressure politicians into accepting, my fourth prescription, the setting up of a unified teaching body with real influence. Of course, were the teaching unions able to submerge their differences, they could establish a skeletal body, which if not able to control entry, length of training or internal discipline, could at least act as the unified voice for the profession. From such beginnings, and with other prescriptions, could come an acceptance of teachers' need for autonomy, for a continued lengthy period of training, for trust in their non-routine application of skills. And only when this happens will they be in a position to argue for teacher control over entry to the profession, and for an internal control of discipline.

## Crucial social function

Of course, convincing the general public that you require a considerable degree of expertise and autonomous reflection in carrying out your occupation is of little consequence if the general public feel they can get by without it. Few people have the ability to walk the high wire in a circus, but few would grant those who do this the status of professionals, for they do something which is of little social consequence. Doctors and teachers are rather different. Both groups can claim to have a crucial social function. The one ministers to the health of the nation, the other is responsible for the induction of the next generation into the values, norms and required knowledge and skills of that society. At first sight, then, there seem to be grounds for optimism here.

However, the manner in which doctors and teachers perform these functions is likely to bolster or undermine this second claim. Whilst there *is* criticism of the performance of the medical profession, it still has an overwhelming degree of public support. Teachers, on the other hand, are regarded much less favourably. This is a shift in public opinion, because for many years they were regarded as exemplary stable and trustworthy pillars of society. This image of the teaching profession stemmed from a number of factors: its nineteenth-century public school origins; the non-political nature of education; its perceived involvement in national greatness; its contribution to a relatively accepted, if class-ridden, status quo. Britain was great: its armed forces, the church, its educational system, were what made it great. Teachers basked in this reflected glory.

Much of this has disappeared. Education has become intensely politicized; Britain's former greatness has waned; answers to economic, political and moral questions seem less clear; economic and social ills have increased, and schools have taken much of the brunt. In an age of questions and decline, schools have been blamed for not providing the answers to the citizens of tomorrow, and of not reversing the trend. Teachers' competence to fulfil their crucial social functions has been questioned.

In such a climate, it is relatively easy for a government to argue that, even though teachers perform a vital social function, they are not to be trusted to do it autonomously, particularly when the government could strengthen its case by drawing on the work of free-market economists like Milton Friedman and Friedrich Hayek to suggest that the welfare state has created a large number of producer groups, such as teachers, who, protected by nationalization and paternalist bureaucracy, have come to control the institutions of the state, rather than to service them for the benefit of the recipients. In so doing, it is argued, schools (and hospitals) have listened less and less to the customer and have more and more become agencies to satisfy the wants of the producers.

So if a well-worked social and political philosophy is allied to a proactive government and a general public perception of an ailing educational system and widespread professional incompetence, the solution is likely to be one of legislative imposition. This characterizes the Education Acts of 1986, 1988 and 1993. They were not so much about consultation as about the effective removal of curricular control from teachers and local authorities and its location with the Secretary of State and his appointees. At the same time, the devolution of financial responsibility to the school periphery, in the name of greater responsibility and the creation of local initiative, also had the effect of distancing blame for underfunding from the centre. Finally, and in the name of parental choice, increased powers were vested in governing bodies, not only in terms of financial control but in the general running of the school. Henceforth, the argument went, schools would look and act like mini-businesses, with the head and staff as chief executive and officials, the governing body the chairman and board of directors exerting local oversight and control on day-to-day running, while central government controlled national strategy. In Handy's (1985) terms, Dionysians, by legislative imposition, became much more like Apollonians, the implementers of national bureaucratic curricular prescriptions. Teachers may well perform a crucial social function, but one now dictated by those more competent and knowledgeable. The post-Fordist agenda is then complete.

## Prestige and power

If teachers are to reassert their autonomy, it becomes crucial that the general public should see them less as members of squabbling unions and more as like-minded serious professionals. An initial step to this would be the creation of something similar to the General Teaching Council argued for by Maclure (1993a and 1993b), which, like the Scottish GTC set up in 1966, minimally controls entry qualifications and maintains internal discipline. When teachers are seen to speak with one voice, they will be perceived as more authoritative.

When such circumstances are generated, teachers will be in a better position to argue their case for the need for a systematic knowledge base. But to do this they need to develop, as argued above, a much more coherent strategy for the education of parents. This is a re-politicization of their role, though in a non-party-political sense, affirming as it does the belief that both parents and children need to be educated citizens to be effective citizens, and that part of that citizenship involves a familiarity with and understanding of educational issues. Teachers, better than anyone else, are in a position to help them do this. Here I disagree with Warnock (1988: 114), who argues that teachers will not be respected by parents until they can draw a distinction 'between the political and the moral', by which she seems to mean that teachers must eschew action over matters of overt societal nature and dwell instead upon matters of school behaviour and manners. This seems a needless and dangerous distinction. Teachers by their very nature as citizen educators cannot afford to ignore the societal: what they need to do is avoid party dogma or ideology in their efforts. Explaining the complexities of such issues is a crucial role for teachers, not only for their own status but, more importantly, for the good of the society in which they work.

So, following from this, teachers need to re-emphasize a neglected characteristic of professionalism, an ethic of service to the community. This ethic of service can be developed and publicized in a number of ways. Firstly, and following on from the setting up of a unified teacher body like a GTC, an explicit statement of an ethical code could be formulated. Attempts at this have already been made (see Sockett, 1983), and it would not take much ingenuity to produce and publicize one which could then form the basis for teacher training institutions and schools in the socialization of individuals into the ethics of the profession, and would provide a clear reference point for matters of internal discipline. Its publication would provide the general public with the message that the teaching profession was beginning to get its act together. It would then be for the profession to prove that it could continue to do so.

A second means is one already laboured – initiatives by schools to educate parents in the complexities of educational issues. If there is a commitment at the outset to draw parents into a genuine discussion on educational issues, and to invite their comments and evaluation rather than their agreement with the school's point of view, then this will be perceived as an attempt by schools to help parents, as part of an ethic of service and not, as it could so easily be, an attempt by teachers to complain about their lot. Schools will enlist parents' help only if parents feel that teachers' practice is undergirded by an ethic of service to the community and the country as a whole.


## THE FUTURE OF TEACHERS' PROFESSIONALISM

It is crucial that professionals should accept that there are many aspects of quality practice which can be sensibly criticized by non-professionals. As indicated above, questions of quality can be divided into two kinds. Those relating simply to service are obvious candidates for a first, non-professional, kind. It needs no degree to know if you are dealt with promptly, and with a smile, and whether what is happening to you or your child is explained in non-technical language. It does, however, take expertise to know the possible methods of treatment and likely outcomes, and to be able to implement and evaluate such methods. It is knowing which is which, and defending real expertise, which is the key to the professional's future. In practice, the defence of the indefensible only ushers in constraint from above and below. In claiming too much to themselves, professionals do neither themselves nor the public any favours.

It is doubtful if teachers will ever be regarded as being as 'professional' as doctors. Nevertheless, one need not be as dismissive as Goode (1969) when he consigns teaching for ever to the 'semi-professions'. It has, after all, considerably extended the length of initial training; it is clinging to the principle of an all-graduate profession; financially, it has, despite a recent slowdown, become a reasonably attractive occupation. At the same time, teaching will for the foreseeable future be an occupation which takes place within a bureaucratic structure, necessarily limiting the autonomy of its practitioners. Perhaps, then, a better description than 'semi-profession', and one which recognizes its limitations, would be Leggatt's (1970: 160) term of one of the 'bureaucratic professions'. Within bureaucracies, the teaching profession needs to prevent a damaging 'rationalization' and de-skilling, with a consequent reduction in autonomy and quality of service. As part of this, the general public need to recognize the teaching profession's expertise, competence, and quality of service. The principal way teachers can bring this about is to *show* the public, to be seen to be willingly accountable. If teachers fail in this, public perceptions of them will be as yet another group in society attempting to carve out a monopoly to service itself rather than the community.

Underpinning this chapter, then, is a vision of a symbiotic relationship between a teaching profession and a future society. If we can distance ourselves from the 1980s rhetoric of there being 'no such thing as society', and can develop a vision which sees people not living as economic Robinson Crusoes but achieving their identity and fufilment in and through contribution to their communities, the result will be that teachers have perhaps *the* crucial role to play. For it is they who can weave the web of incorporative citizenship with the young, and explain and expand this to their parents. In such communities, teachers' expertise would be acknowledged, their ethic of service would be central, their social usefulness would be without question. In such a society, the future of teachers' professionalism would be assured.

# Chapter 7

# The Convergence of Management Codes

## INTRODUCTION

This book, so far, has tended to argue that there is an increasing convergence of practices between all forms of organizations, partly as a result of political ideologies, partly as a result of industrial trends, partly as a result of individuals within one kind of organization looking over the fence to see how other kinds are run. Much of this can be seen as helpful to the better understanding and better running of different kinds of institutions. Nevertheless, a cautionary note needs to be sounded here. Whilst, for example, the commercial sector is adopting many of the practices and strategies of the non-profit sectors, they are doing this, as this and the final chapter will suggest, at least in part, for different reasons: as another means of achieving better results. It is predicted that should such strategies fail to achieve what is envisioned, they will probably be dropped for other methods. In such circumstances, non-profit organizations like schools and hospitals, unlike commercial organizations, should be very wary of surrendering their mission statements and practices because they must be treated as first-order ethical commitments, not second-order strategic options. The conclusion, then, is one of a welcome for the increased dialogue which is likely to take place between the sectors, but the sounding of a cautionary note in any final description of the kind of ethically challenging role which schools may play for other – and particularly commercial – organizations.

If one looks at the history of management theory, most of it has been the product of work in commercial organizations. This is not surprising: such organizations were willing to pay for their services, and so were instrumental in producing much of the data which would make up the nascent management schools. Organization theory became almost synonymous with for-profit theory. Whether it was Taylor at Bethlehem Steel, the Human Relations Group at Western Electric, McGregor at Union Carbide or the Tavistock Institute in British coal mines, the point is the same: commercial organizations financed much of the development of organization theory, and so it should not be surprising if they – and their values – dominated the field. Indeed, and as Hollway

(1991) describes, whilst these writers present a wide variety of the faces of industrial management in the twentieth century, from the extreme autocracy of Taylorism through the sympathetic psychologizing of the Human Relations group to the seemingly democratic proposals of McGregor and recent 'culture theorists', the principal aims have invariably been economic and commercial.

In such circumstances, two things have tended to happen. The first is that much which might have been of value to management scholars has tended to be overlooked. As Moyer (quoted in Leat, 1993: 6) has argued, ' historically, management scholars have tended to neglect those organisations that are not companies, that are not profit seeking, that are not large, that have high ideological content, that offer services rather than products, and that are led by women'. The second is that the imperative for such research has been inspired largely by commerce and management. So whilst there are strong reasons for believing that there is at present an increasing convergence of codes – what some writers have called 'institutional isomorphism' – and that, because of this, much can be learnt by commercial organizations and non-profit organizations (including schools) from each other, their different reasons for the development of such practices need to be kept strongly in mind.

Two examples of this problematic isomorphism will be given here. A first example of this apparent narrowing of differences can be seen in one of the most popular studies in the business sector in the 1980s – Peters and Waterman's (1982) *In Search of Excellence*. In this study, the authors suggest eight attributes which characterize excellent American commercial companies. These are:

- a bias for action
- staying close to the customer
- autonomy and entrepreneurship
- productivity through people
- a hands-on and value-driven approach
- sticking to the knitting
- simple form and lean staff
- simultaneous loose-tight properties

Many practitioners in non-profit organizations, including schools, might wish to claim that *their* institutions would be excellent exemplars of some of these qualities, and might thus argue that the two sectors have rather more in common than many might imagine. Nevertheless, a close reading of the text might also leave reservations. Excellence is seen predominantly in terms of company productivity. Visionary leadership is seen as the key to this excellence: and the provision of visionary meaning by such a leader to his or her followers is the means to the team members's self-regulation. The authors (p. 16) – apparently approvingly – quote one commentator on 3M's commitment to 'simultaneous loose-tight properties', who suggests that 'the brainwashed members of an extremist political sect are no more conformist in their central beliefs'. Even without this, the message is clear – meaning is to be given to employees in order that they will perform better. There is a Pandora's box of questions waiting to be opened here which, in the management literature, seldom is opened. The questions would include the following:

- Is leadership really about the imposition of vision?

- Does an organization have the right to manipulate individuals through imposed visions to achieve their goals?
- To what extent should management writers present the side of management uncritically?
- Has the management literature sold its soul by so frequently and so uncritically writing from a management perspective?
- What damage would school management writers do to schools if they as uncritically disseminate the standard management writing as 'good practice' for schools?

A second example comes from the work of writers like Drucker (1988) and Handy (1989), who argue that the typical business of the future will be characterized by being essentially knowledge-based, with many specialists working in a collaborative and autonomous manner, whilst Peters and Austin (1985) and Kanter (1989) argue that commercial companies, in order to manage well, will increasingly have to promote more egalitarian and participative practices in the workplace.

These descriptions of the businesses of the future – as knowledge-based and collaborative, encouraging autonomy, egalitarianism and participation – are good descriptions of the kind of school and its management for which writers on ethical educational management have increasingly been arguing. This would seem to be an intriguing case of institutional isomorphism if ever there was one!

Yet a note of caution is needed again. As Leat (1993) says, such structures and practices are no longer part of a politically driven ideological imperative but are seen as necessary if companies are to survive in the marketplace of the future, and she states bluntly (p. 39) that 'achieving greater "worker control" is no longer a matter of improving the quality of life – an optional "add on" – but is rather one of matching management practice to process in order to ensure maximum efficiency and minimum waste'.

In other words, whereas non-profit organizations (and particularly schools) might wish to see such practices instituted precisely because they are seen as beneficial to the political, social and ethical development of its members and of society in general, here they are being used in a purely instrumental manner. And what if they fail to succeed in their aims? Hollway's (1991) book is particularly good for indicating that throughout the history of management practice here and in America, strategies that don't work get changed. Taylorism was instituted because it allowed the management to dominate the workforce by singling out the individual, and to thereby circumvent unionized responses – and failed because it produced such resentment. Human Relations was instituted because it again focused on the individual, and gentled individuals along to do what management wanted them to do. It has been modified to forms like organizational development and culture theories, as senior management has perceived that managers need to be changed just as much as workers, that organizations and their values have to change to survive in a different competitive environment.

The message is clear. As Hollway (1991: 137) puts it, when talking of the standard management literature, 'what purports to be a neutral body of knowledge and practice has been produced principally at the behest of management'. This does not make the standard management literature bad. It simply means that it has been instituted for purposes which might not be those of non-profit organizations like schools, and may actually be damaging to them if they are adopted uncritically. We need therefore to look more closely in this chapter at the supposed differences between commercial and non-profit organizations and see whether these differences are in fact narrowing. Schools will initially be classed with other non-profit organizations, in order to examine ways in which, at a macro level, they, as well as other non-profit organizations, may be experiencing institutional isomorphism. The final chapter will then argue that schools are in some ways unique, and that this uniqueness may well make them a challenging and prototypical type of organization for others to follow.

## SIX SUGGESTED DIFFERENCES

Initially, then, I will suggest that six possible differences have been posited as indicating a gulf between commercial and non-profit organizations. These are as follows:

- Commercial organizations tend to rely on material *incentives* to maintain impetus; non-profit organizations tend to rely on non-material rewards such as prestige, or job satisfaction, to maintain impetus.
- Commercial organizations are dominated by the motive of *profit*; profit serves little or no part in the determination of a non-profit organization's goals, or its definition of success.
- Commercial organizations exist in a *competitive* market; non-profit organizations are bounded by an ethos of co-operation.
- Commercial organizations vary their *mission*, depending on the climate and market; non-profit organizations have clearly defined missions from which they wander at their peril.
- Commercial organizations are characterized by *hierarchy* and degrees of delegation; non-profit organizations are characterized by (or at least pay lip service to the ideals of) equality, egalitarianism and participation.
- Commercial organizations have a limited number of *goals and constituencies* to which they must answer; non-profit organizations have numerous and conflicting goals and constituencies.

It is necessary to examine each of these questions in turn.

### Different incentives

An early attempt at differentiation between non-profit and commercial organizations came from Clark and Wilson (1961), who suggested that while commercial organizations relied upon financial incentives, the non-profit sector relied upon incentives of sociability, enjoyment and prestige.

There can be little doubt that the typology is now very dated. Whilst non-profit organizations have increasingly realized that, to attract the best people, they must increasingly attempt to match the kinds of salaries which the commercial sector offers, the commercial sector has similarly realized that a good salary is insufficient to attract, motivate and retain employees – for many, a degree of job satisfaction which salary alone cannot supply is an essential to job fulfilment.

A difference which extends this initial idea is that of the difference between 'expressive' and 'instrumental' organizations, the former being created to satisfy the wants of members, the latter also to satisfy the wants of others. A bowls club is an example of the former, in that if it fails to satisfy the wants of its members, it ceases to exist. A supermarket, on the other hand, would be a good example of the latter. Nevertheless, it has already been indicated that, according to much recent management theory, one of the hallmarks of a successful commercial organization is precisely that it gives expressive satisfaction to membership – that members feel that working for the organization in some way fulfils personal needs. As Peters and Waterman state (1982: 56), 'we need meaning in our lives, and will sacrifice a great deal to institutions that provide it'. They describe, for instance, managers who pull expensive built-in barbecues out of their patios to install a much inferior version simply because it was a recognition by the company of their achievements, just as they recount the commitment of Frito-Lay, a potato crisp manufacturer, to a 99.5 per cent service level (p. 164), which inspires an almost fanatical devotion in its 25,000 employees to product delivery within a short period to customers, no matter where they are in the country, and no matter what factors might impede such deliveries.

Much of this, then, might suggest that the issue of incentives could be seen as an example of convergence between commercial and non-profit organizations. The problems, however, have been noted above. Is it ethical for senior management to implant its desired ideology into its workers and middle manager by means of T-groups, therapy sessions and training programmes? And then to change this ideology – and therefore the mental functioning of the workforce – when the achievement of a competitive edge demands a change in company values?

Non-profit organizations are not immune from this, of course. Nevertheless, the provision of meanings is usually given by the nature of the organization. Schools, for example, may be seen as examples of an organization which provides meaning to its employees through its very function. Education, like medicine, is seen by many as a 'calling' which not only benefits the client but in many ways benefits the practitioner as well. The 'meaning' of the school is provided for teachers by the subject matter and the children: for most, this is a major 'incentive' for teaching. Can commercial organizations claim the same thing? Whilst they may wish to provide meaning for their employees (it provides one strand of motivation which is beneficial to the company), it is doubtful if there is anything *intrinsic* to the nature of the organization which helps them do this. Meanings have, then, to be manufactured, and then recycled and used in a different form when new challenges face the company. In these circumstances, the conclusion must be that whilst businesses have recognized the motivational aspects of employees having a 'calling', they will fail to match the non-profit sector, and schools in particular, precisely because their 'callings' are manufactured. The gap between the two sectors, then, may narrow, but it is doubtful if it can ever completely close.

## Profit

It is hardly surprising that many people believe that the major difference between a for-profit and a non-profit organization is profit! Indeed, for some, it hardly needs commenting upon, it being simply assumed that profit is the driving force for the commercial sector, and therefore clearly differentiates it from organizations with other motivations.

Whilst few, I think, would disagree that profit is the bottom line for commercial organizations, the situation is still not that simple. For a start, whilst profit may be a bottom line, it is not necessarily an overwhelming preoccupation. We saw this above, particularly in the chapters on Marks & Spencer and Fabricast. More broadly, Shipley (1981), in a survey of 728 UK firms, found that only about one-sixth had as their central aim the maximization of profit, though about nine-tenths of them included the achievement of profit as one of their goals. Profit, then, may be important, but it is not all-consuming – it allows for the exploration of aims which may be very much in accordance with the aims of non-profit organizations.

Moreover, while profit may be the bottom line, it is not clear much of the time where that bottom line is. Organizations may, for instance, engage in a policy of portfolio planning where lack of profit is tolerated on a particular line, and indeed is supported by funds from more profitable lines, as the company attempts to bring the unprofitable product to maturity and profitability. So whilst profit may be an ultimate consideration, it is by no means obvious at what stage it becomes a determining factor in the life of a product.

Further, managing without profit as a performance indicator is more common in businesses than one might assume. There are, after all, plenty of areas within a company which cannot be measured by simple calculation of profit. How does one assess the comparative contribution of an information service, a complaints department, even the advertising department, to a company? Kanter and Summers (1987) suggest that profit is favoured by many simply because it can be so easily measured, but it still does not avoid the problem of apportioning the respective contributions within a company to the achievement of profit (or lack of it). As commercial companies eschew the simplistic, they increasingly realize that measurement of a company's success needs to focus on other features of company functioning. This argument too was supported above, particularly in the chapters on Marks & Spencer and BP Chemicals, and is supported more widely in the literature by the writers on total quality management (like Deming (in Walton, 1989) or Crosby, 1979) who, apart from arguing that an essential feature of the successful company is its devotion to customer satisfaction, suggest that an attention to quality comes before profit. The logic, says West-Burnham (1992: 50) is simple: 'If customer needs are met, then profitability is inevitable.'

Here, then, is a good example of an attention not only to features less quantitative than profit, but also, and importantly, to the processes rather than the end results. As total quality management writers argue, by the time the finished product arrives, it is already too late: the damage is done. One needs to go back to the initial point and start changes from there.

So, curiously, a supposedly crucial and distinguishing feature of for-profit organizations may not, on the face of it, be all that distinguishing. There may be other features which are seen as much more central to the company's functioning, such as total quality management and client satisfaction, which are shared with non-profit organizations. There could be real possibilities of code convergence here.

It would be ironic, then, if schools, through legislation at least since 1988, felt impelled to assess themselves in terms of profit and loss. Many heads, and chairs of governing bodies, may feel that their ultimate measure of success, alongside their published results, is in terms of a simple calculation of whether there are more children attending the school than last academic year. It would then become ironic if educators and politicians were to need reminders from the business world that, whilst the calculation of profit may be the simplest and most convenient form of assessment, it is certainly not the most accurate or most important determinant of organizational success.

## Competition

Again, a fairly standard assumption of the commercial company is that it engages in unceasing competition with others in the same business, whilst non-profit organizations (and especially charities), because of their basically altruistic nature, are fundamentally co-operative, even when two of them are in the same field.

Now, whilst there is truth in this remark, the reality is rather more complex. One can begin by questioning whether the statement is altogether factually correct. In big business, after all, the existence of monopolies and oligopolies means that some companies co-operate as much as compete in order to keep prices high and to exclude others from entering the marketplace.

Further, Kanter (1989), among others, argues that the existence of such co-operation is becoming one of the central features of business management, as success will be based less on 'segmentalist' structures, and more on ones of flexible, co-operative teams. Of course, the argument about incentives holds good here as well: co-operation is, on this view, but a tool for the achievement of (competitive) organizational ends, rather than a system of social relationships perceived as beneficial in themselves. It would, on this analysis, be substituted for something much more corrosively competitive if it was felt desirable – as, for instance, Harold Geneen did at ITT (see Sampson, 1973).

In real terms, though, with the increased hiring of management from one sector to the other, one can expect that some cultural assumptions will be transferred along with the individuals moving between sectors. If this is the case, then individual decisions, leading through to general policy, will probably experience a different kind of approach – more co-operation in the commercial sector, more competition in the non-profit sector. Of course, this may be the reality: whether it is desirable that non-profit organizations should engage in competition is another matter entirely, and much more debatable. Whether a strong dose of co-operation will alter the character of commercial organizations is an interesting debating point as well.

On the non-profit side, it has been argued that competition occurs naturally when charities come into existence through the inadequacies of others in the same field to supply a need; and that co-operation and competition are as much a function of personalities as policies. Genuinely bitter rivalries can exist in the non-profit sector as much as in the for-profit sector based on little more than the personal enmity between two organization leaders. Both of these points are undoubtedly true: but it is doubtful whether either affects the principal point that non-profit organizations are of their nature primarily concerned with others' well-being, and are therefore much more co-operatively oriented than the for-profit sector. In such circumstances, it is very debatable whether these principal orientations of the two sectors can or ought to change fundamentally, despite recent initiatives in both sectors.

It is therefore worth reflecting that schools find themselves being drummed into the competitive market upon a tidal wave of free-market theory. Open enrolment, LMS, comparative published results, opting out, are all designed to allow the client or customer to compare products and choose between them. Now client accountability and genuine choice are no bad things: whilst Shaw's observation that all professions are conspiracies against the laity may be a little too sharp, there are too many examples of closed markets where the customer gets a raw deal to believe that schools would not do a better job in having to respond to client wishes. Nevertheless, and as Titmus (1968) pointed out some time ago with regard to blood donors, the production of a commercial relationship can be extremely detrimental to the provision of a public service, a problem which becomes transparent when one compares a public provision like the BBC with the fully developed competitive material served up on American TV. It is not apparent that a better service is provided: in fact there is much evidence to the contrary. Increase in competition can lead to a diminution not only in efficiency but in quality as well. Schools need to avoid cutting each other's throats in the process of surviving, to avoid being seduced by the cut and thrust of the marketplace. A case of politically inspired isomorphism is occurring, and schools, whether they like it or not, are entering the world of business values. They may find that courses in business ethics become germane to their activities in a way they never conceived of ten years ago. Whether this is good for them and society is again highly debatable.

## Mission

It may come as a surprise to some to find it suggested (as by Drucker, 1989) that non-profit organizations tend to be better managed than their commercial counterparts. His argument is fairly straightforward: the non-profit organization is more likely to have a well-defined purpose or mission, and so will tend to be guided and steered by it. Organizations starting and being driven merely by the likes of profits, budget statements and projected sales growth, suggests Drucker, are less likely to provide the structures within which a carefully formulated plan will be followed and implemented.

Of course, exactly the reverse conclusions could be and are drawn. Kanter and Summers (1987), for instance, suggest that it is precisely this centrality of specific goals which increases the likelihood of the non-profit organization being inflexible. In a changing climate, it may find it difficult if not impossible to come to terms with new demands and to change direction. The business organization, precisely because its mission statement is more flexible, is more likely to be able to adapt to the new situation.

This is the argument. Again, the reality is more complex. Commercial organizations are owned and run by individuals with many different 'missions'. Marks, Cadbury and Rowntree were all interested in the welfare of their employees for more than just being the best means of turning a profit. Commercial organizations can have non-profit goals which drive their owners, and from which they will not be deflected, just as much as many non-profit organizations. Similarly, even charity mission statements can be and are phrased in a deliberately broad manner to allow for flexibility, or may simply change with the times and current demands. As Leat (1993: 29) points out, 'the Young Men's Christian Association has managed to transform itself into an organisation serving non-Christian men and women!'.

Nevertheless, there is still a problem, and one which has already been highlighted. It concerns a current management preoccupation with the development of an organizational 'culture', synonymous in many respects with the development of an organizational mission. Yet we have already seen how such cultures, such missions, are not, as they are with non-profit organizations, a primary goal but rather a second-order, instrumental goal: if the culture suits, keep it. If it doesn't prove successful, change it. Deal and Kennedy (1988: 25), for instance, in talking about the values of a company's culture, say that 'they mostly come from experience, from testing what does and does not work in the economic environment'.

It seems clears what is happening: if particular values work in developing a company which is successful in the search for profit and growth, then these values should be promoted. If they don't, then they should be dispensed with. They do not derive, as I suggest they should do in education, from first-order considerations of the development of individual, social and political potentials and the building of a just society.

Yet schools are already changing their colours in the light of recent legislation. Faced with a choice between retaining their mission intact, and changing to survive, some heads and governors are beginning to alter, some would say surrender, their mission statement. Letters go out to parents suggesting that an area is within a school's catchment area, when it has always been acknowledged to be within another's; children with behavioural or discipline problems are discouraged from joining a school, or are made the subject of procedures to hasten their exit; travellers' children are not welcomed in case other parents withdraw their children; teachers are hired because they are cheaper than others; schools withdraw from local authority arrangements, even though they support the principle of mantaining local authority provision, in order to balance their budget at the end of the year. These and many more policies suggest that survival is a more pressing consideration than ethical commitment. For many in the business sector, this has always been a dilemma. It is at least debatable whether this is a form of isomorphism which is desirable or necessary. The conscious construction of systems which institute such dilemmas – and the conscious destruction of systems which allowed for the pre-eminence of ethical decisions – is surely to be deplored.

## Hierarchy

Another proposed difference between the non-profit and business sectors lies in the belief that the non-profit sector may experience greater pressure, stemming partly from its more ethically driven approach, and from the large proportion of professionals and knowledge workers within it, to achieve greater equality and participation within the workforce. Certainly, in charities, where a large proportion of workers may be voluntary, and in organizations created for the benefit of the participants, equality of status, might well be a very important feature if volunteers are to be retained and the participants are to stay with the organization. No one, it might be argued, will stay within a hierarchial structure for the sake of it: it is simply an evil which is tolerated.

People in businesses, on the other hand, precisely because they are hired to do a job, and remain financially viable through their salary, will tolerate a form of organization, and accept inferior status, of being used as a means to an end, precisely in exchange for financial rewards.

Again, reality suggests that whilst there may be truth in such assertions, the two sectors are closer than many might acknowledge, and are becoming closer. Clearly, volunteers can withdraw their labour with little or no penalty to themselves, and yet this does not stop many from accepting hierarchical structures. One reason for this may be through a need to help: it may be worth putting up with overblown authoritarian attitudes to be part of a caring organization. Another reason may be a lifetime of bureaucratic conditioning: people who spend their lives working within hierarchical structures may simply accept that this is how organizations work. They may even feel insecure if greater equality and participation are encouraged, and may welcome the sense of security given by formal hierarchies and structures of authorities. Certainly, Fromm's (1960) seminal work, suggesting that people shun taking personal responsibility for their lives, and Milgram's (1964), depicting the degree to which volunteers will accept instructions from those in superior positions, both argue that an acceptance of hierarchy may be part of the 'hidden curriculum' of a bureaucratized society which infiltrates the running of organizations which have no actual need of it. This, of course, is not a very good argument for isomorphism but rather a condemnation of the society in which we live. If a convergence of management codes is occurring because of these factors, it is not an encouraging but a fairly depressing feature of organizational behaviour today.

Similarly, the fact that commercial organizations are increasingly coming to accept that participative approaches are a hallmark of the successful firm may not actually be much to cheer about. Writers like Handy (1989), Drucker (1988) and Walton and Susman (1987) all argue for a change in workforces and organizations to emphasize professionalism, knowledge workers, flexibility, networks rather than hierarchies, high levels of autonomy, but commitment to core values. Part of this acceptance stems from the post-Fordist recognition that financial incentives are insufficient to generate commitment to an organization, that motivation stems as much from developing within the individual a commitment to company values. Much of this can be derived not from the imposition of standards but from participation in the planning of strategies and practices. Part also stems from the changing nature of the workplace, which sees ideas generated as usefully from lower as from upper levels, thus tending towards a decrease in hierarchies, and more towards solutions like quality circles. Inevitably, then, the successful organization of the future will rely less and less on hierarchies and more and more on the kinds of organization supposedly the province of the non-profit sector.

Nevertheless, such commitment is still second-order commitment, an instrumental attachment to values and practices which serve a greater company end, rather than a commitment generated by the nature of work and an ethical commitment to it and its clients. And, again, if the commercial climate changes so that hierarchy is seen as more competitively advantageous, there is little to suggest that hierarchies and levels will not be resurrected.

Schools, curiously, seem to fall between the two sectors. Supposedly full of professionals and knowledge workers, committed to the development of a citizenship education for their pupils, and thus having many of the ingredients for a flat, democratic and participative system of management, the state school system in the UK has instead been characterized, since its inception, more by a mixture of hierarchy, paternalism and bureaucracy. Partly explained by its inheritance of private school authoritarianism and patriarchy, developments towards egalitarian and participative structures like the GRIDS initiatives (Abbott *et al.*, 1988) have been stifled by the legislation of 1988 and after. This has instituted massive bureaucracy through a National Curriculum and its attendant testing, and instituted hierarchy through hugely increased ministerial powers, Department of Education involvement and the creation of uneasy nexuses of power between headteachers and governing bodies. We may then have a situation, once again, as with the question of profit, where it takes the business sector to remind politicians (and senior educational managers) of the benefits of participation and more egalitarian forms of management, even if they do so for (educationally) the wrong reasons.

## Limited constituencies

A final factor suggested as differentiating the two sectors is that the non-profit sector has varied and, in many cases, conflicting constituencies, all of whom need to be taken account of when policy is formulated. In a charity, for instance, one has not only the recipient to satisfy but also the donor, the trustees, public opinion, even the volunteer force. It is suggested that such varied pressures are not the case in the business sector, in that the customer is seen to dictate policy. If the customer is satisfied, then other pressure groups will be satisfied as well.

Again, the above description is probably simplistic. For a start, in an era of monopolies and oligopolies, it may well be that the producer rather than the customer dictates policy. When the customer's choice is non-existent, or severely limited, then his or her influence is necessarily muted.

Secondly, whilst the non-profit sector *has* many constituencies to answer, the same is increasingly true of the business sector. For a start, there is a problem with the definition of 'customer'. Much of the recent literature on quality defines the customer as being that individual or group which directly receives the product or service from you. This means that the 'customer' can be someone inside the organization, as well as outside of it. If this is the case, then saying that the customer dictates policy, even where true, necessarily means responding to a huge variety of actors in the commercial process, not simply some individual purchasing over the counter. This expanded notion of 'customer' then suggests a much more assorted set of constituencies than the simpler relationships of old.

This point corresponds very well with another recent change in for-profit thinking, highlighted in the chapter on BP Chemicals. Increasingly, argue writers like Carroll (1989), and Schein (1966), companies are accepting that they are accountable no longer to shareholders, but to *stakeholders* in the company. Stakeholders are not necessarily people who have a direct financial interest in the company, such as shareholders, though they often are. They can also be those who have a personal stake through involvement, such as employees, suppliers and customers (in the more usual sense of the word). However, further than this, they can be those individuals, groups or constituencies whom the company, by its actions, may affect at a distance. This then brings in such interested parties as the local community, the local environment and even future generations. Such a sense of accountability, if acted upon, would be a clear acceptance by commercial organizations of an ethical responsibility to the society and world within which they trade, and would reject the freewheeling, self-interested and self-absorbed attitude characteristic of some businesses and politicians of the 1980s. Such 'stakeholder' management would draw commercial organizations into the same kinds of problems and duties that, it has been suggested, are part and parcel of being in the non-profit sector – issues of varied goals and constituencies and of societal responsibilities. On this analysis, then, the commercial sector is increasingly coming to realize societal and global interdependence and to accept its share of responsibility, and is thus taking on board and dealing with the same kinds of diverse challenges.

Such claims seem to run counter to the above-mentioned kind of analysis described by Hollway (1991), for they present a quite radical departure from the general prioritization of introspective company success detailed throughout the history of for-profit organizations. If such claims are acted upon, there may be real and optimistic isomorphism. The reality might be, of course, that this is a new strategy for company success: it is, after all, good business at present to be seen as green and caring. The test for such mission statements will come when they conflict with the economic and commercial priorities of the companies, and continue to do so.

Schools will increasingly have to face such tensions. Whilst they have always been institutions having to answer to the demands of different constituencies and to questions of value, they now have economic pressures to address in a much more prominent way than before. Schools have always been at the forefront in debates about the 'good' society and the needs for the next generation; now they must balance them with commercial considerations. There may be an interesting exchange of ideas here: whilst schools may claim, with charities, a necessary awareness of varied ethical obligations, the business sector may have much to teach them in terms of such things as financial viability. Again, the notion of constituencies highlights the way in which sectors can learn from one another.

## ISOMORPHIC CONCLUSIONS

Despite different assumptions and different aims, there does seem to be a convergence of issues and interests, an increasing isomorphism between the non-profit and commercial sectors. If this is the case, four initial conclusions can be drawn. The first is that it would be foolhardy in the extreme for one sector to ignore the problems and solutions of the other. If the commercial sector has tended to ignore the non-profit sector in the past because of the lack of academic interest in this area, it would be dangerous for the non-profit sector to ignore the commercial sector for whatever reason now. The two sectors have much to teach each other, and much that, through dialogue, they can more easily see should remain their own province. The implications for education are obvious: it cannot ignore the lessons of other organizations, but it should continue to defend those areas which are unsuitable for the invasion of techniques foreign to educational philosophies and values.

If a first conclusion is the danger of sticking one's head in the sand, a second conclusion is that schools can *exchange* lessons with many other organizations. The school, for example, is but one example of a widespread twentieth-century phenomenon – the professional in a bureaucratized organization. A comparison of opportunities and pressures between, say, doctors in the health service and teachers in schools might produce insights for both parties. Similarly, the school could learn much from the manner in which charities use volunteers, as they increasingly induct the volunteer into their organization. And as commercial organizations accept the need to assess qualitative aspects of their organization, schools can provide valuable insights for them.

A third conclusion is one suggested by Leat (1993). This is that it may be as useful to study organizational types as to study sector differences. Thus, to use one of her examples, whilst a market stall and ICI are both commercial organizations, and Oxfam and a village playgroup are both non-profit organizations, ICI may have more in common with Oxfam through problems of size, the use of professionals and knowledge management, whilst the market stall and the village playgroup may have more in common through their similar size and relatively untrained workers. Further, one may go beyond size, and say that Apple and Oxfam have as much in common as Apple and Pepsi, because of the professional and specialized nature of the work of Apple and Oxfam, the commercial nature of Apple and Pepsi. If this is the case, there may be much ground in transcending sectoral stereotypes and developing a form of organizational analysis which sees sectoral differences as only one of many differences which may, depending on the occasion, be among the less interesting and important. Such an attitude might make for genuinely interesting and novel studies which can only add to the health of all organizations studied.

A final conclusion is that many organizations are coming to face some very similar problems, and so may well benefit from comparing and contrasting strategies and results. Whilst differing in their ultimate aims, both commercial and non-profit sectors increasingly accept the need to establish common core values, to build consensus rather than manage by imposition, to effect a balance between the autonomy of the individual and/or branch, and control from the centre. Any specialist in comparative studies realizes that simple transfer is never possible, indeed is positively dangerous; but the very study itself enriches one's understanding of the limits and possibilities of one's own area of interest. Organizations are no different. The benefits may not be immediate or quantitative: but the qualitative difference over a period of time will be apparent even to the most hardened sceptic.

If these conclusions are correct, educational managers are entering an intellectually challenging era, one in which they can not only learn from others but share common problems, defend what is unique to their sector and begin to teach others of and in what they are specialists. Educational management, and much of the non-profit sector, are then no longer the poor relations in the management field. There is then an egalitarian acknowledgement and sharing between the sectors which will be healthy for all.

# Chapter 8

---

# Questions for Education, Lessons from Schools?

## INTRODUCTION

Chapter 7 was concerned with describing how organizations are increasingly moving towards, and borrowing from, organizations in other sectors. It argued that, because of this movement, schools have much to be wary of, much to learn from, and much to offer other kinds of organizations.

This complexity stems to a large extent from the recognition that organizations have different purposes and play different roles in society. Nevertheless, it has been argued in this book that they are seldom so totally different from each other that nothing can be gained by their comparison. Notions of stakeholder management suggest that some interest groups will have a concern for a variety of different kinds of organization. Moreover, the aims of many different kinds of organization will coincide at some point. Whilst schools may not see themselves as principally concerned with wealth generation, one of their functions must be to provide the youth of today with the understanding and skills necessary to be able to contribute to the development of a successful economy. Schools may then have much to learn from these different kinds of organizations.

In like manner, and stemming from their role as pivotal in the dissemination of knowledge and values within advanced societies, schools could be front runners in the discussion of other features central to the running of most institutions. This potential pre-eminence will be illustrated in this final chapter by the raising of a set of six questions, the answers to which, it will be argued, must logically affect the manner in which an educational institution is run. Whilst these questions are at face value of either an epistemological or a political nature, it will be suggested that fundamentally they are ethical questions, for they argue for the manner in which schools *ought* to be run. By extension, they ask questions about how the management of all organizations ought to be approached.

## IS VALUE-FREE MANAGEMENT POSSIBLE?

Organizations are not 'things', in some physical sense. Buildings do not manage, do not make decisions: buildings are not organizations but the shells within which organizations are run. People do these things, and people do these things through their values. Greenfield stresses the deliberateness of such values when he argues (Greenfield and Ribbins, 1993: 217) that 'Organisations are not objects in nature; an organisation is a moral order invented and maintained by human choice and will'.

Greenfield goes on to stress the different value-bases from which people come, but his picture is still probably a little too simple and a little too strong. For a start, whilst people bring their values to organizations, they bring them to *something*, which is normally a complex amalgam of perceptions of the accepted set of existing values for the organization ('We do it this way here'), as well as of resident individuals' own personal agendas.

Perhaps more importantly, much activity in organizations, even if it is value-laden, is not deliberate. Many values are created and maintained by structures and practices the original intentions for which are now forgotten, even if the effect is the same; or they may have unintended and probably unrecognized effects beyond those originally planned for. Toffler (1970: 354) gives a good example of this in the structures and practices of early schools:

> Mass education was the ingenious machine constructed by industrialism to produce the kind of adult it needed . . . the most criticised features of education today – the regimentation, lack of individualisation, the rigid systems of seating, grouping, grading and marking, the authoritarian role of the teacher – are precisely those that made mass public education so effective an instrument of adaptation for its time and place.

The intentions may no longer be there, but the effects are. Originally designed to gentle the masses, such practices can continue to influence people long after the reasons for their creation are forgotten. They can also impair creativity and sociability in a manner probably never contemplated. So whilst the effects of such structures may no longer be deliberate, they still change people's behaviour and thinking: they are still value-laden.

Finally, Greenfield's picture may be deficient in that it focuses upon the intentions of the individual actor, and in so doing fails to capture the fact that many of these actors perform roles within a socially devised script. Now whilst the standard Marxist view – that individuals are prisoners of the class into which they are born – may be too strong, it has its point. By focusing upon the individual, one may fail to see the larger picture which constrains or impels individual views, judgements and actions in one direction rather than another.

Indeed, one may go further, and say that not only does a focus upon the individual limit perception, so does a focus upon the institution. Organizations must be depicted within a societal context to understand their purpose fully. As mentioned in the chapter on Fabricast, this is the nub of many of the criticisms of Caldwell and Spink's (1988) book *The Self-Managing School*. Whilst very clear, and persuasive of the need and benefit of whole-school participatory planning, it fails to locate such planning within a context which, in many countries, has been described as an agenda of budget cuts, and power held by central government, with only participation on tactics possible at the school level. By failing to discuss this wider picture, I would argue, the book obliquely provides support for this pattern of events.

An organization, then, cannot be value-free; it is, intentionally or unintentionally, an expression of individuals, or groups of individuals, past and present, bringing to it opinions, orientations, world views and values. They may act out of their own point of view, or because they have been hired to implement another persons's or group's point of view, but they cannot avoid the fact that they are implementing a particular view of what that organization should be doing, of how people should be behaving, an expression which is necessarily subjective, and therefore, necessarily contestable, even if not always contested.

The great danger, then, is to forget that organizations are such expressions, to take these expressions as 'objective' and incontestable, and then merely to debate the most efficient and effective means to achieve these ends. This, of course, was Max Weber's point, and fear: that we become so bound up with 'formal' rationality, with the devising of the most 'rational' means, that we lose sight of 'substantive' rationality, of the fact that someone is responsible for the ends of the organization, and, if that someone is not us, it is someone with whom we may disagree (even if that someone, as in Toffler's example, has been dead 150 years). As Kelman and Hamilton (1989: 324) say, 'authorities also function as partisans': they have their own agenda, their own interests. Management, then, cannot be value-free. Only if we wish to become moral eunuchs can we take such a point of view. And even then we abnegate our responsibility to others affected by managerial decisions.

Now educational management is triply value-laden. Firstly, and as just argued, all management is a matter of decision-making between alternative choices. Educational management is subject to this as much as any other kind of organization. Secondly, whilst this book has argued that a long-term vision of society must include the concept of businesses looking beyond their own profitability and well-being to that of society in general, it is a notion which in the short to medium term would seem to sit much more comfortably with schools. Finally, educational institutions are, by their nature, also much more centrally concerned than others with epistemological issues. This leads to our second question.

## ARE THERE OBJECTIVE FACTS AND VALUES IN EDUCATIONAL MANAGEMENT TO WHICH ALL CAN OR SHOULD AGREE?

It would be little more than philosophical nitpicking to argue whether notions of 'schools' or 'headteachers' were or were not objective facts. There clearly *is* a level at which people within a culture share a common understanding of terms. Of course, precisely what schools *ought* to be doing, or what the role of a headteacher *ought* to be, is another matter entirely, and is much more problematical. So much may initially be agreed, but once the ground rules are established, real disagreements are almost bound to ensue. Should not such disagreements be given a forum in which differences can be debated rationally and educationally?

Similarly, there is much agreement about the common values by which any civilized society must abide. Popper (1945) focused upon the adoption of rationality as in actuality a *moral* decision by a society, for its rejection – the surrender to irrationality or blind obedience to others' decisions – invites all the brutalities of totalitarian regimes. Peters (1966) expanded this by arguing that the adoption of reason involves the making of various second-order moral commitments – such as impartiality, willingness to listen to others' points of view, and fairness. More recently, Webster (1993) has argued for an objective framework of values based upon freedom, knowledge, rationality, happiness and co-operation. Few would disagree with these lists; most people in actual fact would probably argue that they are non-negotiable. Yet, once agreed, the balance between different values is very much negotiable. What, for instance, should be the balance between equality and freedom in a society? To what extent should people be encouraged to pursue their own interests, to what extent should they be encouraged to see their development as only possible through an identification with the needs of their community? What should be the balance in society between competition and co-operation? Clearly, here is fertile ground for difference, dissent and debate. Should this not be encouraged?

Finally, and again at a commonsense level, there is usually little argument about general issues on a school management agenda. The curriculum, the finance, the strategic deployment of individuals within the institutions, are going to figure large on any school management agenda in this society. Nevertheless, there will still be differences regarding the kinds of curricula that should be taught, and how much of each. There will be differences regarding how a limited budget ought to be spent. And, similarly, not all will agree upon the kinds of talents the teachers within a school possess, and how they can be most effectively utilized.

The problem lies in that, even granting that there is some single reality of which we are a constituent part, this does not avoid the conclusion that there will be a variety of views as to precisely what that reality is or should be. And the perception of it will be conditioned by such factors as age, sex, social class, race, physiological equipment, psychological background, historical period and geographical location. The understanding of this reality, then, is arrived at with the lenses of subjective perception. We are limited in what we can perceive by the quality of our equipment; and from that selection we tend to limit ourselves to what we value, to the value-scheme we adopt. Even at the epistemological level, even in the 'hard' sciences, the result is a genuine degree of uncertainty:

> The empirical base of objective science has thus nothing 'absolute' about it. Science does not rest upon solid bedrock. The bold structure of its theories rise, as it were, above a swamp. It is like a building erected on piles. The piles are driven down from above into the swamp, but not down to any natural or 'given' base; and if we stop driving the piles deeper, it is not because we have reached firm ground. We simply stop when we are satisfied that the piles are firm enough to carry the structure, at least for the time being.
> (Popper, 1982: 111)

As it is true in the physical sciences, so it is in the human sciences, only more so, where the 'truth' of an action depends upon individuals' perceptions and values of it. As Carr (1982: 23) says of historical facts:

> they are like fish swimming about in a vast and sometimes inaccessible ocean; and what the historian catches will depend, partly on chance, but mainly on what part of the ocean he chooses to fish in and what tackle he chooses to use – these two factors being, of course, determined by the kind of fish he wants to catch.

Inevitably, then, as Greenfield (in Greenfield and Ribbins, 1993: 107) says, 'Facts, whatever they are, are less important to us than our judgement of them . . . facts decide nothing; it is people who decide about the facts'.

Management, educational or not, is about the decision as to whether certain 'facts' and values are to be counted as important. Organizations, then, are inevitably going to be the focus for competing choices, for individual subjectivities. So, because of our limitations in the perception of relevant 'facts', and because such facts are grounded in particular theories about the world, many judgements in organizations about what is to be done are going to be contestable.

We have then, three separate issues, one epistemological, the second political, the third moral. The *epistemological* argues that much of what counts as knowledge is predetermined by what a person is capable of perceiving, and what he or she counts as valuable. The *political* argues that, precisely because such knowledge is subjective, it is contestable, and at the organizational level almost certainly a function of the power relations within that society and that organization: in other words, those in charge will probably suggest that theirs is the objective, and therefore legitimate, definition of what an organization should be doing. The *moral* argues that, precisely because such knowledge is subjective and contestable, *if* a major purpose of a school is to contribute to the democratic functioning of that society, then these epistemological and political issues need to be pointed up and debated. It will be clear, then, that they need to become part of the fabric not only of a school's curriculum but also of its managerial decision-making, through an acceptance of this subjectivity and contestability, and through this to a greater participation in decision-making. Of course, if one wishes to inculcate values of hierarchy and deference, then presenting only one curricular version of 'reality', and creating management structures in schools which replicate the authoritarian political structures of the country, are excellent means of doing so!

## DO EDUCATIONAL AND BUSINESS MANAGEMENT DIFFER IN THEIR AIMS AND OBJECTIVES?

We have already seen that the most common approach to this question is to assume that they differ very little, save in that businesses and business management tend to be more professional, driven as they are by the imperatives of the marketplace. The result is that from an assumption of commonality derives the question of what *they* can do for education and educational management. It is from such an approach that innovations in appraisal, staff development, total quality management, customer care and related issues are usually introduced to educational institutions. Such developments have been attended to by schools in much the same way as sectors of business and industry have attended to innovations from other sectors: with some interest, some scepticism and a fairly rapid adoption if legally prescribed, a more gradual and considered adoption to their own circumstances when they are seen to further organizational ends.

Another approach is to suggest that much of the development of western societies can be seen in terms of business and industry driving societal agendas. As with a Fordist approach to industry, and the transposition of such techniques to education, so with post-Fordist approaches to business and industry, and their extension to non-profit organizations. This book, and specifically this chapter, questions the unproblematic acceptance of such an approach, assuming as it does a one-way transfer of interests.

A third way of looking at this question is to examine rather more systematically, as the previous chapter did, the possible commonalities between different kinds of organizations, and areas where there is increasing institutional isomorphism. Through such a procedure it was concluded that an approach in which the managements of educational and other non-profit organizations were viewed less and less as junior partners, and more and more as equals in the enterprise of organizational analysis, has much to commend it.

However, it is possible to suggest a final approach: that through the particular epistemological, political and moral demands made upon educational management, *it* has much to teach other organizations. Thus, if one of the central functions of schools should be to teach a curriculum as fairly and accurately as possible, then that curriculum should be taught in a manner which attempts to reflect the reality of the world beyond it. Now, as argued above, because an appreciation of the reality underlying the curriculum is necessarily to some degree subjective, schools should make a specific focus upon this subjectivity, and therefore upon the areas of contestability within their curricula. From there schools must examine various models for the resolution of this contestability. Where, because of the plurality of viewpoints, an ultimate resolution is not possible, an appreciation of the problem, and the structuring of rational means of resolution, can still be seen as valuable, for they can help towards a tolerance, even a celebration, of difference. Here, clearly, approaches inspired by the different perspectives of culture, gender, age, background and (dis)ability can all foster greater appreciation.

Further than this, though, educators should look at the management of their own organizations and accurately depict its nature, which, like the curriculum, will have degrees of subjectivity and contestability. However, as with the curriculum, they must go further than merely pointing out differences; they must also begin to tread the path to resolution. This means they have a responsibility to structure the management of their organizations in such a way as to help their inhabitants to decide on the best means of the resolution of the different visions of the function of the school. It will *not* do, as argued above, for a senior management team to see its job as the most efficient and effective implementation of governmental directives: its organization should be one which encourages the enunciation of different perspectives and the best ways of resolving such differences. This inevitably turns the school into a political organization, for part of its duty, stemming from the ethical duty of providing an accurate description of reality, is to act as the institution within which young people come to appreciate different visions, and begin to formulate ways of resolving such contestations. If the best way is a variant of democracy, then the school has a social responsibility to move its structure and functioning as far as possible, given the limited experience and maturity of many of its participants (but limitations, I suggest, hugely overestimated) towards some variant of democracy. Schools then accurately reflect epistemological and political realities, and educate their charges towards a peaceful resolution of inevitable differences.

How does this affect business and industry? It affects business and industry by asking them what their societal role is. Do they merely have to be efficient wealth-producers, or should they be contributing to other societal aims, including the development of individuals and the quality of life in a wider than economic sense; and do they, like educational organizations, have a social responsibility to reflect epistemological and political realities accurately?

Certainly, some businesses recognize the subjectivities, the differences, of perception, and then harness them. The quality initiative at BP Chemicals, and the more general total quality management initiative, with specific applications like quality circles, recognize that the delivery of a high-quality service depends on all levels of the organization, and the best suggestions for change and improvement do not always, or even most of the time, come from the top. Nevertheless, the encouragement of such subjectivities is located within a post-Fordist agenda: they are invariably for the purpose of increasing the likelihood of the success of management policies. It is specifically recognized in most companies (and accepted in most management literature) that the function of senior management is to provide a vision for the company, and to provide others with the motivation to achieve that vision. It is generally not seen as the responsibility of a company to encourage different perceptions of the direction of the organization to further any notions of workplace or societal participative democracy.

From most companies' point of view, then, only one perception of reality is encouraged, and that is the shareholder's or management's perception of it. Free-market perspectives do nothing to dispel such a view, for, minimally, they depict society as made up of entrepreneurs whose only responsibility is to envision and design institutions to compete in a market for customers, and who hire and develop other individuals to implement this vision. Milton Friedman puts it most succinctly when he says (1962: 133): 'If businessmen do have a social responsibility other than making maximum profits for stockholders, how are they to know what it is? Can self-selected individuals decide what the social interest is?'

Yet whilst, paradoxically, much of this kind of argument stems from a subjectivist philosophical position (see Gray, 1992), one need not assume that an individual is being asked to decide on a definition of social good and social interest by him- or herself. Rather, if one adopts the kind of stakeholder model for businesses described above, then no one shareholder, manager or management team is being called upon to decide on the public good by themselves. Rather they are being asked:

- to accept that general societal norms of truth-telling, justice, fairness etc., apply to them, as much as to others in society;
- to accept that their businesses have effects beyond their own concerns, which affect many different groups in this society and beyond, and that they have to accept some responsibility for these effects;
- to accept that there are *different* perceptions of the good, and that, if business and industry are to be seen as integral and vital parts of society, they cannot withdraw from the debate of such issues and simply do their own thing;
- to accept that it is debatable whether strategies for running business and industry should provide the agenda for driving other institutions like schools.

If this is accepted, they may then argue that their actions had *unintended* consequences on others in society; but it will be much harder to argue that such consequences were *unforeseeable*, for, had they adopted a stakeholder approach, they would have consulted others and would probably have learned of such consequences.

A stakeholder approach, then, suggests a re-orientation and re-ordering of businesses' and society's priorities. Society's judgement of the success of a business or industry would then be *partly* determined by its profitability, but it would also be determined by the extent to which it acknowledged its effect upon the community, the extent to which it listened to, and integrated, the views of other interested stakeholders into the development of its vision. A list of such stakeholders would certainly include shareholders, and companies would still be concerned with generating a profitable return on investments, but the list of stakeholders would include other parties directly or indirectly affected by the company's activities. The list might also then most directly include managers, employees, customers, and suppliers, but also local, national and global communities, and representatives for future generations and the natural environment.

In adopting a stakeholder approach, then, the workplace is inevitably politicized, for a decision is thereby made to hear other voices besides those of the owners and management. However, in so doing, organizations are not entering the political arena for the first time: they have always been there. The free-market position, by arguing for organizations' value-neutrality, has not made them value-neutral: it merely passively supports the status quo within them and in society at large. As this book has argued throughout, organizations are created by human beings to achieve certain values. Reflection upon such values may lead to their restatement, or to their re-assessment, and from there to a change in an organization's structures and practices to reflect the increased importance of other values. The managers of educational organizations should feel obliged by the demands of an accurate epistemology, and of an acceptable political education, to do precisely this. Shareholders, and through them managers, of businesses and industries, from considerations of the physical and ideological effects of business and industry upon the development of society, might begin to do so as well.

## WHAT DEGREES OF PARTICIPATION AND DISSENT SHOULD EDUCATIONAL ORGANIZATIONS ENCOURAGE?

Such approaches are going to be at variance with the views of individuals and groups running companies along traditional business lines; such interested parties would need to accept the right of a variety of stakeholders to express their perceptions of the organizational vision, and increasingly of the right to have the means to contribute to the organization's vision. The prospects for such a realization are clearly not bright unless individual companies are persuaded by the morality of such a move, or see a competitive advantage in it for themselves, or legislation facilitates its introduction. None of these seems likely at present, in the UK at least. Nevertheless, such considerations should not drive such principles from an agenda.

Not only will such approaches be antithetical to many businesses: they will also be uncomfortable to authoritarian Secretaries of State for Education, and paternalist headteachers. Yet here, at the level of the school, notwithstanding the non-negotiability of the values of certain issues, and of the existence of legislation which simply excludes the concept of contestability from much decision-making, there is a genuine chance of beginning such a process. Schools could begin to provide an education which was overtly political at the level of the resolution of different visions. Within an accepted framework, such an organization would accept the place of contestability of the balance of values, including management values. Participation and dissent would be part of a currency spent in the articulation of a political vision, probably that of a democratic nature.

Where this vision *is* democratic in nature, the question then becomes one not so much of 'how much' participation and dissent is permissible, but rather, 'how, given that they are essential components of a genuine political involvement, are they to be incorporated into the management framework of the school?' They become no longer elements the inclusion of which is debatable, but rather elements essential to a complete education. They are, as described above, constrained by areas of non-negotiability, by legislative imperatives, and also by the age and expertise of participants. This latter caveat, as I have argued elsewhere (Bottery, 1992), is largely a matter of guesswork at present, though what little evidence there is suggests that a more optimistic attitude should be adopted for their extensive inclusion than is normally held. Within the framework adopted, and to paraphrase Downey and Kelly (1986: 124), the teacher's, and the organization's authority must contain within them the seeds of their own change. This could become the watchword for the development of democratic institutions, not only within schools, but ultimately within society as well.

## TO WHAT EXTENT SHOULD PRACTITIONERS BE REGARDED AS MEANS TO ENDS IN EDUCATIONAL ORGANIZATIONS?

Here, in many ways, we have the nub of the dilemma. Kantian morality inveighs against the treating of people as means to ends, and yet, if one assumes that the organization has primacy over the individual, this legitimates such actions. The person becomes the servant of the organization, to do very much as the organizational vision demands. The difficulty with a rigid Kantian view, on the other hand, is precisely the opposite of the collective imperative: it fails to recognize that individuals are not islands: they live in societies, and this inevitably necessitates the need for give and take within and through institutions designed for the general benefit, rather than an absorption in the total prosecution of individual visions. A participative, stakeholder approach resolves many of these difficulties, in that individuals are consulted, are allowed to participate in any vision. The final vision would almost certainly not be their own, but it would partly be theirs. They may thus be 'used' in its prosecution, but in such a system of education, most would be willing to be so 'used', to be participants. They would not see themselves as being 'used' in the hard sense because their own judgement would not be eliminated or ignored by others absorbed with the prosecution of *their* vision.

This is a sensitive issue in British education at present. Despite the claim, discussed in the previous chapter, that business organizations are increasingly encouraging the development of individual contributions through the move to the small and the flexible, education in the UK reflects not only this tendency, through strategies like the use of LMS and increased powers of governing bodies, but also a continuing process of bureaucratization, rationalization and centralization of power, particularly through the prosecution of the National Curriculum and its attendant testing procedures. Indeed, Ritzer (1993) in a highly readable and persuasive book, argues that Weberian bureaucratization is still alive and well through the 'McDonaldization' of western societies; and the more educational operations become 'rationalized' in the Weberian sense, the more individuals see themselves and are seen as purely instruments to instrumental ends.

Of course, small and flexible does not necessarily mean more participative, more humane. As mentioned above, the contributors to Smyth (1993) argue that much of the movement towards the Local Management of Schools, seen across much of the western world, is in actuality a device to devolve responsibility and problems down to schools, while still retaining control of aims and purposes at the centre. Similarly, Sewell and Wilkinson (1992), from the business sector, argue that the bureaucratic *and* the small and flexible may both be little more than different instruments for managerial and social control in the workplace. The latter accomplishes this, they argue, firstly by means of sophisticated technologies which provide managers with huge volumes of information about the worker's performance, and secondly by peer review through autonomous workgroups and quality circles – by 'collegiality'. This is certainly one interpretation of many of the measures described in Chapter 5 on new legislation in the NHS. Finally, it is worth mentioning the work of Hargreaves (1992) who suggests that collegial approaches in schools are increasingly being 'contrived' by those beyond the school, the purposes of which are then imposed by the group upon the individual. The result is that all are made to walk to the same drummer, regardless of whether this improves individual practice or not.

Either way, centralized or decentralized, this will, for some, still be stating the obvious, the incontestable: that organizational visions must come before individual visions. Yet it is neither obvious nor incontestable that organizational imperatives should inevitably take precedence over individual wants. Organizations can be created to reflect the diversity and to structure the resolution of these wants and visions. To repeat, organizations are cultural artefacts, given value and meaning by the people who create them. It is not obvious that schools (and other organizations) should not have power devolved to them, and be devoted at least as much to the development of individuals within them as to the furtherance of causes beyond them.

If this is the case, then it is a matter of (political) choice as to whether schools are designed primarily to enhance a country's gross national product; whether teachers and pupils are only to be efficient, calculable, predictable and controllable; whether teachers are all herded into collegialities which then constrain their, and ultimately their pupils', initiative. It is also a matter of (political) choice as to whether schools are there as much because education is a good in itself, which develops individuals for no further reason than that it expands their consciousness of themselves and their potentials, and most directly contributes to society by providing citizens who, rather than being simply efficient and calculable, are instead deep and complex, who are truly human and therefore both responsible and unpredictable, and who are the antithesis of controllable. We can *choose* to have such schools, such a society.

## WHAT ROLE SHOULD A LEADER TAKE IN AN EDUCATIONAL ORGANIZATION?

The role of an educational leader follows logically from all of the above. Clearly it must be accepted that there are parameters within which all must work: the legislative imperatives, the non-negotiable values. Nevertheless, at the same time, it must be recognized that there can be no value-free management in schools: that the facts and values which a leader draws on share degrees of subjectivity and hence contestability. Therefore, whilst an essential function of a leader is to present to pupils and teachers their own personal vision of where the school and society should be going, another is to provide a forum in which other visions are debated and resolved. Participation and dissent are then essential features of any educational organization worthy of the name. In such cases, their leaders are no longer linchpin heads, driving others by various means towards their – or others' – personal visions. They, and others beyond the school, *will* have their plans, their ideals for the future, and valuable and important they will be; but they must include within them the belief that others need to be encouraged and inspired towards their own visions, and that they need to generate the framework within which such visions may be raised, debated and resolved.

## CONCLUSION

People of most political hues would probably agree that the function of a school is to provide a training ground and partial model for the society within which it works, and that the management of schools is to facilitate that process. My argument has been that it should be concerned less with efficiency, calculability, predictability and control, and the implementation of agendas set elsewhere, and more with empowerment, consciousness-raising and participation. For some concerned with educational management this will be uplifting, for others disquieting; the reactions to such prospects in the commercial sector will be similarly diverse.

Because all organizations are human creations, moral orders, we can choose to develop a society which provides its citizens with an education in participation, a belief in their abilities to affect and restructure the affairs of state and society. We can choose to develop a society which provides institutions like schools which respond to and make fact this belief. We can also develop places of work which see them as contributing to such developments, by developing the stakeholder model much more systematically than has been done so far. In so doing, we strengthen democracy, firstly by acknowledging the acceptance of key values, secondly by acknowledging the contestability of visions inspired by such values, and then by dispersing power within society's institutions to reflect this diversity. Educational institutions can be the beginnings of such a process.

Schools, then, need not stick their heads in the sand and ignore what other kinds of organizations are doing. Nor need they develop an inferiority complex. They can and should be front-runners in the development of democratic structures in society. Through their appreciation of their epistemological, political and moral responsibilities, this can be their distinctive managerial contribution. Whilst one character in

Brecht's *Galileo* said 'pity the country that has no heroes', another argued 'No, pity the country that needs heroes'. The challenge for school management is to begin the process of building a land that has no place for heroes, or makes everybody a hero. They amount to much the same thing.

# Bibliography

Abbott, R., Steadman, S. and Birchenough, M. (1988) *GRIDS: Primary Schools Handbook*, 2nd edition. London: Longman.

Abrahamsson, B. (1993) *Why Organisations?* London: Sage.

Aldrich, H. E. (1993) 'Incommensurable paradigms? Vital signs from three perspectives', in M. Reed and M. Hughes, *Rethinking Organization: New Directions in Organization Theory*. London: Sage.

Alexander, R. J. (1984) *Primary Teaching*. London: Holt.

Anthony, P. D. (1977) *The Ideology of Work*. London: Tavistock.

Ball, S. (1993) 'Culture, cost and control: self-management and entrepreneurial schooling in England and Wales', in J. Smyth (ed.), *A Socially Critical View of the 'Self-Managing School'*. Lewes: Falmer Press.

Barry, C. H. and Tye, F. (1975) *Running a School*. Hounslow, Middlesex: Temple Smith.

Becker, H. S. (1962) 'The nature of a profession', in N. B. Henry (ed.), *Education for the Professions*. Chicago: National Society for the Study of Education Yearbook.

Belbin, R. M. (1981) *Management Teams – Why They Succeed or Fail*. London: Heinemann.

Bell, A. and Sigsworth, A. (1987) *The Small Rural Primary School: A Matter of Quality*. London: Falmer Press.

Bernbaum, G. (1976) 'The role of the head', in R. S. Peters, *The Role of the Head*. London: Routledge & Kegan Paul.

Bottery, M. (1992) *The Ethics of Educational Management*. London: Cassell.

Brown D. and Solomon, D. (1983) 'A model for prosocial learning: an in-progress field study', in D. L. Bridgeman (ed.), *The Nature of Prosocial Development*. New York: Academic Press.

Bush, A., Coleman, M. and Glover, D. (1993) *Managing Autonomous Schools*. London: Paul Chapman Publishing.

Butler, J. (1992) *Patients, Policies and Politics*. Milton Keynes: Open University Press.

Caldwell, B. and Spink, J. (1988) *The Self-Managing School*. Lewes: Falmer Press.

Campbell, R.J. (1985) *Developing the Primary School Curriculum*. Eastbourne: Holt.

Carr, E. H. (1982) *What Is History?* Harmondsworth: Penguin.

Carroll, P. (1989) *Business and Society: Ethics and Stakeholder Management*. Cincinnati: South-Western Publishing.

Clark, P. B. and Wilson, J. Q. (1961) 'Incentive systems: a theory of organisations', *Administrative Science Quarterly*. **6**, 129–166.

Codd, J. A. (1993) 'Managerialism, market liberalism and the move to self-managing schools in New Zealand', in J. Smyth (ed.), *A Socially Critical View of the 'Self-Managing School'*. Lewes: Falmer Press.

Collins Publishers (1986) *Dictionary of the English Language*, ed. P. Hanks. London: Collins.

Coulson, A. (1986) 'The role of the primary head', in T. Bush, R. Glatter, J. Goodey and D. C. Riches (eds), *Approaches to School Management*. London: Harper & Row.

Crosby, P. (1979) *Quality Is Free*. New York: Mentor Books.

Culyer, A. J. (1989) *Competition in Health Care*. Occasional Paper 3. York: University of York Centre for Health Economics.

Culyer, A. J. (1990) *The Internal Market: An Acceptable Means to a Desirable End*. Discussion Paper 67. York: University of York Centre for Health Economics.

Deal, T. and Kennedy, A. (1988) *Corporate Cultures*. Harmondsworth: Penguin.

Department of Health and Social Security (1989) *Working for Patients*, Cm 855. London: HMSO.

Department of Health and Social Security (1993) *NHS Management Enquiry (Griffiths Report)*. London: HMSO.

Downey, M. and Kelly, V. (1986) *Theory and Practice of Education*, 3rd edition. London: Harper & Row.

Drucker, P. (1968) *The Practice of Management*. London: Pan.

Drucker, P. (1977) *Management*. London: Pan.

Drucker, P. (1988) 'The coming of the new organisation', *Harvard Business Review*, Jan. – Feb., 45–53.

Drucker, P. (1989) 'What business can learn from non-profits', *Harvard Business Review*, July – Aug., 89–93.

Drucker, P. (1990) *Managing the Non Profit Organisation*. London: Butterworth Heinemann.

Eisner, E. (1985) *The Art of Educational Evaluation*. Lewes: Falmer Press.

Enthoven, A. (1985) *Reflections on the Management of the National Health Service*. London: Nuffield Provincial Hospitals Trust.

Ford, H. (1923) *My Life and Work*. London: Heinemann.

Friedman, M. (1962) *Capitalism and Freedom*. Chicago: University of Chicago Press.

Fromm, E. (1960) *The Fear of Freedom*. London: Routledge.

Fullan, M. (1991) *The New Meaning of Educational Change*. London: Cassell.

Galton, M. and Patrick, H. (1990) *Curriculum Provision in the Small Primary School*. London: Routledge.

Gilbert, N., Burrows, R. and Pollert, A. (eds) (1992) *Fordism and Flexibility*. London: Macmillan.

Goode, W. J. (1969) 'The theoretical limits of professionalization', in A. Etzioni (ed.), *The Semi-Professions and Their Organization*. New York: Macmillan.

Gouldner, A. (1954) *Patterns of Industrial Democracy*. Glencoe, Ill.: The Free Press.

Gray, J. (1992) *The Moral Foundations of Market Institutions*. London: IEA Health and Welfare Unit.

Greenfield, T. and Ribbins, P. (eds) (1993) *Greenfield on Administration*. London: Routledge.

Griffiths, D. E. (1957) 'Towards a theory of administrative behaviour', in R. F. Campbell and R. T. Gregg (eds), *Administrative Behaviour in Education*. New York: Harper.

Griffiths, D. (ed.) (1964) *Behavioural Science and Educational Administration*. Chicago: University of Chicago Press.

Griffiths, D. (1977) 'The individual in the organisation: a theoretical perspective', *Educational Administrative Quarterly*, **13**(2), 1–18.

Hadow Report (1931) *Report of the Consultative Committee on the Primary School*. London: HMSO.

Halmos, P. (1971) *The Professions and Their Prospects*. Beverly Hills: Sage.

Ham, C. (1992) *Health Policy in Britain*, 3rd edition. London: Macmillan.

Handy, C. (1985) *Gods of Management*. London: Pan.

Handy, C. (1989) *The Age of Unreason*. London: Business Books.

Handy, C. and Aitken, R. (1986) *Understanding Schools as Organisations*. Harmondsworth: Penguin.

Hargreaves, A. (1992) 'Contrived collegiality: the micropolitics of teacher collaboration', in N. Bennett, M. Crawford and C. Riches (eds), *Managing Change in Education*. London: Paul Chapman Publishing.

Hartley, D. (1993) 'The evaluative state and self-management in education: cause for reflection?', in J. Smyth (ed.) *A Socially Critical View of the 'Self-Managing School'*. Lewes: Falmer Press.

Hillgate Group (1986) *Whose Schools? A Radical Manifesto*. London: Hillgate Group.

Hodgkinson, C. (1978) *Towards a Philosophy of Administration*. Oxford: Basil Blackwell.

Hodgkinson, C. (1983) *The Philosophy of Leadership*. Oxford: Basil Blackwell.

Hollway, W. (1991) *Work Psychology and Organisational Behaviour*. London: Sage.

Hoyle, E. (1980) 'Professionalization and de-professionalization in education', in E. Hoyle and J. Megarry (eds), *World Yearbook of Education 1980: The Professional Development of Teachers*. London: Kogan Page.

Hoyle, E. (1983) 'The professionalization of teachers: a paradox', in P. Gordon (ed.), *Is Teaching a Profession?* London: Bedford Way Papers, no. 15.

Kanter, R. M. (1989) *When Giants Learn to Dance*. London: Simon & Schuster.

Kanter, R. M. and Summers, D. V. (1987) 'Doing well while doing good: dilemmas of performance measurement in non-profit organisations and the need for a multiple-constituency approach', in W. W. Powell (ed.), *The NonProfit Sector: a Research Handbook*. New Haven: Yale University Press.

Keeble, S. P. (1992) *The Ability to Manage: A Study of British Management 1890–1990*. Manchester: Manchester University Press.

Kelman, C. and Hamilton, V. L. (1989) *Crimes of Obedience*. New Haven: Yale University Press.

Klein, R. (1989) *The Politics of the NHS*, 2nd edition. London: Longman.

Kohn, M. (1977) *Class and Conformity*. Chicago: University of Chicago Press.

Lapham, L. H. (1991) 'Notebook: opening the mail', *Harper's*, 28 Feb.

Lawn, M. and Ozga, J. (1987) 'The educational worker? A re-assessment of teachers', in L. Barton and S. Walker (eds), *Schools, Teachers and Teaching*. Lewes: Falmer Press.

Leat, D. (1993) *Managing across Sectors*. London: City University Business School.

Leggatt, T. (1970) 'Teaching as a profession', in J. A. Jackson (ed.), *Professions and Professionalism*. Cambridge: Cambridge University Press.

LeGrand, J. and Robinson, R. (1992) *The Economics of Social Problems*, 3rd edition. Basingstoke: Macmillan.

Levitt, T. (1960) 'Marketing myopia', *Harvard Business Review*, Jul. – Aug., 45–46.

Lipsky, M. (1980) *Street-Level Bureaucracy*. New York: Russell Sage Foundation.

Lortie, D. C. (1969) 'The balance of control and autonomy in elementary school teaching', in A. Etzioni (ed.), *The Semi-Professions and Their Organization*. New York: Macmillan.

Maclure, S. (1993a) 'Wise hand needed on the wheel', *The Times*, 18 January.

Maclure, S. (1993b) 'A General Teaching Council for England and Wales?', *NCE Briefing Paper No. 11*. London: Paul Hamlyn Foundation.

Macquarrie, J. (1972) *Existentialism*. London: Hutchinson.

Marris, P. (1975) *Loss and Change*. New York: Anchor Press/Doubleday.

Maynard, A. (1992) *Competition in Health Care*. Basingstoke: Macmillan.

Merton, R. K. (1952) 'Bureaucratic structure and personality', in R. K. Merton, A. P. Gray, B. Hockey and H. C. Selvin (eds), *Reader in Bureaucracy*, Glencoe, Ill.: The Free Press.

Meyenn, R. J. (1980) 'Peer networks among middle school children', in A. Hargreaves and L. Tickle (eds), *Middle Schools: Origins, Ideology and Practice*. London: Harper & Row.

Milgram, S. (1964) *Obedience to Authority*. London: Tavistock.

Morgan, G. (1986) *Images of Organisation*. London: Sage.

Morgan, G. (1993) *Imaginization*. London: Sage.

Mullen, P. M. (1991) 'Which internal market? The NHS White Paper and internal markets', in G. Thompson, J. Frances, R. Levacic and J. Mitchell (eds), *Markets, Hierarchies and Networks*. London: Sage.

Murgatroyd, S. and Morgan, C. (1993) *Total Quality Management and the School*. Milton Keynes: Open University Press.

Peddiwell, J. A. (1939) *The Sabre Tooth Curriculum*. New York: McGraw-Hill.

Peters, R. S. (1966) *Ethics and Education*. London: George Allen & Unwin.

Perkins, H. (1983) 'The teaching profession and the game of life', in P. Gordon (ed.), *Is Teaching a Profession?* London: Bedford Way Papers, no.15.

Peters, T. and Austin, N. (1985) *A Passion for Excellence*. London: Collins.

Peters, T. and Waterman, R. (1982) *In Search of Excellence*. New York: Harper & Row.

Plowden Report (1967) *Children and Their Primary Schools*. Central Advisory Council for Education. London: HMSO.

Popper, K. (1945) *The Open Society and Its Enemies*, 2 vols. London: Routledge & Kegan Paul.

Popper, K. (1982) *The Logic of Scientific Discovery*. London: Hutchinson.

Reed, M. (1989) *The Sociology of Management*. Hemel Hempstead: Harvester Wheatsheaf.

Rees, G. (1969) *St. Michael: A History of Marks and Spencer*. London: Weidenfeld & Nicolson.

Reiff, P. (1971) 'The dangers of the techni-pro: democratising the human science professions', *Social Policy*, **2**, 62–4.

Ritzer, G. (1993) *The McDonaldization of Society*. London: Pine Forge/Sage.

Sampson, A. (1993) *Sovereign State: The Secret History of ITT*. London: Hodder and Stoughton.

Schein, E. (1966) 'The problem of moral education for the business manager', *Industrial Management Review* **8**(1), 3–14.

Schon, D. (1983) *The Reflective Practitioner: How Professionals Think in Action*. New York: Basic Books.

Selznick, P. (1949) *TVA and the Grassroots*. Berkeley, Cal.: University of California Press.

Sewell, G. and Wilkinson, B. (1992) ' "Someone to watch over me": surveillance, discipline and the just-in time labour process', *Sociology*, **20**(2), 271–89.

Shiell, A. (1991) *Self-Governing Trusts: An Agenda for Evaluation*. Discussion paper 78. York: University of York Centre for Health Economics.

Shipley, D. D. (1981) 'Primary objectives in British manufacturing industry', *Journal of Industrial Economics* **29**, 429–44.

Sieff, I. M. (1970) *Memoirs*. London: Weidenfeld & Nicolson.

Sieff, M. (1990) *On Management: The Marks and Spencer Way*. London: Weidenfeld & Nicolson.

Simon, H. A. (1957) *Administrative Behaviour: A Study of Decision-Making Process in Administrative Organizations*, 2nd edition. New York: Free Press.

Smyth, J. (ed.) (1993) *A Socially Critical View of the 'Self-Managing School'*. Lewes: Falmer Press.

Sockett, H. (1993) 'Towards a professional code in teaching', in P. Gordon (ed.), *Is Teaching a Profession?* London: Bedford Way Papers, no. 15.

Strong, P. and Robinson, J. (1990) *The NHS – Under New Management*. Buckingham: Open University Press.

Sullivan, M. (1991) *Marketing Your Primary School*. London: Longman.

Titmus, R. M. (1968) *Commitment to Welfare*. London: Simon Shand.

Toffler, A. (1970) *Future Shock*. London: Bodley Head.

Tse, K. K. (1985) *Marks and Spencer: Anatomy of Britain's Most Efficiently Managed Company*. Oxford: Pergamon.

Walton, M. (1989) *The Deming Management Method*. London: Mercury Books.

Walton, R. and Susman, G. (1987) 'People policies for the new machines', *Harvard Business Review*, Mar. – Apr., 98–196.

Warnock, M. (1988) *A Common Policy for Education*. Oxford: Oxford University Press.

Waugh, D. (1991) 'Implementing educational change in the small primary school', in D. Waugh (ed.), *Small Primary Schools*. Aspects of Education, no. 44. University of Hull.

Webster, D. (1982) 'Spiritual growth in religious education', in M. F. Tickner and D. H. Webster (eds), *Religious Education and the Imagination*. Aspects of Education, no. 28. University of Hull.

Webster, D. (1985) 'Commitment, spirituality and the classroom', *British Journal of Religious Education*, **8**(1), 20–9.

Webster, D. (1993) 'Mystery and education: morality and the gas chamber', *Curriculum*, **14**(2), 97–103.

West-Burnham, J. (1992) 'Total quality management in education', in N. Bennett, M. Crawford and C. Riches (eds), *Managing Change in Education*. London: Paul Chapman Publishing.

Williams, A. (1989) *Creating a Health Care Market: Ideology, Efficiency, Ethics and Clinical Freedom*. Occasional Paper 5. York: University of York Centre for Health Economics.

Williams, M. (1990) *In-Service Education and Training*. London: Cassell.

Willower, D. (1980) 'Contemporary issues in theory of educational administration', *Educational Administration Quarterly* **16**(3), 1–25.

Wragg, E. D. (1984) *Classroom Teaching Skills*. London: Croom Helm.

# Index